Re

CW00327065

Criminal Law

Fourth edition edited by
John Herrmann LLB, LLM

HLT Publications

HLT PUBLICATIONS
200 Greyhound Road, London W14 9RY

First Edition 1990
Reprinted 1991
Second Edition 1992
Reprinted 1992
Third Edition 1994
Fourth Edition 1995

ISBN 0 7510 0601 7

British Library Cataloguing-in-Publication.

A CIP Catalogue record for this book is available from the British Library.

Printed and bound in Great Britain by
Hartnolls Limited, Bodmin, Cornwall

CONTENTS

Acknowledgement — v

Introduction — vii

How to Study Criminal Law — ix

Revision and Examination Technique — xi

Table of Cases — xv

Table of Statutes — xxvii

1   Criminal Conduct — 1

2   State of Mind — 6

3   Participation — 25

4   Non-Fatal Offences against the Person — 40

5   Homicide — 59

6   Theft, Burglary and Deception — 85

7   Other Theft Act and Related Offences — 129

8   Criminal Damage — 146

9   Inchoate Offences — 157

10 Defences — 165

11 University of London LLB (External) 1994
    Questions and Suggested Solutions — 186

ACKNOWLEDGEMENT

Some questions used are taken or adapted from past University of London LLB (External) Degree examination papers and our thanks are extended to the University of London for their kind permission to use and publish the questions.

Caveat

The LLB answers given are not approved or sanctioned by the University of London and are entirely our responsibility.

They are not intended as 'Model Answers', but rather as Suggested Solutions.

The answers have two fundamental purposes, namely:

a) To provide a detailed example of a suggested solution to an examination question, and

b) To assist students with their research into the subject and to further their understanding and appreciation of the subject of Law.

INTRODUCTION

This WorkBook is based on examination papers set by the University of London over the last twelve years. Unlike the *Criminal Law Suggested Solutions Pack* published by HLT Publications, this book has been divided into syllabus topics under broad headings eg 'automatism' appearing under 'Defences' (Chapter 10). Such classification has been done to assist students in their revision in a more structured way whilst, at the same time, providing students studying this subject with another Examination Board with ease of access to the topics they wish to revise.

As none of the topics exists in isolation there is necessarily some overlap between them, and so questions focussing on mens rea may include offences of murder or theft. Similarly, all the questions will involve some examination of mens rea and actus reus as there would be no crime without them.

The suggested solutions are just that – they are not intended to be model 'examination answers', indeed some of them could never be written in their entirety in the time allowed, nor are they endorsed by the University of London. They do, however, represent a very useful and effective revision medium, providing examples of previous examination questions, suggested answers and an up-to-date review of relevant cases and statutes.

In this revised 1995 edition the final chapter contains the complete June 1994 University of London LLB (External) Criminal Law question paper, followed by suggested solutions to each question. Thus the student will have the opportunity to review a recent examination paper in its entirety, and can, if desired, use this chapter as a mock examination – referring to the suggested solutions only after first having attempted the questions. This 1995 edition has also expanded the content of the WorkBook to give a fuller summary of the key ingredients of the main offences with particular emphasis on the most examinable areas.

References for London University examination papers

Following each question is a reference to the University of London LLB Examination (for External Students) in which it was set for examination purposes. To focus more clearly on the chapter topic the Editor has generally amended or shortened the wording to some extent. To indicate this, the words 'Adapted from' are used in the reference. Some questions were specially written by the Editor.

Paper currency

Occasionally, in a question, a possible misdemeanour depends on confusion between a one-pound note and a note of higher value (eg five or ten pounds). These questions were prepared before Britain dispensed with the one-pound note in favour of a coin only for this amount. To make sense of the problem or issue involved the references to pound notes have not been changed.

HOW TO STUDY CRIMINAL LAW

Unlike many other 'compulsory' areas of law, Criminal Law is generally remembered by students as being one of the most interesting and therefore studying it becomes so much easier than some other disciplines. That is not to say, though, that it is an 'easy' subject, and there are certain crucial aspects of it which require a great deal of attention in order to understand them fully.

A considerable amount of Criminal Law appears in statutes and it is vital to be familiar with these enactments and their more important sections. Students must have a good working knowledge of which statutes create certain offences and which sections lay down criteria for determining questions arising from alleged offences (eg ss1–7 Theft Act 1968). You must know the ingredients of all the main offences covered by their respective syllabuses together with any defences.

Care should be taken not to confuse elements from one offence with those of another, such as 'reasonable excuse', 'lawful authority' and 'dishonesty'. One of the most difficult areas of Criminal law is that of mens rea. Which type of mens rea is applicable in a given case? The different types of mens rea must be clearly understood together with the various objective and subjective tests which have been developed by the courts.

Problems in this area are nowhere more apparent than in the area of murder – still governed by the Common law – and the epithet 'malice aforethought' which most laymen associate with 'pre-meditation' has had a turbulent and confusing passage through the courts over recent years.

When considering an accused's liability, one must not be blinkered; the facts will often reveal several (sometimes overlapping) offences. Some instances of criminal damage may also amount to theft. Separate offences of burglary and robbery may be disclosed on the same facts. Consider, too, how an offence has been committed; were any instruments, disguises, or 'props' used? If so, then other offences may have been made out. How many people were involved? Were they all acting voluntarily? Are they equally culpable? Were they acting in concert?

If you were able to defend the accused what possible defences, however remote, may be available? How restrictive are they and how have the courts interpreted them? Is there an essential element missing from the facts as presented thereby obviating the need for a defence?

In asking these questions one must establish the elements required in order to attract liability, and then consider each individual part in the light of statutory guidance and case law.

So, in an alleged burglary one should proceed logically through the facts to discover whether there has been an 'entry'; whether it was into a 'building'; whether it was made as a 'trespasser'; whether the accused had the requisite 'intent' and so on. One must then look at the attendant (possibly mitigating) circumstances, eg the accused had got drunk, he had been drugged, he was mistaken, he was acting under duress, he did it for a joke, etc. In other words, once the basic principles have been grasped from a thorough reading of the textbooks and cases, one should approach specific instances of alleged criminal conduct from the point of view of both prosecutor and defence counsel, finally weighing up the respective merits of each argument and coming to a conclusion.

As with any other legal topic, students should have a sufficient number of authorities in their 'armoury' to support the arguments they propose and by repeatedly practising the application of what they have learned to hypothetical cases, students can become competent and confident in answering problem questions favoured by examiners, and also in discussing broader concepts of Criminal Law such as impossibility and strict liability.

Finally it is suggested that students read the *Criminal Law Review* which, apart from containing the most recent cases on the subject, also has regular articles of interest to academics and practitioners alike.

REVISION AND EXAMINATION TECHNIQUE

In tackling any examination one must first know the extent of the syllabus and although it seems a fairly obvious observation, a lot of valuable study time can be wasted on topics that are of little importance or oblique relevance in that syllabus. This pitfall is particularly hazardous to part-time external candidates who can labour for hours over points that will earn only a fraction of the marks for an examination question. Students must be aware primarily of the major areas of their subject such as those which are embraced by the topic headings in this WorkBook. With Criminal Law, it is fortunate that one is able to predict with some accuracy what areas are almost certain to be examined.

Revision

An inescapable part of learning the law is the committing of facts to memory and, despite the very large proportion of problem questions used in Criminal Law papers which test a candidate's ability to apply posited principles and opposing arguments, there is still a considerable amount of 'rote learning'.

Although everyone develops their own style of revision, there are certain universal features of learning that are worthy of note, particularly for those in their first year of degree-level study. The first is that repeatedly transcribing information from books and notes, and effective learning, are not by any means synonymous. In fact the converse can well be the case and mechanical duplication of written texts can be distracting, time-wasting and counter-productive in that it may give one the feeling of having done 'a lot of work'. Such time could be far better utilised by re-reading textbooks and concise annotations, which brings us to the second point. Legal tomes can seem extremely obscure and require sustained concentration which is best broken up into short but determined bouts. In this way the reader proceeds piece by piece until the whole area has been covered and, therefore, it is essential that students re-read their main textbooks (at least three times) in order to gain a sound overall view of the subject and, at the same time, to increase their retention of the salient points.

Unlike re-writing notes and texts, there is a direct correlation between the number of times one reads an article and the amount that is digested and retained.

Few of us have sufficient time to do all that we would like and when studying, especially part-time, it is essential that time is used to the best effect. What should be borne in mind when revising is that examination time limits are very restrictive and it is virtually impossible for the well-read student to rehearse all that he has learnt, which is relevant, in the examination room. Therefore the key points in each topic area should be grasped, together with the established current authorities. In reading cases and other textbooks it must be asked whether or not the expenditure of valuable time and effort is warranted by the potential improvement in understanding and learning. Even if students were allowed to take all their notes, textbooks, and law reports into the examination, it is unlikely that they would have time to refer to them – unless they were hopelessly unprepared.

A very important exercise in revision is to practise writing answers under examination conditions. It will quickly be seen that the forty or so minutes allowed for each question go very rapidly. More importantly, one can develop the knack of unravelling complex sets of facts and apportioning liability, and setting down arguments and opinions in a logical and persuasive manner while 'under pressure'.

A good way to test one's knowledge is to apply the principles learnt to everyday events – newspaper and television reports, films, occurrences at work, for example. If you read a story in the paper about an alleged 'robbery' or 'burglary', stop and consider the facts and call up the authorities you have learnt – it is surprising how often the nomenclature used in the press is misleading.

In more structured revision it is important to organise the time spent on each aspect of the subject, with 'goals' at the end. Concentrate primarily on what you do know and don't label one topic as 'easy' or 'done' and then ignore it until the examination. Learning the law is like juggling with, at first one, then many, different topics and keeping them 'in the air' until you sit the examination.

Examination technique

There are several crucial areas which students must bear in mind during examinations.

a) *Time*

After allowing time to review all the questions on the paper and selecting those that you intend to tackle, you will be left with just over half an hour – in a 3 hour examination of four questions – to do the actual writing of your answer. Given the amount of detail involved in most problem questions, this presents quite a hurdle in itself hence the need to practise writing specimen answers beforehand.

b) *Relevance*

If there is one thing that antagonises examiners it is the regurgitation by students of all they know on a topic. Unless the answer is directly relevant to the question, and addresses it in the manner required, you will be wasting your time and the examiner's.

c) *Structure*

Try to make your answers balanced and structured. In answering problem questions it is useful to follow the pattern:

i) Introduction – concise – maybe a few lines.

ii) Principles – look at the principles of law raised by the question – along the lines of the skeleton solutions used here.

iii) Application – apply those principles to the facts and consider any counter-arguments. Discuss any ways in which those facts differ from the decided cases.

iv) Conclusion – having applied the principles and weighed the arguments, arrive at some conclusion which is supported by your discussion.

Remember, it is the argument upon which you base your conclusion that is the most important part of the answer.

Also, if the examiner asks you to 'advise X' then do just that.

Finally, when studying for the London University LLB degree remember to follow their study guide and READ THE EXAMINER'S COMMENTS FROM THE PREVIOUS YEAR. These are obtainable from the University and will often indicate areas which were poorly covered in the examination. Quite often those areas are examined again the following year.

Remember too that Criminal Law papers carry few surprises and a good knowledge of the topics covered here will provide a very sound foundation for your revision.

Good luck!

TABLE OF CASES

Abbot *v* R [1977] AC 755   *55, 168, 182*
R *v* Adomako [1994] 1 WLR 15; [1994] NLJ 936   *51, 61, 62, 63, 66, 68, 70, 72, 81, 156, 189*
R *v* Ahluwalia [1993] Crim LR 63   *60, 62*
Airedale NHS Trust *v* Bland [1993] 1 All ER 821   *2*
Albert *v* Lavin [1981] 1 All ER 628; (1981) 72 Cr App R 178   *11, 177, 178*
R *v* Ali [1995] Crim LR 303   *168, 169*
R *v* Allen [1985] AC 1029; [1985] 3 WLR 107; [1985] 2 All ER 641   *87, 90, 101, 103, 104, 116*
R *v* Allen [1988] Crim LR 698   *172*
Alphacell Ltd *v* Woodward [1972] AC 824; [1972] 2 All ER 475   *7, 16, 17, 18*
R *v* Anderson [1986] AC 27   *25*
Anderton *v* Ryan [1985] AC 560; [1985] 2 WLR 968; [1985] 2 All ER 355   *160*
Andrews *v* DPP [1937] AC 576   *68, 80*
R *v* Andrews and Hedges [1981] Crim LR 106   *87*
R *v* Ashford and Smith [1988] Crim LR 682   *146, 152*
Atkinson *v* Sir Alfred McAlpine & Son Ltd [1974] Crim LR 668   *16, 18*
Attorney-General for Northern Ireland *v* Gallagher [1963] AC 349   *166, 173*
Attorney-General's Reference (No 1 of 1974) [1974] 2 WLR 891   *131*
Attorney-General's Reference (No 1 of 1975) [1975] QB 773; (1975) 61 Cr App R 118   *185*
Attorney-General's References (Nos 1 and 2 of 1979) [1979] 3 WLR 577   *33, 35, 93, 111, 118, 136*
Attorney-General's Reference (No 4 of 1979) (1980) 71 Cr App R 341   *194*
Attorney-General's Reference (No 6 of 1980) [1981] QB 715   *40, 46*
Attorney-General's Reference (No 1 of 1983) [1985] QB 182; [1984] 3 All ER 369   *85, 125, 128*
Attorney-General's Reference (No 2 of 1992) [1993] 3 WLR 982   *167, 168*
R *v* Austin (1973) 58 Cr App R 163; [1973] Crim LR 778   *54*
R *v* Ayres [1984] AC 447; (1984) 78 Cr App R 232   *34*

R *v* Bailey (1800) Russ & Ry 1, CCR   *177*
R *v* Bailey (1977) 66 Cr App R 31   *60*
R *v* Bailey [1983] 2 All ER 503; (1983) 77 Cr App R 76   *63, 64, 166, 171, 172, 184*
R *v* Bainbridge [1960] 1 QB 129; [1959] 3 WLR 356; [1959] 3 All ER 200; (1960) 43 Cr App R 194   *26, 30, 190, 201*
R *v* Baker [1994] Crim LR 445   *26, 202*
R *v* Ball [1989] Crim LR 730   *62, 66*
R *v* Banks (1873) 12 Cox CC 393   *162*
R *v* Bannister [1962] Crim LR 119   *182*
Barker *v* R (1983) 153 CLR 338   *121*
R *v* Barr, Kenyon and Heacock (1989) 88 Cr App R 362   *63, 71, 75, 78*
R *v* Bashir (1982) 77 Cr App R 59   *20*
R *v* Bateman [1925] All ER 45; (1925) 19 Cr App R 8   *64*

R v Becerra (1975) 62 Cr App R 212   *202*

Beckford v R [1988] 1 AC 130; [1987] 3 WLR 611; [1987] 3 All ER 425   *11, 168, 178, 179, 192*

R v Belfon [1976] 1 WLR 741   *3, 44, 53, 66, 70, 110, 163, 185*

R v Bernhard (1938) 26 Cr App R 137   *98*

R v Betts and Ridley (1930) 22 Cr App R 148   *28*

R v Bird [1985] 2 All ER 513   *44*

Bird v Jones (1845) 7 QB 742   *47*

R v Blaue [1975] 1 WLR 1411; [1975] 3 All ER 446; (1975) 61 Cr App R 271   *1, 10, 44, 50, 61, 63, 65, 70, 75, 189, 193*

R v Bloxham [1983] 1 AC 109; [1981] 1 WLR 859   *131, 194*

R v Bogacki [1973] QB 832   *11, 126, 129, 132, 134*

R v Boshears (1961) The Times 8 February   *170*

R v Boulton (1871) 12 Cox CC 87   *29*

R v Bow [1977] Crim LR 176; (1976) 64 Cr App R 54   *11, 126, 129, 132, 134, 139, 142*

R v Bradish [1990] Crim LR 723   *7, 17*

Bratty v Attorney-General for Northern Ireland [1963] AC 386; [1961] 3 WLR 965; [1961] 3 All ER 523   *167, 170, 184*

R v Breckenridge [1984] Crim LR 174   *20*

R v Brooks and Brooks [1983] Crim LR 188; (1982) 76 Cr App R 66   *87, 104, 116*

Broome v Perkins [1987] Crim LR 271   *184*

R v Brown (1776) Leach 148   *82, 84*

R v Brown [1969] 3 WLR 370   *130*

R v Brown [1985] Crim LR 212   *88, 121, 136*

R v Brown [1985] Crim LR 398   *56*

R v Brown [1993] 2 WLR 556 HL; [1992] 2 WLR 441 CA   *40, 46, 69, 203, 204*

Brown v Dyerson [1969] 1 QB 45   *12*

Buckoke v GLC [1971] 1 Ch 655; [1971] 2 All ER 254   *12, 167*

R v Bundy [1977] 1 WLR 914; [1977] 2 All ER 382   *130*

R v Burgess [1991] 2 All ER 769; [1991] Crim LR 548   *167*

R v Burke [1987] Crim LR 336   *76, 182*

R v Byrne [1960] 3 All ER 1   *60*

C v S [1988] QB 135   *51*

C (a minor) v DPP (1995) The Times 17 March; [1994] Crim LR 523   *23, 133, 150, 165, 198, 200*

C (a minor) v Eisenhower [1984] QB 331   *41, 197, 198*

R v Calcutt and Varty (1985) 7 Cr App R(S) 385   *98, 99*

R v Campbell [1991] Crim LR 268   *161*

Campbell and Cosans v United Kingdom [1982] 4 EHRR 293   *41*

R v Carberry [1994] Crim LR 447   *26, 28, 38, 202*

R v Cato [1976] 1 WLR 110; [1976] 1 All ER 260; (1976) 62 Cr App R 41   *42, 53, 185*

R v Cavendish [1961] 1 WLR 1083   *130*

R v Chan Fook [1994] Crim LR 432   *9, 30, 41, 42, 44, 46, 52, 55, 66, 69, 74, 192, 198, 201, 203*

Chan Wing-Siu v R [1985] AC 168; [1984] 3 All ER 871   *28, 30, 73*
R v Cheshire [1991] 3 All ER 670; [1991] Crim LR 709   *1, 61, 70*
Chief Constable of Avon and Somerset v Shimmen [1986] Crim LR 800; (1987) 84
   Cr App R 7   *8, 196*
R v Church [1966] 1 QB 59; [1965] 2 All ER 72; (1965) 49 Cr App R 206   *2, 62,*
   64, 66, 70, 71, 153, 156, 189, 193
R v Clarence (1888) 22 QBD 23   *3, 20, 23, 110*
R v Clarke [1972] 1 All ER 219   *166, 170*
R v Clarkson [1971] 3 All ER 344; [1971] 1 WLR 1402; (1971) 55 Cr App R 445
   4, 26, 32, 119–120, 183
R v Clarkson [1987] AC 417   *182*
R v Clear [1968] 1 QB 670   *134, 153*
R v Clegg [1995] All ER 80   *168, 169*
R v Clotworthy [1981] RTR 477   *127*
R v Clouden [1987] Crim LR 56   *201*
R v Clucas [1949] 2 KB 226   *90, 96, 102, 139*
R v Codere (1916) 12 Cr App R 21   *170*
R v Cole [1994] Crim LR 583   *167, 168, 182*
Cole v Turner (1705) 6 Mod Rep 149   *137*
R v Collins [1973] QB 100; [1972] 2 All ER 1105   *35, 81, 82, 88, 100, 108, 111,*
   118, 121
Collins v Wilcock [1984] 3 All ER 374   *198*
R v Collis-Smith [1971] Crim LR 716   *86, 93*
Comer v Bloomfield (1970) 55 Cr App R 305   *161*
R v Coney (1882) 8 QBD 534   *4, 26, 32, 40, 72, 96, 119, 141, 183*
R v Conway [1988] 3 All ER 1025   *12, 167, 182*
R v Cooke [1986] 2 All ER 985; [1986] AC 909   *34*
Corcoran v Anderton [1980] Crim LR 385; (1980) 71 Cr App R 104   *129*
R v Court [1987] 1 All ER 120   *81, 83*
Cox v Riley [1986] Crim LR 460; (1986) 83 Cr App R 54   *153, 155*
R v Culyer (1992) The Times 17 April   *81, 83*
R v Cunningham [1957] 2 QB 396; [1957] 2 All ER 412   *5, 7, 20, 28, 46, 47, 51,*
   54, 55, 57, 66, 69, 163, 185, 191, 195, 197, 204
R v Cunningham [1982] AC 566; [1981] 2 All ER 863   *78*
R v Curr [1968] 2 QB 944   *25, 163*

R v D [1984] AC 778   *188*
R v Dalby [1982] 1 WLR 425; [1982] 1 All ER 916   *4, 50*
Davies v DPP [1954] AC 378; [1954] 1 All ER 507   *28, 38, 202*
R v Dawson (1985) 81 Cr App R 150   *189*
R v Dawson and James (1976) 64 Cr App R 170   *129*
R v Denton [1982] 1 All ER 65   *146*
Dip Kaur v Chief Constable for Hampshire [1981] 1 WLR 578   *122, 124*
Dobson v General Accident, Fire & Life Assoc plc [1990] 3 WLR 1066; (1989) The
   Guardian 5 October   *126*
R v Donovan [1934] 2 KB 498; (1934) 25 Cr App R 1   *40, 47, 69, 72, 203*
Doodeward v Spence (1908) 6 CLR 406   *110*
R v Doughty [1986] Crim LR 625; (1986) 83 Cr App R 319   *64, 76*

DPP v Camplin [1978] AC 705; [1978] 2 All ER 168   60, 64, 76
DPP v Harris (1994) The Times 15 March   167, 168
DPP v Huskinson [1988] Crim LR 620   85, 92
DPP v Lavender [1994] Crim LR 297   86, 88
DPP v Little [1992] 1 All ER 299   198, 203
DPP v Majewski [1977] AC 142; [1976] 2 All ER 142; [1976] Crim LR 374   14, 15, 21, 166, 172, 173, 184, 192
DPP v Morgan [1976] AC 182; [1975] 2 All ER 347   11, 177, 178
DPP v Newbury and Jones [1977] AC 500; [1976] 2 WLR 918   10, 62, 68, 70, 71, 73, 76, 80, 156
DPP v Nock [1978] AC 979; [1978] 2 All ER 654   159, 161
DPP v Pittaway [1994] Crim LR 600   168, 169
DPP v Ray [1974] AC 370   86, 96, 101, 126, 127
DPP v Smith [1961] AC 290; [1960] 3 All ER 161   3, 41, 48, 52, 54, 66, 69, 78, 80, 197, 198
DPP v Stonehouse [1978] AC 55; [1977] 2 All ER 909   93, 104, 107, 117, 161
DPP for Northern Ireland v Lynch [1975] AC 653; (1975) 61 Cr App R 6; [1975] 1 All ER 913   175, 182, 183
DPP for Northern Ireland v Maxwell [1978] 3 All ER 1140; (1978) 68 Cr App R 128   201, 202
R v Dudley [1989] Crim LR 57   199
R v Dudley and Stephens (1884) 14 QBD 273   167, 181, 182
R v Duffy [1949] 1 All ER 932   60, 75
R v Duffy [1967] 1 QB 63   45
R v Dunbar [1988] Crim LR 693   30
R v Duncalf [1979] 2 All ER 1116   27
R v Dyson [1908] 2 KB 454   59, 71, 78
R v Dytham [1979] QB 722; [1979] 3 All ER 641   2, 5, 74

R v Easom [1971] 2 QB 315   33, 93
Edwards v Ddin [1976] 1 WLR 942; [1976] 3 All ER 705   86, 89, 104
Edwards v Toombs [1983] Crim LR 43   119
R v Ellames [1974] 3 All ER 130   142
Elliott v C (a minor) [1983] 1 WLR 939; [1983] 2 All ER 1005   150, 196
Eley v Lytle (1885) 50 JP 308; (1885) 2 TLR 44   148

Fagan v Metropolitan Police Commissioner [1969] 1 QB 439; [1968] 3 All ER 442   4, 30, 40, 46, 52, 74
R v Fancy [1980] Crim LR 171   148
Farrell v Secretary of State for Defence [1980] 1 All ER 166   180
Faulkner v Talbot [1981] 3 All ER 468   46
R v Feely [1973] 1 QB 530   35, 92, 93, 95, 101, 103, 106, 108, 114, 116, 141
R v Ferguson (1970) 54 Cr App R 410   98, 99
R v Fitzmaurice [1983] 2 WLR 227; [1983] 1 All ER 189; [1983] QB 1083   25
Frankland and Moore v R [1987] AC 576   82, 83–84
R v Franklin (1883) 15 Cox CC 163   65, 73

Gammon (Hong Kong) Ltd v Attorney-General of Hong Kong [1985] AC 1; (1984) 80 Cr App R 194   7

R v Garwood [1987] 1 All ER 1032; [1987] Crim LR 476   *129, 154*
Gayford v Chouler [1898] 1 QB 316   *148, 155*
R v Ghosh [1982] 1 QB 1053; [1982] Crim LR 608   *4, 35, 86, 89, 90, 92, 93, 95,*
    96, 98, 99, 101, 103, 106, 108, 109, 112, 114, 116, 118, 119, 120, 122, 124, 125,
    128, 135, 137, 139, 141, 153, 154, 194
R v Gibbens and Proctor (1918) 82 JP 287; (1918) 13 Cr App R 134   *1*
R v Gilbert (1977) 66 Cr App R 237   *76*
R v Gilks [1972] 3 All ER 280; [1972] 1 WLR 1341   *95, 106, 108, 114, 120*
R v Gillard (1988) 87 Cr App R 189   *42, 199*
R v Gittens [1984] QB 698; [1984] 3 All ER 252   *60*
R v Gomez [1993] 1 All ER 1   *85, 86, 88, 113, 125, 137*
R v Goodfellow [1986] Crim LR 468; (1986) 83 Cr App R 23   *62, 66, 81*
R v Gorrie (1918) 83 JP 136   *23, 133, 150, 165*
R v Gotts [1992] 1 All ER 832   *168, 176*
R v Graham (1982) 74 Cr App R 235; [1982] 1 All ER 801   *56, 167, 175, 176,*
    182, 183, 190
Grant v Borg [1982] 2 All ER 257   *80*
R v Grundy (1989) The Times 9 February   *73*
R v Gullefer [1990] 3 All ER 882   *124, 157, 161, 163, 164*

R v Hale (1978) 68 Cr App R 415   *4, 112, 129, 138, 139*
R v Hall [1973] 1 QB 126; [1973] 3 WLR 381; [1972] 2 All ER 1009   *85, 92, 110*
R v Hall (1985) 81 Cr App R 260   *130*
R v Halliday (1876) 61 LT 701   *41*
R v Hammond [1982] Crim LR 611   *87*
R v Hancock and Shankland [1986] AC 455; [1986] 2 WLR 257; [1986] 1 All ER
    646; (1986) 82 Cr App R 264   *8, 10, 59, 63, 65, 68, 71, 73, 75, 78, 79, 80, 148,*
    181, 189, 193
R v Hanson (1849) 4 Cox CC 138   *53*
R v Hardie [1985] 1 WLR 64; [1984] 3 All ER 848   *64, 166, 172, 184*
Harding v Price [1948] 1 KB 695   *17*
Hardman and Others v Chief Constable of Avon and Somerset Constabulary [1986]
    Crim LR 330   *57, 151*
R v Harris (1987) 84 Cr App R 75   *130*
R v Harry [1974] Crim LR 32   *129, 134*
R v Harvey, Ulyett and Plummer (1980) 72 Cr App R 139   *129, 143*
Haughton v Smith [1975] AC 476   *28, 131, 158, 159, 161*
R v Hayward (1833) 6 C & P 157   *60*
R v Hennessy (1989) 89 Cr App R 10   *167*
R v Hensler (1870) 22 LT 691   *1, 86, 107*
R v Hill; R v Hall [1989] Crim LR 136   *152*
Hill v Baxter [1958] 1 QB 277   *14, 170*
R v Holden [1991] Crim LR 471   *93, 106*
R v Holland (1841) 2 Mood R 351   *70*
R v Howe [1987] AC 417; [1987] 2 WLR 568; [1987] 1 All ER 771; (1987) 85 Cr
    App R 32   *56, 168, 176, 182, 190*
R v Hudson and Taylor [1971] 2 QB 202   *55, 168, 175, 190*
R v Hunt [1977] Crim LR 740   *146*

R v Hurley and Murray [1967] VR 526   *55, 167, 175*
Hyam v DPP [1975] AC 55; [1974] 2 All ER 41   *8, 59*

Invicta Plastics v Clare [1976] RTR 251   *25, 37*
R v Ibrams and Gregory [1982] Crim LR 229; (1981) 74 Cr App R 154   *76*
R v Instan [1893] 1 QB 450   *2, 4*

JJC (a minor) v Eisenhower [1984] QB 331; (1983) The Times 3 May   *3, 30, 52, 54*
JM v Runeckles (1984) 79 Cr App R 255   *199*
R v Jackson [1983] Crim LR 617   *87*
Jaggard v Dickinson [1981] QB 527; [1981] 2 WLR 118; [1980] Crim LR 717   *81, 82, 146, 166*
R v Jakeman [1983] Crim LR 104   *173*
R v Jenkins [1983] 3 All ER 448; [1983] 1 All ER 100   *38*
Johnson v Youden [1950] 1 KB 544   *4, 96, 141, 183*
R v Johnson [1968] SASR 132   *81, 83*
Johnson v DPP [1994] Crim LR 672   *146, 147*
R v Jones [1987] Crim LR 123   *54*
R v Jones and Smith [1976] 3 All ER 54   *35, 87, 94, 111, 118, 124, 154*
R v Jordan (1956) 40 Cr App R 152   *70*

Kaitamaki v R [1985] AC 147   *20*
R v Kanwar [1982] 1 WLR 845   *130*
R v Kelly [1993] Crim LR 763   *88*
R v Kemp [1957] 1 QB 399; [1956] 3 All ER 249   *166, 170*
R v Khan [1985] RTR 365   *14*
R v Kimber [1983] 1 WLR 1118; [1983] 3 All ER 316   *20, 177*
R v King [1938] 2 All ER 662   *131*
R v King and Stockwell [1987] Crim LR 398   *92*
R v Kingston [1994] Crim LR 846 HL; [1993] 3 WLR 676 CA   *166, 168, 192*
R v Kohn (1979) 69 Cr App R 395   *98, 99*
R v Kovacs [1974] 1 All ER 1236; [1974] 1 WLR 370   *92, 93*

R v Lamb [1967] 2 QB 981; [1967] 2 All ER 1282   *40, 62*
R v Lambie [1981] 1 All ER 332   *86, 90*
R v Langford (1842) Car & M 602   *82*
R v Larsonneur (1933) 97 JP 206; (1933) 149 LT 542; (1933) 24 Cr App R 74   *7*
R v Latimer [1886–90] All ER 386; (1886) 17 QBD 359   *8, 23, 72*
R v Lawrence [1982] AC 510; [1981] 1 All ER 974; [1981] 2 WLR 524   *12, 13, 14, 61, 68*
Lawrence v Metropolitan Police Commissioner [1972] AC 626; [1971] 3 WLR 225; [1971] 2 All ER 1253   *85, 102, 105, 113, 119, 125, 135, 137*
R v Lawrence and Pomroy [1971] Crim LR 645   *143*
Laws v Eltringham (1881) 8 QBD   *148*
R v LeBrun [1991] 4 All ER 673   *2*
R v Letenock (1917) 12 Cr App R 221   *172*
R v Lipman [1970] 1 QB 152; [1969] 3 All ER 410   *171, 172*
Lloyd v DPP [1991] Crim LR 904   *146*

R *v* Lloyd and Ali [1985] 3 WLR 30   *86*
Logden *v* DPP [1976] Crim LR 121   *40, 57*
Low *v* Blease (1975) 119 Sol Jo 695   *109*
R *v* Lowe [1973] QB 702; [1973] 2 WLR 481; [1973] 1 All ER 805; [1973] Crim LR 238   *73*

McC *v* Runneckles [1984] Crim LR 499   *23, 133, 150, 165*
McCluskey *v* HM Advocate [1989] RTR 182   *68*
R *v* McDavitt [1981] Crim LR 843   *87, 104*
R *v* McDonough (1962) 47 Cr App R 37   *158*
R *v* McGill [1970] RTR 4   *130, 132*
R *v* M'Growther (1746) Fost 13   *55, 154*
R *v* McIvor [1982] 1 All ER 491; [1982] 1 WLR 409   *95*
R *v* M'Loughlin (1838) 8 C & P 635   *54*
M'Naghten's Case (1843) 10 Cl & F 200   *77, 166, 169, 172*
R *v* McNamara (1988) The Times 16 February   *17*
R *v* McPherson [1973] Crim LR 191   *113*
R *v* Madigan [1983] RTR 178   *14*
R *v* Malcherek and Steel [1981] 2 All ER 422; (1981) 73 Cr App R 173   *1, 70*
R *v* Manning and Rodgers (1871) 12 Cox CC 106; (1871) 25 LT 537   *121*
R *v* Marchant (1985) 80 Cr App R 361   *129–130*
R *v* Marcus [1981] 1 WLR 774; [1981] 2 All ER 833   *42, 49, 53, 185*
R *v* Marriott (1838) 8 C&P 425   *4*
R *v* Martin (1881) 8 QBD 54   *3, 23, 41, 75, 155, 163, 198*
R *v* Martin [1989] 1 All ER 652   *182*
R *v* Martindale [1986] 1 WLR 1042; [1986] 3 All ER 25   *17*
R *v* Mayers (1872) 12 Cox CC 311   *204*
R *v* Meade and Belt (1823) 1 Lew CC 184   *43, 57*
Metropolitan Police Commissioner *v* Caldwell [1982] AC 341; [1981] 2 WLR 509; [1981] 1 All ER 961   *5, 7, 8, 13, 15, 21, 22, 45, 57, 58, 69, 89, 147, 149, 151, 155, 173, 188, 185, 195, 196, 197, 199, 204*
Metropolitan Police Commissioner *v* Charles [1977] AC 177; [1976] 1 All ER 659; [1977] Crim LR 615   *86, 90, 105, 194*
R *v* Miller [1954] 2 QB 282; (1954) 38 Cr App R 1   *47, 184*
R *v* Miller [1983] 2 AC 161; [1983] 2 WLR 539; [1983] 1 All ER 978   *2, 14, 150*
R *v* Mills [1963] 1 All ER 202; [1963] 1 QB 522   *50*
R *v* Minor (1987) 52 JP 30   *130*
R *v* Mitchell [1983] QB 741; [1983] 2 WLR 938   *62*
R *v* Mohan [1975] 2 All ER 193   *157*
R *v* Moloney [1985] AC 905; [1985] 2 WLR 648; [1985] 1 All ER 1025   *8, 10, 59, 63, 65, 68, 71, 73, 75, 78, 79, 80, 82, 83, 148, 181*
Moriarty *v* Brooks (1834) 6 C&P 684   *54*
Morphitis *v* Salmon [1990] Crim LR 48; (1990) 154 JPN 186   *89, 146*
R *v* Morris [1984] AC 320; [1983] 3 WLR 697; [1983] 3 All ER 288   *4, 35, 85, 105, 112, 113, 118, 119, 124, 125, 135, 137, 138, 144*
R *v* Morrison (1988) The Times 12 November   *45, 69*
R *v* Mowatt [1968] 1 QB 421; [1967] 3 All ER 47   *23, 28, 48, 163, 185*
Moynes *v* Cooper [1956] 1 QB 439   *122, 125, 128*

R v Murphy [1980] QB 434; [1980] 2 All ER 325; (1980) 71 Cr App R 33   *12, 14*

Neal v Gribble [1978] RTR 409; (1977) 64 Cr App R 54   *130*
R v Nedrick [1986] 1 WLR 1025; [1986] 3 All ER 1; [1986] Crim LR 742   *8, 10,*
   59, 63, 65, 68, 71, 73, 75, 79, 80, 82, 83, 148, 181
R v Newell (1980) 71 Cr App R 331   *60, 64, 76*
R v Nicholls (1874) 13 Cox CC 75   *4*
R v Nkosiyana (1966) 4 SA 655   *56*

R v Oatridge [1992] Crim LR 205   *168, 192*
R v O'Connor [1991] Crim LR 135   *166*
R v O'Grady [1987] 3 WLR 321; [1987] 3 All ER 420; (1987) 85 Cr App R 315
   166, 178
R v O'Leary (1986) 82 Cr App R 341   *88*
R v Orpin [1980] 2 All ER 321   *15*
Oxford v Moss [1979] Crim LR 119   *85*

R v Page [1954] 1 QB 170; [1953] 3 WLR 895; [1953] 2 All ER 1355   *77*
R v Pagett (1983) 76 Cr App R 279   *66*
Palmer v R [1971] AC 814   *11, 67, 77, 168*
R v Parker [1993] Crim LR 856   *147*
R v Parmenter (1991) Cr App R 68; see also R v Savage; R v Parmenter   *50, 55,*
   57, 66
R v Peart [1970] 2 QB 672   *130, 132, 140*
R v Pembliton (1874) LR 2 CCR 119; (1874) 12 Cox CC 607   *23, 67*
Pharmaceutical Society of Great Britain v Logan [1982] Crim LR 443   *7*
R v Pigg [1982] 1 WLR 762; [1982] 2 All ER 591   *20*
R v Pitchley [1972] Crim LR 705   *130*
R v Pitham and Hehl (1976) 65 Cr App R 45   *143, 144*
R v Pittwood (1902) 19 TLR 37   *2*
R v Poulton (1832) 5 C&P 329   *77*
R v Price [1990] Crim LR 200; (1990) 90 Cr App R 409   *92, 96, 141*
Price v Cromack [1975] 1 WLR 988; [1975] 2 All ER 113   *54*

R v Quick and Paddison [1973] QB 910; [1973] 3 All ER 347   *167, 170, 171*

R v Rabey (1977) 37 CCC (2d) 461 (Ont)   *167*
Race Relations Board v Applin [1973] QB 815   *25, 35, 37, 56, 174, 188*
R v Rahman (1985) 81 Cr App R 349   *47*
Rance v Mid-Downs Health Authority (1990) 140 NLJ 325   *42*
R v Ransford (1874) 13 Cox CC 9   *37, 162*
R v Rashid [1977] 1 WLR 298; [1977] 2 All ER 237   *86, 96, 130, 142*
R v Raven [1982] Crim LR 51   *76*
Read v Coker (1853) 13 CB 850   *44*
R v Reid [1992] 3 All ER 673   *8, 14, 196*
Riley v DPP (1989) The Times 13 December   *179*
R v Ring (1892) 56 JP 552; (1892) 17 Cox CC 49   *159*
R v Roberts (1971) 56 Cr App R 95; (1971) 115 Sol Jo 809   *61, 185*
R v Roberts [1992] NLJ 1503   *26, 190*

R v Robinson [1977] Crim LR 173   *129, 138*
R v Rolfe (1952) 36 Cr App R 4   *46*
R v Rose (1884) 15 Cox CC 540   *45, 177*
R v Rothery [1976] RTR 550   *110*

R v Sainthouse [1980] Crim LR 506   *141, 145*
R v Sangha [1988] 2 All ER 385; [1988] Crim LR 371   *23*
R v Satnam [1983] 3 All ER 316   *204*
R v Saunders [1985] Crim LR 230   *48, 54, 80, 163, 184*
R v Savage; R v Parmenter [1991] 3 WLR 914 HL   *9, 10, 21, 23, 28, 41, 44, 46, 47, 48, 52, 55, 69, 74, 153, 155, 185, 191, 192, 197, 198, 201, 203*
R v Scarlett (1993) The Times 18 May   *44*
R v Scott [1967] VR 276   *170*
Scott v Metropolitan Police Commissioner [1975] AC 819   *27, 34*
Scott v Shepherd (1773) 2 Wm Bl 892   *40, 198*
Scudder v Barret [1979] 3 WLR 591   *123*
R v Senior [1899] 1 QB 283   *51*
R v Seymour [1983] 2 AC 493; [1983] Crim LR 742; 76 Cr App R 211   *63, 64*
R v Shannon (1980) 71 Cr App R 192   *11, 44, 76–77*
R v Shelton (1986) 83 Cr App R 379   *141*
R v Shendley [1970] Crim LR 49   *4*
R v Shepherd [1987] Crim LR 686; (1988) 86 Cr App R 47   *175*
R v Shivpuri [1987] AC 1; [1986] 2 WLR 988; [1986] 2 All ER 334   *28, 50, 123, 157, 160, 162*
R v Sibartie [1983] Crim LR 470   *32, 87*
Simpson v Peat [1952] 2 QB 24   *12, 13*
R v Slack [1989] 3 WLR 513   *28, 73*
Smedleys Ltd v Breed [1974] AC 839   *7*
R v Smith (1850) 1 Den 510   *130*
R v Smith [1959] 2 QB 35; [1959] 2 All ER 193   *1, 61, 70*
R v Smith [1961] AC 290   *21, 30, 47*
R v Smith [1974] QB 354; [1974] 1 All ER 632   *81, 82*
R v Smith and Jones [1976] 3 All ER 54   *136*
Southwark London Borough v Williams [1971] 2 All ER 175   *167, 181*
R v Spencer and Turner (1989) unreported   *96*
R v Spratt [1991] 2 All ER 210; (1990) 91 Cr App R 362   *57, 66*
R v Steane [1947] KB 997; [1947] 1 All ER 813   *55, 78*
R v Steer [1988] AC 111; [1987] 2 All ER 833; [1986] 3 All ER 611   *57, 199*
R v Stephenson [1979] QB 695   *22*
Stevens v Gourley (1859) 7 CBNS 99   *136*
R v Stewart (1982) The Times 14 December   *86*
R v Stokes [1982] Crim LR 695   *134*
R v Stone and Dobinson [1977] 1 QB 354; [1977] 2 All ER 341; [1977] Crim LR 166   *1, 4, 74*
R v Sullivan [1984] AC 156; [1983] 1 All ER 577   *167, 169*
Sweet v Parsley [1970] AC 132; [1969] 1 All ER 347   *7, 17, 18*

R v T [1990] Crim LR 256   *167*
R v Taaffe [1984] AC 539   *160, 162*

R v Tandy [1989] 1 WLR 350; [1989] 1 All ER 267; [1988] Crim LR 308   60,
172
R v Taylor (1869) LR 1 CCR 194   54
Thorne v Motor Trade Association [1937] AC 797   143
R v Thornton [1992] 1 All ER 306   60
R v Tolson (1889) 23 QBD 168   178
Treacy v DPP [1971] AC 537   129, 134
Troughton v Metropolitan Police Commissioner [1987] Crim LR 138   87
Tuberville v Savage (1669) 2 Keb 545; (1669) 1 Mod Rep 3   40, 43
R v Turner (No 2) (1971) 55 Cr App R 336   98

R v Valderrama-Vega [1985] Crim LR 220   167
R v Velumyl [1989] Crim LR 299   86, 140
R v Venna [1976] QB 421; [1975] 3 All ER 788; (1975) 61 Cr App R 310   3, 40,
44, 46, 57, 66, 112, 185, 191, 195, 198, 201, 203
R v Vickers [1957] 2 QB 664; [1957] 2 All ER 741   68, 78
R v Vinagre (1979) 69 Cr App R 104   60

W (a minor) v Dolbey [1983] Crim LR 681   3, 48, 66, 69, 75
R v Waites [1982] Crim LR 369   86
R v Walker [1962] Crim LR 458   36
R v Walker and Hayles (1990) 90 Cr App R 226   199
R v Walkington [1979] 2 All ER 716; (1978) 68 Cr App R 427   87, 118
R v Waltham (1849) 13 JP 183; (1849) 3 Cox CC 442   54
R v Wakeley and Others [1990] Crim LR 119   28
R v Ward [1987] Crim LR 338; (1987) 85 Cr App R 71   28
R v Waterfield [1964] 1 QB 164   48, 179
R v Welsh [1974] RTR 478   110
R v West (1848) 2 Cox CC 500   51
Westminster City Council v Croyalgrange [1986] 2 All ER 353   178
R v White [1910] 2 KB 124   1
R v Whitefield (1984) 79 Cr App R 36   26
R v Whitehouse [1977] QB 868; (1977) 65 Cr App R 33   56
Whittaker v Campbell [1984] QB 318; [1983] 3 WLR 676   130, 139
R v Whybrow (1951) 35 Cr App R 141   67, 163
R v Whyte [1987] 3 All ER 416   11, 44, 77, 180
R v Willer (1986) 83 Cr App R 225   167, 182
R v Williams [1983] 3 All ER 316   192
R v Williams (Gladstone) [1987] 3 All ER 411; [1984] Crim LR 163; (1984) 78 Cr
App R 276; [1983] 3 All ER 316   11, 44, 165, 168, 176, 178, 179, 195
Williams v Phillips (1957) 41 Cr App R 5   85
R v Wilson [1955] 1 All ER 744   40, 43
R v Wilson [1984] AC 242; [1983] 3 WLR 686   9, 21, 23, 41, 47, 48, 52, 54, 55,
75, 155
R v Windle [1952] 2 QB 826   170
R v Wood (1830) 4 C&P 381; 1 Mood. CC 278   54
R v Woodman [1974] 2 All ER 955   85
R v Woolven [1983] Crim LR 632   93

R *v* Wootton and Peake [1990] Crim LR 201   *93, 106*
Wrothwell (FJH) *v* Yorkshire Water Authority [1984] Crim LR 43   *7*

Yeandel *v* Fisher [1966] 1 QB 440   *17*
Yip Chiu Cheung *v* R [1994] Crim LR 824   *25, 26*

TABLE OF STATUTES

Abortion Act 1967   *42*
Accessories and Abettors Act 1861
   s8   *4, 26, 27, 28, 32, 56, 120, 176, 190*
Animals Act 1911
   s1(1)   *66*

Computer Misuse Act 1990   *97, 98, 99*
   s2   *98*
Criminal Attempts Act 1981   *28, 33, 107, 123, 158, 159, 160, 161*
   s1   *4, 27, 31, 33, 35, 67, 104, 117, 151, 157, 161, 174, 175, 198*
   s1(1)   *28, 111, 137, 158, 159, 161, 164*
   s1(2)   *27, 28, 33, 50, 117, 157, 158, 159, 160, 161, 162*
   s1(3)   *33, 93, 118, 161, 162*
   s5(1)   *159*
   s9   *155*
Criminal Damage Act 1971   *15, 22, 146, 147, 148, 149, 151, 155*
   s1   *13, 89, 90, 188, 195, 196, 199*
   s1(1)   *14, 15, 21, 22, 57, 82, 148, 149, 150, 151, 173, 184*
   s1(1)(b)   *22*
   s1(2)   *14, 15, 21, 22, 57, 149, 150, 155, 173, 188, 199*
   s1(3)   *14, 147, 149, 188*
   s3   *13, 147, 150, 151, 152*
   s5   *151*
   s5(2)   *148, 152, 167*
   s5(2)(a)   *146*
   s5(2)(b)   *146, 152*
   s5(3)   *146, 152*
   s10(1)   *146, 148, 181*
   s10(2)   *146, 148*
   s27   *147*
Criminal Justice Act 1967
   s8   *63, 78, 80*
   s91   *81, 82*
Criminal Justice Act 1987
   s12   *34*
Criminal Justice Act 1991
   s1(2)(b)   *156*
Criminal Law Act 1967
   s1   *50, 56*
   s3   *9, 10, 11, 31, 42, 43, 44, 45, 65, 67, 74, 76, 168, 179, 180, 183, 184*
Criminal Law Act 1977   *27, 35, 38, 133*
   s1   *25, 27, 29, 31, 36, 133, 200*
   s1(1)   *27, 29, 33, 37, 159, 164*
   s1(1)(a)   *163*
   s1(1)(b)   *25*
   s2(2)(c)   *36*

Criminal Law Act 1977 (continued)
    s5   *37*
    s5(7)   *35, 163, 164*
    s16   *174*
    s54   *158*
Criminal Procedure (Insanity) Act 1964
    s1   *170*

Family Allowance Act 1945
    s9(b)   *37*
Firearms Act 1968   *53*
    s5(1)(b)   *7, 17*

Homicide Act 1957
    s2   *10, 60, 76*
    s3   *60, 75–76, 76*
Human Tissue Act 1961   *110*

Infant Life (Preservation) Act 1929   *42*
    s1   *51*
    s1(1)   *51*

Misuse of Drugs Act 1971   *17, 18, 161*
    s5(3)   *6*

Offences Against the Person Act 1861   *9, 41, 52, 53, 74, 112*
    s18   *3, 4, 5, 10, 14, 20, 21, 23, 27, 28, 29, 30, 38, 41, 42, 43, 44, 48, 49, 50, 52, 54, 55, 65, 66, 67, 68, 69, 70, 71, 72, 83, 110, 155, 163, 174, 175, 183, 184, 192, 197, 198, 201*
    s20   *3, 4, 5, 7, 9, 10, 13, 14, 20, 21, 23, 27, 28, 29, 30, 38, 41, 43, 44, 46, 47, 48, 49, 50, 52, 53, 54, 55, 58, 65, 66, 69, 71, 72, 74, 75, 110, 153, 155, 163, 183, 184, 192, 197, 201*
    s23   *42, 49, 50, 51, 53, 185, 198, 199*
    s24   *42, 49, 50, 51, 53, 185, 198, 199*
    s47   *3, 4, 5, 9, 10, 13, 20, 29, 41, 43, 44, 45, 46, 47, 49, 50, 52, 54, 55, 57, 58, 65, 66, 69, 71, 72, 74, 75, 179, 183, 184, 191, 192, 198, 201, 203*
    s58   *42, 49, 50, 51*
    s59   *49, 50*

Police Act 1964
    s51   *42, 48, 177, 179*
    s51(2)   *48, 179*
Police and Criminal Evidence Act 1984
    s24   *67*
Public Order Act 1986   *36*

Regulation of Railways Act 1889
    s5(3)(a)   *32*

Road Traffic Act 1972
  s1   *61, 63*
  s9   *110*
Road Traffic Act 1988   *13*
  s1   *61, 63, 68*
  s2   *11, 12, 13, 68*
  s3   *11, 12, 13, 14*
  s4   *7*
  s5   *157*
  s22A   *24*
  s170   *2*
Road Traffic Act 1991   *12, 63, 163*

Sexual Offences Act 1956   *204*
  s1   *20, 204*
  s14   *83*
Sexual Offences Act 1985   *83*
Suicide Act 1961   *49, 51*

Theft Act 1968   *85, 91, 92, 97, 101, 106, 109, 146*
  ss1–7   *91, 95, 100, 103, 109, 142*
  s1   *3, 4, 30, 33, 35, 86, 89, 90, 91, 93, 95, 96, 97, 100, 102, 104, 105, 106, 107, 108, 109, 112, 113, 114, 115, 116, 117, 119, 122, 129, 132, 135, 138, 140, 142, 143, 189, 193, 194*
  s1(1)   *98, 144*
  s2   *92, 93, 94, 95, 101, 102, 106, 108, 109, 114, 117, 118, 122, 124, 140, 141, 153*
  s2(1)   *137*
  s2(1)(a)   *85, 98, 125, 128, 138, 194*
  s2(1)(b)   *85, 127, 154*
  s2(1)(c)   *85*
  s3   *4, 35, 96, 108, 112, 113, 114, 115, 116*
  s3(1)   *101, 105, 120, 124, 137, 144*
  s4   *102, 122*
  s4(1)   *85, 98, 109, 124*
  s4(4)   *114*
  s5   *116*
  s5(1)   *85, 98, 108, 110, 113, 114, 115, 117, 120, 122, 124*
  s5(3)   *85, 91, 110*
  s5(4)   *95, 96, 105, 106, 108, 113, 114, 117, 120, 122, 123, 125, 126, 127, 128*
  s6   *101, 106*
  s6(1)   *86, 92, 101, 140, 154*
  s8   *3, 4, 30, 112, 129, 134, 135, 138, 139, 142, 201*
  s9   *31, 33, 81, 82, 91, 93, 100, 107, 108, 124*
  s9(1)(a)   *6, 33, 34, 35, 37, 38, 87, 88, 94, 100, 111, 112, 117, 118, 121, 122, 127, 136, 194, 200, 201, 204*
  s9(1)(b)   *33, 34, 35, 37, 38, 83, 87, 88, 100, 109, 111, 112, 117, 118, 127, 136, 137, 154, 201*
  s10   *201*

Theft Act 1968 (continued)
  s11   *111, 130*
  s12   *11, 126, 127, 128, 129, 132, 133, 138, 139, 141*
  s12(1)   *126, 140*
  s12(3)   *142*
  s12(6)   *11, 12, 127, 133, 140, 142*
  s15   *86, 90, 91, 92, 95, 96, 98, 100, 102, 103, 104, 105, 117, 119, 126, 132, 134, 135, 136, 194*
  s15(1)   *99*
  s15(2)   *86*
  s15(4)   *32, 86, 92, 93, 96, 101, 102, 104, 105, 107, 113, 115, 119, 135, 139, 194*
  s16   *86, 91, 93*
  s16(1)   *93, 99, 113, 114*
  s16(2)   *99, 113, 114, 115*
  s16(2)(b)   *93*
  s17   *99, 117, 119*
  s17(1)(a)   *98*
  s21   *129, 134, 135, 142, 143, 153, 201*
  s22   *90, 97, 140, 141, 189, 193, 194*
  s22(1)   *99, 144, 145*
  s24   *194*
  s24(2)   *131, 141*
  s24(3)   *158*
  s25   *123, 130, 140, 142*
  s28   *98, 99*
  s30(1)   *92*
  s32   *194*
Theft Act 1978   *85, 91, 92, 97, 101, 146*
  s1   *31, 32, 86, 91, 93, 100, 101, 102, 107, 127, 132, 133, 138, 139*
  s1(1)   *93, 98, 99, 139*
  s1(2)   *32, 93, 101, 107, 139*
  s2   *31, 32, 102, 103, 105, 107, 115, 116*
  s2(1)   *86, 87, 102*
  s2(1)(a)   *32, 87, 102*
  s2(1)(b)   *32, 87, 102, 105*
  s2(1)(c)   *32, 87, 107, 127*
  s2(3)   *87*
  s3   *87, 89, 100, 101, 102, 103, 104, 115, 116, 127, 137*
  s3(1)   *137*

1 CRIMINAL CONDUCT

1.1   Introduction

1.2   Key points

1.3   Recent cases

1.4   Analysis of questions

1.5   Question

1.1 Introduction

In most offences, certainly the more serious ones, there is a requirement that the accused has voluntarily brought about the proscribed consequences or/and circumstances and in doing so his 'actions' may be positive and deliberate, or they may take the form of an omission.

The acts/omission to act, together with the required consequences or/and circumstances make up the 'actus reus' or criminal conduct element of the offence.

In all cases there must be a causal link 'joining' the accused to the 'conduct' and the consequences/circumstances.

1.2 Key points

The following points must be understood.

a) *Acts and omissions*

   The accused must voluntarily act or pursue a course of conduct which brings about the proscribed consequences/circumstances. If what he does fails to bring those consequences/circumstances about, there is no actus reus (although there may be a charge of attempt): *R v Hensler* (1870) 22 LT 691; *R v White* [1910] 2 KB 124.

   If the accused's conduct initiates a sequence of events which are overtaken by a subsequent supervening event, then he has not caused the circumstances/consequences that follow that event and they cannot form part of the actus reus: *R v Smith* [1959] 2 QB 35; *R v Blaue* [1975] 3 All ER 446; *R v Malcherek and Steel* [1981] 2 All ER 422. The accused's acts need not be the sole cause of the proscribed result (for example, death or serious injury), it being sufficient if the accused's acts contribute significantly to that result: *R v Cheshire* [1991] 3 All ER 670.

   Although generally a failure by the accused to act will not be sufficient to establish the actus reus for an offence, there are occasions where an omission will suffice:

   i)   where the accused's relationship with another imposes a duty to act, eg parent-child (*R v Gibbens and Proctor* (1918) 13 Cr App R 134) or where an accused has taken it upon himself to look after another: *R v Stone and Dobinson* [1977] 1 QB 354;

1

ii) where the accused has a duty by virtue of his office to act (eg police officer): *R* v *Dytham* [1979] QB 722;

iii) where a statute imposes such a duty eg the duty to stop after a road traffic accident (RTA 1988 s170) or where the accused is under a contractual duty (eg by virtue of his terms of employment: *R* v *Pittwood* (1902) 19 TLR 37) or other agreement: *R* v *Instan* [1893] 1 QB 450;

iv) where a subsequent duty follows the accused's actions eg where he accidentally set fire to a room and, on realising what he had done went to sleep elsewhere and omitted to put the fire out: *R* v *Miller* [1983] 2 AC 161.

b) Cases of strict liability and involuntary conduct are dealt with in later chapters.

c) *Coincidence of actus reus and mens rea*

As a general rule the accused must commit the act or omission at the same time as he has the requisite mens rea. Thus, an acused who knocks a victim unconscious and then, wrongly believing her to be dead, throws her in the river where she drowns would apparently not be guilty of murder because at the time of doing the act which actually caused death the accused no longer intended to kill since he believed his victim to be already dead. The obvious injustice of this rule has been avoided by use of the 'continuing act' doctrine where all of the accused's acts are seen as part of a series of acts, it being sufficient if he had the requisite mens rea *at any stage* in that series: see *R* v *Church* [1966] 1 QB 59 and *R* v *LeBrun* [1991] 4 All ER 673.

1.3 Recent cases

Airedale NHS Trust v *Bland* [1993] 1 All ER 821 – the House of Lords confirmed that a doctor who did a positive act to acelerate the death of a patient would be guilty of murder no matter how good his motives were. However, it was judicially confirmed for the first time in English criminal law that a doctor may withhold life-saving treatment, allowing a patient to die of natural causes, without being exposed to a charge of murder, providing the doctor did not 'breach his duty to the patient'.

1.4 Analysis of questions

As the concept of actus reus is crucial to all criminal offences in assessing liability, almost every question will, to some degree, involve an examination of the required elements. The question that follows enables students to concentrate primarily on the criminal liability of the actors.

1.5 Question

K was attacked in a street by a group of youths. L, who was the leader, caused K to be thrown to the ground where several of the gang kicked him until he became unconscious. They then left the scene. Whilst K was on the ground M passed by and removed K's wallet to see if there was anything worth stealing. M took five pounds from the wallet and kicked K twice before leaving causing severe bruising. N who was next to pass the scene saw that K was seriously ill but did nothing, deciding that he did not want to become involved. O, a doctor, also passed by without rendering assistance. P finally came over to K's aid but because of his inexperience in such matters, he moved K which in turn caused K's internal injuries to become severe.

Advise the parties of their criminal liability.

University of London LLB Examination
(for External Students) Criminal Law June 1987 Q4

General Comment

Although primarily concerned with the offences of assault and theft, this question is a good illustration of some of the different types of mens rea in criminal law.

It is a complicated question involving a number of parties and students should take care not to get bogged down in generalities.

Skeleton Solution

L   Meaning of cause – assault, incitement, accomplice.

Youths Sections 47, 20, 18 OAP 1861 – causation.

M   Section 1 TA, s8 TA and ss47, 20, 18.

N   Causation, assault, omission.

Suggested Solution

Mens rea need be shown as to the consequences of actual bodily harm *R* v *Venna* (1975).

Section 20 Offences Against the Person Act 1861 provides that it is an offence unlawfully and maliciously to wound or inflict any grievous bodily harm upon any person. There is nothing to indicate that K has suffered a wound – which requires a break in the external skin: *JJC* v *Eisenhower* (1983). However it seems likely that there has been an 'infliction' of grievous bodily harm. 'Grievous bodily harm' means 'really serious bodily harm': *DPP* v *Smith* (1961). In order to inflict such harm there must be an assault of some kind, ie a use of force against the victim. In *R* v *Clarence* (1888) it was stated that the force had to be directly applied. However, in *R* v *Martin* (1881) an indirect assault was allowed.

The mens rea for s20 requires not only that the accused is intentional or reckless as to the act. In addition he must foresee the possibility of at least a little harm: *W* v *Dolbey* (1983).

Section 18 OAP 1861 contains the offence of wounding or causing any grievous bodily harm with intent to do grievous bodily harm. This is obviously the most serious of the assaults and it has a very high mens rea. Intention to do grievous bodily harm is required and recklessness will not suffice: *R* v *Belfon* (1976). On the facts in question there is nothing to indicate this high mens rea is satisfied.

The youths who performed the assaults would be the principal offenders as they are closest to the performance of the actus reus. Sections 47 and 20 are the most likely offences but it must be recalled that s20 requires a higher mens rea than s47. L would be an accomplice to these offences.

An aider and abettor is a person present assisting or encouraging at the scene of the offence: *R* v *Coney* (1882); *R* v *Clarkson* (1971). He must have full knowledge of the circumstances of the offence: *Johnson* v *Youden* (1950).

Section 8 of the Accessories and Abettors Act 1861 provides that for the purposes of trial and punishment accomplices are to be treated as principal offenders.

When M removes K's wallet to see if there is anything worth stealing he may commit an attempted theft. Section 1 Theft Act 1968 provides that theft is committed where an accused dishonestly appropriates property belonging to another with intention to permanently deprive the other of it.

In order to establish attempted theft the prosecution must show that M has done an act 'more than merely preparatory' (s1 Criminal Attempts Act 1981) with full mens rea. M takes the wallet to see if there is anything worth stealing. This is an example of 'conditional intention'. Provided the indictment is drafted broadly without reference to particular items, eg M attempted to steal from the contents of the wallet, the mens rea for attempted theft will be satisfied. In practice as M proceeds to the full offence it is unlikely the prosecution would pursue an attempted charge.

The full offence will be complete when M removes £5 from the wallet – at that time there is an assumption of the rights of an owner (s3 TA 1968) and this would amount to an appropriation. It is undoubtedly an act by way of adverse interference with or usurpation of an owner's rights: *R* v *Morris* (1983). There seems no doubt that the mens rea is satisfied. He has an intention to permanently deprive and he is clearly dishonest. Were there to be any difficulties in relation to dishonesty the jury should be directed in line with: *R* v *Ghosh* (1982). After he has stolen M kicks K twice causing severe bruising. At that point M commits an assault either under s47, s20 or possibly s18, depending on mens rea. The offences have already been outlined and on the assumption that the bruising amounts to grievous bodily harm M's criminal liability would depend on how high is mens rea.

It should be noted that he is not liable for robbery. Section 8 Theft Act 1968 provides that a person commits robbery if he steals and immediately before, or at the time and in order to do so he uses force on any person or puts any person in fear of being then and there subjected to force. M undoubtedly uses force. However this occurs after the theft is complete. Even allowing for the prosecution to argue that there is a continuing actus reus (*R* v *Hale* (1978)) it could still not amount to robbery as the force used is gratuitous force and not force in order to steal: *R* v *Shendley* (1970).

Omission:

N would appear to have no liability in this matter. Undoubtedly certain crimes may be committed by omission. But there can be no liability by this means unless there is a duty to act in law. In these circumstances N has no duty to act in law and therefore would have no liability. It should be noted in relation to matters already discussed that an assault cannot be performed by omission. It must invariably take place by means of a positive act: *Fagan* v *MPC* (1969).

N was under no legal liability to help K. Where English criminal law does impose a duty to act, there must be a close relationship ie family, a business or similar: *R* v *Marriott* (1838); *R* v *Nicholls* (1874); *R* v *Instan* (1893); *R* v *Stone and Dobinson* (1977); *R* v *Dalby* (1982).

Similarly, O would not be liable unless he stood in such a special relationship to K (ie his family doctor). He has a moral duty to act but, in these circumstances that is not automatically translated into a duty under criminal law.

One could argue, on the lines of *R* v *Dytham* (1979) where a police officer was determined to be liable, virtute officii, to intervene and stop an assault, that O has a similar duty to act by virtue of his 'office' in which case his omission would be sufficient to attract liability.

Causation:

When P moves K causing his internal injuries to become severe, he would not become liable in criminal law. There are two main reasons for taking this view. Firstly as a matter of law he would not be regarded as the *legal* cause of the injuries. The chain of causation will not be broken in these circumstances – P would be regarded as an innocent or non-responsible intervener. Where such a person intervenes by an act instinctively done to assist someone he would not break the chain of causation and the harm resulting would not be in law attributable to him but rather to those who started the chain of causation. Furthermore the offences contained in s47, s20, and s18 are crimes of maliciousness and from the facts patently P is not acting in a malicious manner. It would not be sufficient mens rea to allege that P is reckless. Although recklessness may be sufficient mens rea for s47 it is *Cunningham* recklessness and not *Caldwell* recklessness that must be established. On the facts this is not shown.

2 STATE OF MIND

2.1   Introduction

2.2   Key points

2.3   Recent cases and statutes

2.4   Analysis of questions

2.5   Questions

2.1 Introduction

It is a fundamental rule of our criminal law that a man cannot be guilty by his actions unless he also has a guilty mind – '*actus non facit reum nisi mens sit rea*'.

The idea of a 'guilty' mind is not entirely accurate and the required 'state of mind' is a more appropriate way of regarding mens rea.

The requirement for mens rea is subject to some exceptions, notably negligence and strict liability. Furthermore, it is of paramount importance that the actus reus and the required mens rea be shown to have coincided.

2.2 Key points

a)   Traditionally, offences are categorised by the extent of mens rea required for their commission, with those involving a very high degree of mens rea (and therefore being more difficult to prove) including crimes of ulterior or specific intent.

b)   Crimes of general or basic intent require a lesser degree of mens rea, and those crimes which may be committed by negligence even less so.

Finally there are those crimes which may be committed with no 'guilty knowledge' or negligence at all, ie crimes of absolute and strict liability.

   i)   Specific intent crimes require proof of a particular specific intention in the mind of the accused when he acted (eg an intention to kill or cause serious injury for murder).

   Ulterior intent crimes require proof of an intention to do something in addition to the initial actus reus, eg burglary under s9(1)(a) Theft Act 1968 – entering a building as a trespasser with intent to go on to commit further offences therein (rape, steal, inflict gbh, cause damage). Similarly possessing a controlled drug with intent to supply, contrary to s5(3) Misuse of Drugs Act 1971, requires proof of this ulterior intent.

   ii)   Crimes of basic or general intent require proof of mens rea but not a particular 'intention'. They cannot be committed by negligence but, in contrast to crimes of specific intent, recklessness may suffice to prove their commission.

   iii)   Crimes of negligence are almost all statutory in origin, except manslaughter (which may be committed by gross disregard for life), examples of which are driving without due care and attention: s4 RTA 1988, or failing to exercise proper control of a dog.

iv) Crimes of absolute and strict liability: absolute liability is a concept generally at variance with our legal system and is committed by a proscribed 'state of affairs': *R v Larsonneur* (1933) 24 Cr App R 74 and the offences it covers are rare. Strictly liability is less extreme and, unlike absolute liability, general recognised defences (eg automatism) are applicable.

Strict liability offences include – quasi-criminal offences: *Smedleys Ltd v Breed* [1974] AC 839; *Pharmaceutical Society of Great Britain v Logan* [1982] Crim LR 443 and offences aimed at regulating public nuisance: *Alphacell v Woodward* [1972] AC 824, *FJH Wrothwell v Yorkshire Water Authority* [1984] Crim LR 43.

There is also a trend towards strict liability in interpreting statutes which seek to penalize acts that pose a grave social danger: *Gammon (Hong Kong) Ltd v Attorney-General for Hong Kong* [1985] AC 1; *R v Bradish* [1990] Crim LR 723 – possesion of 'prohibited weapon' s5(1)(b) Firearms Act 1968 – no mens rea required.

Note however the presumption against such a construction: *Sweet v Parsley* [1970] AC 132, albeit a rebuttable one.

c) In addition to intention and negligence there is the complicated and very examinable area of 'recklessness', the third aspect of mens rea. Recklessness is insufficient mens rea for the specific and ulterior intent crimes. It is, however, sufficient to prove offences requiring basic intent and negligence.

The two leading cases in this area **must** be known: *R v Cunningham* [1957] 2 QB 396 and *MPC v Caldwell* [1982] AC 341.

Cunningham recklessness requires the conscious taking of a risk. Thus when answering a question involving *Cunningham* recklessness (eg recklessly inflicting grievous bodily harm contrary to s20 of the Offences Against the Person Act 1861) a student should discuss two issues. Firstly, was the accused reckless? – a mere accident is insufficient, the accused must have taken an unjustifiable risk of causing injury. Secondly, did the accused at the time of the act or omission *foresee* the harm or damage charged.

The main difference between *Caldwell* recklessness and *Cunningham* recklessness is that the former does not require that the accused foresee any harm or damage at all. *Caldwell* recklessness is therefore largely (although not totally) objective in nature. When analysing an accused's liability under *Caldwell* recklessness a student should discuss the following two issues. Firstly was the risk of the harm or damage charged so great that it would have been obvious to a reasonable and prudent person? Secondly, what was the accused's state of mind? An accused will be convicted if (i) he foresaw the risk but went ahead to take it anyway, or (ii) he never thought about the possibility of there being any risk in the first place.

When discussing *Caldwell* recklessness students should be aware of the 'lacuna'. The lacuna is the 'gap' between the two states of mind mentioned in the second limb of the *Caldwell* test above. A person may fall within the lacuna in two circumstances: if they have considered that there may be a risk but believe (wrongly) that they have taken adequate precautions to eliminate it, or if they *have* considered the possibility of there being a risk but have erroneously concluded that there is no such risk. Such a person does not fall under the first limb of *Caldwell* recklessness because they believe that there is no risk or that they have eliminated the risk. Neither do they fall under the second limb because they have addressed their mind to the possibility that there may be a risk.

The law is unclear whether a person falling under the lacuna falls within the ambit of *Caldwell* recklessness and may be convicted. However, the cases of *Chief Constable of Avon and Somerset* v *Shimmen* (1986) 84 Cr App R 7 and *R* v *Reid* [1992] 3 All ER 673 indicate (obiter) that a person falling under the lacuna falls outside the ambit of *Caldwell* recklessness and may be acquitted.

d) Intention is a mens rea required of many crimes (such as murder or intentionally causing grievous bodily harm) but has proved elusive of a clear and precise definition.

One thing is now clear; foresight is *not* the same as intention. Therefore, for example, the fact that the accused merely foresaw that his act would kill would be insufficient to sustain a conviction for murder: *R* v *Moloney* [1985] AC 905, overruling *Hyam* v *DPP* [1975] AC 55.

It should be noted that *R* v *Hancock and Shankland* [1986] AC 455 and *R* v *Nedrick* [1986] 1 WLR 1025 do not overrule *Moloney* but clarify the direction which a judge may give to a jury on the *evidential* role of foresight. Under *Hancock* and *Nedrick* a judge may direct a jury that they may infer that the accused intended to kill if the jury believe:

i)   that death was a 'virtually certain consequence of the accused's actions'; and

ii) that the accused was aware that death was a virtually certain consequence.

e) *Transferred malice*

If D's intention to bring about a particular result is directed at a particular target (A) but D accidentally misses and damages target (B), D's intention directed at target A may be transferred to target B. This is known as the doctrine of transferred malice: see *R* v *Latimer* [1886–90] All ER 386. However, note that the consequence of the crime intended must be the same as that of the crime actually caused. Thus transferred malice would secure a conviction for murder where D shoots at A intending to kill but misses and kills B instead, but would not secure a conviction for criminal damage where D shot at A and missed smashing a window (although D may be guilty of recklessly causing criminal damage).

2.3   Recent cases and statutes

There have been no major recent developments in this area.

2.4 Analysis of questions

As with actus reus, all questions will necessarily involve a consideration the relevant state of mind of the accused. There are frequently questions that specifically test the very important areas of intention in relation to murder, and recklessness in its recognised forms. Students are also required to show what category of mens rea will be required by different classes of offence eg recklessness and crimes of basic intent. Occasionally there will be essay questions on eg the rationale behind strict liability.

2.5 Questions

QUESTION ONE

U, who was 22 years but with a mental age of 10 years, was playing in the playground when a fellow pupil, V, shouted abuse at him. U lost his temper and pushed V to the ground. V, who had a thin skull, was concussed by the fall. X, who was U's best friend, tried to pull U away from V whom U was trying to kick. W, a schoolmaster, came on the scene and, misunderstanding what was going on, pulled X off U. Released, U ran and kicked V on the ground.

Advise the parties of their criminal liability on the basis that V had died as a result of concussion and internal injuries.

University of London LLB Examination
(for External Students) Criminal Law June 1987 Q7

General Comment

A good question to tackle. Core elements of the syllabus were examined and all the main aspects were easily recognisable on the facts.

Skeleton Solution

U   assault – s47, s20 OAP 1861 – causation – murder; diminished responsibility; constructive manslaughter.

X   battery – lack of MR – accomplice role – s3 CLA 1967.

W   assault – s3 CLA 1967 – mistake.

Suggested Solution

When U pushes V to the ground and thereafter kicks him he may commit a number of assaults contrary to the Offences Against the Person Act 1861.

Section 47 OAP 1861 provides that it will be an offence to assault occasioning actual bodily harm. 'Actual bodily harm' was defined in R v Chan-Fook (1994) as 'any injury which is more than trivial'. In R v Savage; R v Parmenter (1991) the House of Lords held that the only mens rea required for the s47 offence is that necessary for the assault, and that no mens rea is required as to the actual bodily harm caused. Consequently, by pushing V to the ground and causing him to suffer concussion, U may be guilty of the s47 offence even though he did not intend or foresee that V would be injured by the push.

Section 20 OAP 1861 provides that it is an offence to unlawfully wound or inflict grievous bodily harm. 'Grievous bodily harm' means really serious bodily harm. It was established by the House of Lords in R v Wilson (1984) that although the word 'inflict' as used in s20 does not require an assault, it connotes a narrower meaning

9

than 'cause' as used in s18 in that the former requires the direct application of force. By kicking and pushing V this condition would appear to be met. In *R* v *Savage*; *R* v *Parmenter* (1991) the House of Lords held that in order to secure a conviction under s20 the accused must foresee that he will cause at least some harm, although he need not foresee that he will cause wounding or grievous bodily harm. Although this test is subjective, it is submitted that by kicking V, U must have foreseen that he would cause some harm to V.

Both s47 and s20 are 'result crimes', that is crimes where a consequence must be shown as part of the actus reus. V who had a thin skull was concussed by the fall. In order to establish the actus reus of either s47 or s20 it must be shown that U is the legal cause of the injury sustained by V. However U must take his victim as he finds him, *R* v *Blaue* (1975), and therefore the chain of causation will not be broken because of the victim's special characteristic of a thin skull.

The victim dies as a result of concussion and internal injuries. V's possible liability for murder must be considered. In order to establish this as a very serious offence it must be shown that U is the legal cause of V's death. Furthermore it must be shown that U had the necessary mens rea for murder at the time of the actus reus. The mens rea for murder is very high. The prosecution would have to establish that U killed V intending to kill or intending to do grievous bodily harm. 'Intention' includes both desiring to kill or do grievous bodily harm (direct intent) or knowing that death or grievous bodily harm is certain or virtually certain to occur (oblique intent). Where the prosecution rely on oblique intent it is not sufficient to establish the accused foresaw the result as highly probable. While this may be useful as evidence it is no more than that. Foresight is not to be equated with intention. A jury should be directed that they are not entitled to infer the necessary intention unless they are satisfied that death or grievous bodily harm was virtually certain as a result of the defendant's actions *and* the defendant appreciated that this was the case *R* v *Moloney* (1985); *R* v *Hancock and Shankland* (1986); *R* v *Nedrick* (1986).

On the facts in question there seems little doubt that U is the legal cause of death. If he has intention to kill or intention to do grievous bodily harm at any time when the actus reus is continuing he may be liable for murder.

The statutory defence of diminished responsibility under s2 Homicide Act 1957 may be available. Section 2 provides that where a person kills he shall not be convicted of murder if he was suffering from such abnormality of mind (whether arising from arrested or retarded development or any inherent causes or induced by disease or injury) as substantially impaired his responsibility. Thus murder will be reduced to voluntary manslaughter. On the facts in question this may well be available.

If U lacked mens rea for murder he could be liable for constructive manslaughter. This is established where a person kills as a result of an unlawful act – in this case one of the assaults. Furthermore in addition to an intention to do the unlawful act it must be shown that a reasonable man would foresee the possibility of at least a little harm from the act. *DPP* v *Newbury* (1976).

X has no criminal responsibility on the facts as given. Undoubtedly he uses force against U when pulling him away and this could amount to a common law battery – a direct use of force, intentionally or recklessly committed. However, under s3 Criminal Law Act 1967, a person may use reasonable force in the prevention of a crime. It must be established that X was acting defensively and not aggressively: *R* v *Shannon* (1980). The question of whether the force used was reasonable must be considered by reference to the circumstances the accused found himself in: *Palmer* v *R* (1971); *R* v *Whyte* (1987). There seems little doubt on the facts that this would be available to X as a defence.

A similar approach should be adopted in considering any liability W may have. Undoubtedly he may commit a common law battery when he pulls X off U. However, W's position is complicated because of his mistake. He believed wrongly that X was the aggressor. He will still be able to claim s3 Criminal Law Act 1967 as a defence providing the mistake was honest. In *DPP* v *Morgan* (1975) the House of Lords confirmed that an honest mistake, whether or not it was reasonable, enabled an accused to be judged on the facts as he believed them to be. In *Albert* v *Lavin* (1981) the Divisional Court considered that a mistake in relation to a defence had to be both honest and reasonable before an accused could be judged on the facts as he believed them to be but in *R* v *Williams* (1984) that approach was disapproved of and *DPP* v *Morgan* was applied. Following the Privy Council decision in *Beckford* v *R* (1987), provided W's mistaken belief is honestly held, he will have a defence.

QUESTION TWO

Jane, a young mother, noticed that her child was extremely white and covered in perspiration. Realising that the child was very ill, she picked up the baby and ran outside. She saw an unlocked car parked with its ignition key in it, placed her baby in the car and drove off to hospital. She drove through a red traffic signal. When she arrived at the hospital she discovered that her child was dead.

Discuss Jane's criminal liability.

University of London LLB Examination
(for External Students) Criminal Law June 1981 Q2

General Comment

The question centres around the mens rea required for the offences of taking a conveyance and reckless or careless driving.

Skeleton Solution

Section 12 TA 1968 – 'belief': s12(6) – ss2 and 3 RTA 1988.

Suggested Solution

Jane may have committed an offence of taking a conveyance without the owner's consent or other lawful authority contrary to s12 of the Theft Act 1968.

There is no requirement for her to have an intention 'permanently to deprive' as there is in the offence of theft. All that is required is a 'taking' of the vehicle – completed when she moves it: *R* v *Bogacki* (1973) for her use as a conveyance: *R* v *Bow* (1976). She does not appear to have the consent of the owner, neither can she point any lawful authority for the taking of the car.

However, Jane may be able to avail herself of the provisions of s12(6) of the Act if she can show that she believed that the owner would have consented had he known of the taking and of the circumstances. Given the nature of her urgent need of the conveyance Jane would very likely be able to show that she had such subjective belief.

Jane may have committed a further offence contrary to s3 of the Road Traffic Act 1988 (as amended by the Road Traffic Act 1991) by driving without due care and attention. Alternatively, she may have committed an offence contrary to s2 of the Road Traffic Act 1988 of driving recklessly.

Section 3 contains the lesser offence and is an example of a crime where the mens rea required is that of negligence ie an objective standard. The court has to consider whether the accused was exercising that degree of care and attention that a reasonable and prudent driver would exercise in the circumstances: *Simpson* v *Peat* (1952).

The more serious offence of driving recklessly has been considered by the House of Lords in *R* v *Lawrence* (1981), where it was held that mens rea is required in the offence of driving recklessly and that the mental element required is that, before adopting a manner of driving that in fact involves an obvious and serious risk of causing physical injury to another person using the road, or of doing substantial damage to property, the driver has failed to give any thought to the possibility of there being such a risk, or, having recognised that there was some risk involved, has gone on nonetheless to take it. The House of Lords considered the case of *R* v *Murphy* (1980) was defective in certain respects in that it referred to 'due care and attention' which lowered the standard of care to that of the less serious offence contained in s3 of the Act. Once the 1991 Road Traffic Act comes into force, Jane's driving will be judged against that of a careful and competent motorist in order to determine whether such driving was dangerous.

Jane will not be able to claim a general defence to the offences shown on the basis of the necessity of her situation. The defence of necessity is not one recognised in English law. Lord Denning stated an opinion in *Buckoke* v *GLC* (1971) that the driver of a fire engine who crossed a red light to rescue someone in a blazing house would commit an offence although, in his view the man should be congratulated and not prosecuted. Similarly in *Brown* v *Dyerson* (1969) it was held that a medical emergency was not a defence to a charge of driving with excessive blood alcohol.

However, Jane may claim duress of circumstances caused by the threat of death/serious injury to her child: *R* v *Conway* (1988). (See chapter 10.)

QUESTION THREE

Dan was driving one afternoon and felt increasingly drowsy. He fell asleep and his car mounted the pavement, crashed into a wall and trapped a young boy against the wall, seriously injuring him. The crash woke Dan, who, seeing the trapped boy, decided not to move his car. After some time he did decide to move, reversed and drove away. Jack, a passing pedestrian, witnessed the event and was very upset by the occurrence. In his efforts to erase the memory of the injured boy, Jack drank a large quantity of brandy and became extremely drunk. He stumbled into a hotel and did not realise that he had dropped his cigarette on the the hall carpet. The hotel caught fire and two of the occupants died in the blaze. Jack escaped.

Discuss their criminal liability.

University of London LLB Examination
(for External Students) Criminal Law June 1981 Q3

General Comment

The question centres mainly around the respective mens rea of both Dan and Jack, particularly with regard to their 'recklessness' and thereby tests knowledge of the types of recklessness relating to different offences.

Skeleton Solution

Dan   Sections 2 and 3 RTA 1988 – recklessness – sections 47 and 20 OAP 1861.

Jack   Sections 1 and 3 CDA 1971 – recklessness.

Suggested Solution

Dan may commit a number of offences contrary to the Road Traffic Act when his car mounts the pavement and injures a boy.

Section 3 of the Road Traffic Act 1988 (as amended by the RTA 1991), provides that if a person drives a motor vehicle (or mechanically propelled vehicle) on a road without due care and attention or without reasonable consideration for other persons using the road, he shall commit an offence.

Section 2 of the Road Traffic Act 1988, provides that a person who drives a motor vehicle on a road recklessly shall be guilty of an offence. This offence is, owing to probative difficulties in driving cases, to be replaced by one of dangerous driving, but the discussion of recklessness which follows is instructive. Section 2 creates the more serious offence and because of that it is generally considered that a higher standard of mens rea is required to satisfy the offence. A person could be driving 'without due care and attention' if he fails to exercise the degree of care and attention that a reasonable and prudent driver would exercise in the circumstances: *Simpson* v *Peat* (1952). This is an objective standard and it is an example of one of the few crimes of negligence in English criminal law.

It is not so easy to define the test which will indicate whether a person is driving recklessly. Certainly, recklessness denotes deliberate taking of an unjustifiable risk and mere inadvertence will not be sufficient without there being an essential element of the awareness of the risk involved. The test for deciding whether a person is driving recklessly has been considered by the House of Lords in the case of *R* v *Lawrence* (1982) where, following to the case of *MPC* v *Caldwell* (1982), the House of Lords held that mens rea was an essential element in the offence of driving recklessly, furthermore, the mental element necessary is that before adopting a manner of driving that in fact involves an obvious and serious risk of causing physical injury to another person using the road, or of doing substantial damage to property, the driver has failed to give any thought to the possibility of there being such a risk or having recognised that there was some risk involved, has gone on nonetheless to take it. In

R v *Reid* (1992) the House of Lords recognised (obiter) that a person falling under the 'lacuna' (ie where the accused had considered whether there was a risk but wrongly concluded that there was none) would not be reckless.

Lord Diplock's direction in *R* v *Lawrence* (1982) was approved as a model in *R* v *Madigan* (1983) and the need for the word 'obvious' to be included in such a direction was emphasised in *R* v *Khan* (1985).

In *R* v *Lawrence* the House of Lords considered that the earlier decision of *R* v *Murphy* (1980) was defective in that it referred to 'due care and attention' which in effect lowered the standard of care to that of the less serious offence contained in s3. This was an incorrect approach.

Obviously, it is necessary to consider what mens rea Dan had and whether the fact that he fell asleep may provide him with a defence. The fact that Dan fell asleep does not enable him to claim the defence of automatism. He would be convicted on the basis that at the time when he realised he was sleepy, he should have stopped and therefore, as he did not stop he committed an offence at that time. The defence of automatism could possibly have been claimed if Dan had started driving while concussed or sleep-walking and therefore, the act of driving itself was one which was involuntary in some way. The facts of the question can be distinguished from the situation where, for example, a swarm of bees stung a driver so that his driving became involuntary. In *Hill* v *Baxter* (1958) it was stated that in these circumstances there could be a defence of automatism. However, on the facts in the question, Dan had awareness of feeling drowsy and could have stopped the car and thus avoided the risk. The mental element required for driving recklessly is one which is for almost all purposes objective. It is immaterial that Dan has failed to give any thought to the possibility of there being a risk of causing physical injury to some other person or doing substantial damage to property.

By not reversing away from the boy immediately Dan may have caused further injuries to the boy. Dan may therefore by liable for wounding or causing further grievous bodily harm contrary to ss18 or 20 of the 1861 Act (depending on his mens rea). Although an omission to act cannot generally found criminal liability, this case is likely to fall under the exception stated in *R* v *Miller* (1983) that an accused is under a duty to rectify a danger that he himself has created.

Jack may commit an act of criminal damage contrary to s1(1) of the Criminal Damage Act 1971, where intentionally or recklessly he destroys or damages property belonging to another with intent or being reckless as to whether such property is destroyed. Prima facie, there is the more serious offence within s1(2) of the Criminal Damage Act, in that he destroys or damages property intentionally or recklessly with intention to endanger life or being reckless as to whether life is endangered.

Because the offence is performed by fire, then it will come within s1(3) – arson. However, there may be difficulties in showing that Jack had the necessary mens rea in his drunken state. However, he will not be able to plead this as a defence unless it can be shown that the offences with which he could be charged are crimes of specific intent. In these circumstances, drunkenness may be a defence if it can be shown that the drunkenness totally negatives the mens rea required: *DPP* v *Majewski* (1976). If it is a crime of basic intent, then drunkenness will be no defence even though the accused is incapable of forming mens rea. The House of Lords considered

2 STATE OF MIND

the defence of drunkenness in relation to the Criminal Damage Act in *MPC* v *Caldwell* (1982). The House of Lords considered that the term 'reckless' within s1 of the Act, held a meaning which it bore in in ordinary speech. That meaning included not only deciding to ignore the risk of harmful consequences resulting from one's acts that one recognises as existing but also, failing to give any thought to whether or not there was such risk in circumstances where if any thought were given to the matter, it would be obvious that there was. Therefore, the fact that the defendant was unaware of the risk of endangering lives owing to his voluntary intoxication would be no defence if the risk would have been obvious to him had he been sober. The result is that if Jack was charged under s1(2) of the Criminal Damage Act, with being reckless as to whether life was endangered, then he will not be able to claim drunkenness as a defence. However, if he were charged under s1(2) of the Criminal Damage Act, intending to endanger life, evidence of self-induced intoxication could be relevant as a defence. The result of the decision of *MPC* v *Caldwell* (1982) is, that within s1(2), there are two separate offences where one of which is a basic intent crime within the *DPP* v *Majewski* rule and the other is a specific intent crime. This goes against earlier case law where it has been held that s1(1) of the Act was a crime of basic intention where voluntary intoxication would offer no defence and s1(2) of the Act was a crime of specific intent where voluntary drunkenness could be raised as a defence: *R* v *Orpin* (1980).

The test of 'recklessness' outlined in *MPC* v *Caldwell* is open to quite severe criticism on the ground that it goes against the Law Commission recommendations and introduces a substantial objective element into the test.

Because of this objective element, it will not really be necessary to enquire into the state of mind of the accused even though, Lord Diplock states in *MPC* v *Caldwell* that 'mens rea is, by definition, a state of mind of the accused himself at the time he did the physical act that constitutes the actus reus of the offence; it cannot be the state of mind of some non-existent hypothetical person'.

QUESTION FOUR

'Strict liability must be retained. It provides social benefits which would not be obtained through any of the supposed alternatives to it and the injustice caused by it is often exaggerated.'

Discuss.

University of London LLB Examination
(for External Students) Criminal Law June 1981 Q9

General Comment

A very hard question which admits of detailed discussion. Therefore it is potentially hazardous in that answering essay questions such as this can quickly eat into one's time. Only students who are well-disciplined and well-organised in their examination technique should attempt such a question.

Skeleton Solution

Strict liability and absolute liability compared and contrasted – social benefits of 'no-fault' liability at criminal law – 'negligence' aspect – drawbacks of such liability and apparent inequity thereof.

Suggested Solution

A crime of strict liability is one where mens rea (intention, recklessness or even negligence) is not required as to one or more elements in the actus reus. Such crimes are sometimes referred to as crimes of 'absolute liability'. However, this is a misnomer since apart from one or two exceptional situations, some mens rea must be shown the 'strict' element relating to only one or two elements of the actus reus.

Crimes of strict liability are generally the creation of statute. Under the common law it was, on the whole, accepted that every crime required mens rea of some kind. However, with the industrial revolution, Parliament began to legislate in such matters as safety in factories, selling impure food and the regulation of economic activities of all types. When it did so, it frequently laid down in detail what the prohibited act consisted of, but failed to specify any mental element. It therefore fell to the courts to decide whether this omission was intended to mean that strict liability was to be imposed or alternatively whether such statutes were to be interpreted in accordance with the general principles of criminal law where there is a presumption in favour of mens rea. On the whole, the courts have taken the first view and almost invariably have imposed strict liability when Parliament has omitted words like 'wilfully', 'knowingly'. Occasionally, the courts have even interpreted an offence as one of strict liability where such words have been present.

It is necessary to examine exactly what social benefits arise from imposition of criminal liability without fault before it can be considered whether or not strict liability must be retained. It has been argued particularly by Baroness Barbara Wootton, Social Scientist, that one of the main aims of criminal law must be to protect society from harmful acts. Such an act which must be prevented is one which would be harmful, whether done intentionally, recklessly, negligently or even inadvertently. However, this argument does not apply simply to crimes of strict liability and if it were a correct approach, it is one which could be applied to all crimes, so that simply performing the actus reus of any offence would amount to a crime.

Indeed, one of the very strong arguments against strict liability is that the influence of strict liability does tend to affect the court's attitude to all crimes and undermine greatly the strength of the presumption in favour of mens rea.

A further argument frequently put forward in support of strict liability is that it is generally applied only to offences of a minor nature, those that could be described as 'regulatory' or 'social' rather than 'real crimes'. Originally there may have been some truth in this argument. The first type of strict liability offences did relate to food and hygiene legislation and other social regulatory offences. However, it is not an argument which is supported when one looks at the present areas where strict liability is applied. Legislation relating to pollution is usually interpreted as giving rise to strict liability: *Alphacell* v *Woodward* (1972). However, the consequences of allowing rivers to become polluted can be extremely serious and it would certainly be wrong to say that such crimes have no moral content.

In *Atkinson* v *Sir Alfred McAlpine & Son Ltd* (1974), it was held that the company committed an offence contrary to the Asbestos Regulations 1969 by failing to give written notice that they were going to undertake work involving crocidolite. The company neither knew nor indeed had reason to know that the work did involve crocidolite. However, the court found that where a statute contained an absolute prohibition against the doing of some act, as a general rule, mens rea was not a constituent of that offence. Furthermore, it distinguished the situation from that where the law imposed a duty to act where mens rea was a necessary requirement, for example, failure to report an accident, where the defendant would not be guilty if he was unaware that the accident had occurred: *Harding* v *Price* (1948).

A further example of the application of strict liability in pure criminal law may be seen in the legislation concerning dangerous drugs. This has on occasions in recent years been defined as involving crimes of strict liability: *Yeandel* v *Fisher* (1966). Here the defendant was found guilty of 'being concerned with the management of premises for the purposes of smoking cannabis', even though he did not know and had no means of knowing that such smoking was taking place. However, this case was overruled by *Sweet* v *Parsley* (1969) where a conviction on similar facts to those in the *Yeandel* v *Fisher* case was quashed by the House of Lords. The Misuse of Drugs Act 1971 has to some extent moved away from imposing pure strict liability by allowing a statutory defence for an accused where charged with being in possession of prohibited drugs to show that he neither knew of or suspected nor had reasons to suspect the existence of some fact alleged by the prosecution which it is necessary for the prosecution to prove if he is to be convicted of the offence charged. Thus, if it can be shown that the accused did not know or believe that he has a controlled drug on him, he will have a defence. However, it will not be a defence for the accused to show that he did not know or believe the substance to be the particular controlled drug it in fact was, if he knew or suspected that it was a controlled drug which he was not entitled to have: *R* v *McNamara* (1988).

Neither will the fact that D 'forgets' he has such a drug absolve him: *R* v *Martindale* (1986).

A rather better argument in support of strict liability is one founded in practicality. If the courts were to accept that mens rea had to be proved in every case, the prosecutor's task would often be made impossible. Indeed, this aspect was one stressed by Lord Salmon in *Alphacell* v *Woodward* (1972) and by their Lordships in the Court of Appeal decision in *R* v *Bradish* (1990) where the appellant had been found in possession of a can of CS gas, a 'prohibited weapon' under s5(1)(b) of the Firearms Act 1968. The court held that a balance had to be struck between protecting the innocent possessor of such articles and the underlying policy behind legislation which sought to protect the public from such weapons.

In *Alphacell* v *Woodward* Lord Salmon said:

'If it were held to be the law that no conviction could be obtained of the 1951 Act unless the prosecution could discharge the often impossible onus of proving that the pollution was caused intentionally or negligently, a great deal of pollution would go unpunished, and undeterred to the relief of many riparian factory owners. As a result, many rivers which are now filthy, would become filthier still and many rivers which are now clean, would lose their cleanliness.'

This indeed is probably one of the most important historical explanations for the existence of such offences. However, the consequences of such a situation are very grave. If a prosecutor does not have to prove mens rea, it is unlikely that he will go to the bother of doing so. So, when it comes to sentencing, the court will often find it very difficult to distinguish between the worst cases of a deliberate breach of the law and instances of inadvertant failure to comply with the required standard. It is very difficult to impose a sentence in such a situation and generally the court will want to enquire into which category the convicted person falls. Treating the offence as a crime of strict liability simply removes the decision as to these very important facts, from the jury into the hands of the judge.

It has been argued in support of offences of strict liability that the guilty defendant will, in almost every case, at least have been negligent, otherwise the statute would not have been complied with. However, there are cases where the defendant is absolutely blameless – for example, *Alphacell* v *Woodward* (1972); *Atkinson* v *Sir Alfred McAlpine & Son Ltd* (1974) – so even in the absence of any fault, liability may still be imposed. This point is sometimes argued in a slightly different way by saying that there is a substantial amount of empirical evidence to show that prosecutions are frequently only brought where the prosecuting agency (eg the factory inspectorate) is sure that some degree of fault is present. If this is so, why does Parliament not specify in detail what degree of fault must be proved for the offence to be committed?

Certainly, therefore, there are some arguments that can be put forward in support of strict liability, although on the whole the arguments have rather shaky foundations. However, before it can be considered whether or not strict liability must be retained, it is necessary to look at the arguments against such offences. The two main arguments against strict liability, indeed arguments that have been touched on already in considering supporting arguments to strict liability, are firstly, that it is unnecessary. Strict liability results in the conviction of persons who have been found by the court to have behaved impeccably and who should not be required to alter their conduct in any way. Furthermore, and possibly more importantly, strict liability is unjust. It is no argument to say that strict liability offences are not 'real crimes'. Those convicted of strict liability offences are treated as criminals, they go through a criminal process and the stigma of a criminal conviction attaches to them. Strict liability offences may catch the large number of truly guilty defendants, but it also catches the small number of persons who are absolutely morally innocent.

A conviction in a criminal court in that situation will obviously make the defendant feel rightly aggrieved and have consequences far outside the courts as in *Sweet* v *Parsley* (1969). It is no answer to such an argument to say that where there is no moral guilt, then the penalty imposed by the court will be only nominal. The court's penalty is the least of many penalties which attach to an individual when convicted of an offence. The stigma attached to the conviction may be a much more severe penalty. Where such a sense of injustice arises from a conviction in an offence of strict liability, the aggrieved defendant's attitude to criminal law generally may be affected so that the public respect for the criminal law, which is necessary for its upkeep, is undermined.

A practical argument in favour of strict liability is the most persuasive of all the arguments in support and could possibly outweigh the arguments against strict liability if there were no alternative to such offences. The practical problems of showing mens rea, which is the basis of the argument for strict liability, could to some extent be mitigated by altering the burden of proof in such offences. Indeed, to some extent, this has been seen by the statutory defence contained in the Misuse of Drugs Act as outlined above. However, a simpler approach would be to provide for the imposition of liability for negligence. Thus, a person would be liable if it were shown that they had inadvertently taken an justified risk. However, they would be acquitted if it was found that their conduct was faultless. The imposition of liability for negligence does seem to meet the arguments of most of those who are in favour of strict liability. Roscoe Pound in 'The Spirit of the Common Law' writes that 'the good sense of the courts has introduced the doctrine of acting at one's peril with respect to statutory crimes which express the needs of society. Such crimes are not meant to punish the vicious will, but to put pressure upon the thoughtless and the inefficient to do their whole duty in the interest of public health or safety or morals'.

The 'thoughtless and inefficient' to which Roscoe Pound refers are obviously those who are negligent. They are certainly not those who have done everything they could possibly do and are in no way to blame for the act, omission or state of affairs which constitute the actus reus of the offence.

Furthermore, by providing for liability for negligence, the public will be encouraged to do their duty to the highest possible standard and thus, avoid a possible criminal conviction. The Law Commission Working Paper No 31 The Mental Element in Crime (1970), suggested various reforms in the law relating to the mental element in crime. The basis of the report was that mens rea in some form, be it intention, recklessness or negligence, should be a normal requirement of guilt. In relation to all future offences, the Law Commission considered that the presumption in favour of mens rea must operate unless expressedly excluded. Where intention, knowledge or recklessness is expressly excluded in the statute in respect of any element in an offence, negligence should be required unless the offence is specifically stated to be one of strict liability.

By this means, the burden would be on Parliament to state whether an offence is to be one of strict liability and not merely be a question for the courts. In relation to existing offences, negligence should be substituted for any offences which are at present strictly interpreted. Where negligence is the sufficient mens rea in any offence, it would be treated as being established in the absence of any evidence to the contrary.

Bearing in mind the alternatives available to strict liability in its present form, it is difficult to support a statement that it must be retained. It is certainly true to present a fairly strong argument that it provides social benefits. Furthermore, these social benefits might not be obtained where mens rea in the sense of intention or recklessness were a necessary requirement of every crime. However, in this social regulatory field, where the aim of the criminal law is to encourage the highest possible standards of care, this may be achieved by the imposition of liability for negligence without the very serious consequence of catching those who are blameless.

QUESTION FIVE

David hitched a lift home and was picked up by Gloria. They stopped at a pub for a few drinks and having resumed their journey, David persuaded Gloria to stop the car for sexual intercourse. Whilst participating, Gloria changed her mind asking David to withdraw. David gave Gloria venereal disease.

Advise David about what crimes have been committed.

University of London LLB Examination
(for External Students) Criminal Law June 1983 Q2

General Comment

The question involves consideration of an area which is not specifically covered in the syllabus and it therefore appears to be quite difficult. However, the principles of consent and recklessness are the main feature of the question and students ought to be familiar with the basic elements of rape.

Skeleton Solution

David – rape – recklessness – ss47 and 20 OAP 1861.

Gloria – consent.

Suggested Solution

When David initially has sexual intercourse he commits no offence – assuming Gloria is at least 16 years old – as she consents to it. Such consent must be freely given and not obtained by duress, fear or fraud.

Without such consent he would be guilty of rape contrary to s1 of the Sexual Offences Act 1956 (as amended) if:

i)   he has sexual intercourse with a woman who, at the time, does not consent to it; and

ii)   at that time he knows that she does not consent or is reckless as to whether she consents or not.

Does the consent end when Gloria changes her mind? The Privy Council in *Kaitamaki* v *R* (1985) held that if a man continues intercourse under these circumstances it would amount to rape if he knows or is reckless as to whether the consent has been withdrawn. Here Gloria asks him to withdraw so David may thereafter be guilty of rape.

David's recklessness as to whether Gloria consents or not will be judged on the subjective *R* v *Cunningham* (1957) principles (ie consciously taking the risk) *R* v *Pigg* (1982) and it was held in *R* v *Bashir* (1982) by the Court of Appeal that the test was whether D had acted recklessly and not whether a reasonable man would have so acted. If David is indifferent to Gloria's consent in that he 'could not care less either way' then he is 'reckless' for this purpose: *R* v *Kimber* (1983); *R* v *Breckenridge* (1984).

The question of consent and/or withdrawal of consent is also relevant in deciding whether David bears any criminal responsibility for infecting Gloria with venereal disease. It seems almost certain that venereal disease would be regarded as grievous bodily harm and therefore the offences of s20 and s18 of the Offences Against the Person Act 1861 should be considered.

In *R* v *Clarence* (1888) the accused, who had sexual intercourse with his wife and infected her with veneral disease, was acquitted of the s20 charge on the grounds

2 STATE OF MIND

that the word 'inflict' required an assault. However, this must be read subject to the House of Lords' decision in *R* v *Wilson* (1983) which held that no assault is required. Consequently it is submitted that by infecting Gloria with veneral disease David may be guilty of the s20 offence. The House of Lords in *R* v *Savage*; *R* v *Parmenter* (1991) held that although the accused need not intend or foresee that his act will cause wounding or grievous bodily harm he must intend or foresee that he will cause some injury. Accordingly, David's liability for the s20 offence may depend on whether he was aware that he was infected with veneral disease.

Infecting another with venereal disease may amount to grievous bodily harm (defined as 'really serious harm' in *R* v *Smith* (1961), and if it could be established that David knew he was carrying this disease and that he intended to pass it on to Gloria he could be guilty of intentionally inflicting grievous bodily harm contrary to s18 of the Offences Against the Person Act 1861.

The question refers to David and Gloria having had a few drinks. However, there is nothing in particular to indicate an offence of driving with excess alcohol in the blood. As to the defence of voluntary intoxication David does not appear to be sufficiently affected by drink to be able to claim he lacks mens rea. In *DPP* v *Majewski* (1976) it was stated that voluntary intoxication would afford a defence to a crime of specific intent but only if the intoxication resulted in the accused being unable to form mens rea. However, it would afford no defence to a crime of specific intent. Rape has been categorized as crime of specific intent (*DPP* v *Majewski*) but in *MPC* v *Caldwell* (1982) the House of Lords considered that any crime that included recklessness within its mens rea was a crime of basic intent.

QUESTION SIX

Fitzgerald, aged 13 years, was playing on an embankment near a highway. He threw stones at passing cars. Gordon, who was driving his car very fast hit a stone. The car crashed into the control barrier and Gordon was severely injured.

Fitzgerald who was not very bright had not realized the danger his stone-throwing constituted. He also threw a stone at Dan but it missed him, hitting John.

Advise Fitzgerald.

University of London LLB Examination
(for External Students) Criminal Law June 1983 Q3

General Comment

This question again examines the elements of recklessness, in relation here to criminal damage and offences against the person. Also considered is the doctrine of transferred malice.

Skeleton Solution

Fitzgerald – Sections 1(1) and 1(2) CDA 1971; recklessness;

Sections 20 and 18 OAP 1861; recklessness; doli incapax.

21

Suggested Solution

Fitzgerald should be advised that he may have committed an offence contrary to s1(1) of the Criminal Damage Act 1971 which provides that it is an offence to destroy or damage any property belonging to another, intending to destroy or damage any such property or being reckless as to whether any such property would be destroyed or damaged, without lawful excuse. The mens rea for s1(1) is intention or recklessness as to all the circumstances and consequences that constitute the actus reus of criminal damage under s1(1)(b).

Furthermore, Fitzgerald may have committed the more serious offence contained in s1(2) of the Criminal Damage Act which provides that it will be an offence for a person without lawful excuse to destroy or damage any property, whether belonging to himself or another:

a) intending to destroy or damage any property or being reckless as to whether any property would be destroyed or damaged; and

b) intending by the destruction or damage to endanger the life of another, or being reckless as to whether the life of another would be thereby endangered.

In relation to both of these offences certain aspects need further consideration. Firstly, the question of causation could be a problem. We are told that Gordon was driving very fast when he hit the stone on the road, and it could be argued that he was the cause of the damage to the property and the consequent injuries because of his excessive driving speeds. Only if the jury are satisfied that Fitzgerald was in law a substantial and operating cause of the consequences that occurred will he be held to be liable. It should be noted that it is unnecessary to show that Fitzgerald is the only cause in law. There may be other causes contributing to the consequence which actually flows. The second point requiring consideration is whether Fitzgerald would be viewed as reckless in relation to the circumstances and consequences contained in the actus reus of s1(1) and (2). In *MPC* v *Caldwell* (1982) Lord Diplock considered the meaning of the word in the context of the Criminal Damage Act.

'In my opinion, a person charged with an offence under s1(1) of the Criminal Damage Act 1971 is "reckless as to whether or not any property would be destroyed or damaged" if:

a) he does an act which in fact creates an obvious risk that property will be destroyed or damaged;

b) when he does the act he either has not given any thought to the possibility of there being any such risk or has recognised that there was some risk involved and has nonetheless gone on to do it.'

This definition of recklessness is a departure from the earlier definitions contained in cases like *R* v *Stephenson* (1979) where emphasis was placed on the accused subjectively having appreciated the risk. In Lord Diplock's definition of recklessness many more states of mind would be in decided, ranging from failure to give any thought at all to whether or not there is any risk of those harmful consequences to recognising the existence of the risk and nevertheless deciding to ignore it.

The result of this much wider definition of recklessness is that thoughtless people or people of low intelligence who may not have appreciated a risk that would be obvious to the ordinary person may now be caught within the definition of recklessness and therefore be liable in criminal law.

This 'objective' type of recklessness was confirmed in *R* v *Sangha* (1988) where the Court of Appeal held that in criminal damage cases – here arson of a flat – the test was whether an ordinary and prudent bystander would have perceived an obvious risk that property would be damaged and life endangered thereby.

It could be argued that Fitzgerald has committed an offence contrary to s18 or s20 in the Offences Against the Person Act 1861. Section 18 is the more serious offence and it provides that a person who unlawfully and maliciously wounds or causes any grievous bodily harm to any person with intent to do any grievous bodily harm shall commit an offence.

The actus reus of this offence may well be satisfied providing the jury are satisfied that in law Fitzgerald was the legal 'cause' of the injuries sustained by Gordon. However, the mens rea element of s18 would not be satisfied. There is no 'intention' to cause the grievous bodily harm as Fitzgerald does not desire it nor does he know it is certain to occur.

Under s20 it is an offence for a person unlawfully and maliciously to wound or inflict any grievous bodily harm upon another. The problem on the facts would be whether or not there has been an infliction of grievous bodily harm. In the case of *R* v *Clarence* (1888) it was held that the term 'inflict' implied an assault in the sense of a battery, although this has been interpreted to mean both a direct assault and a more indirectly inflicted injury, *R* v *Martin* (1881) and *R* v *Wilson* (1983). However, even if it were held that there was an 'infliction of grievous bodily harm' it would have to be shown that Fitzgerald acted 'maliciously'. In the case of *R* v *Mowatt* (1968) it was stated that the term 'maliciously' imported upon the part of the person who unlawfully inflicts the wound or other grievous bodily harm an awareness that his act may have the consequence of causing some physical harm to some other person.

Following *R* v *Savage*; *R* v *Parmenter* (1991), in order to secure a conviction under s20 the prosecution would need to establish that Fitzgerald intended or foresaw that he might cause *some* harm to Gordon.

Fitzgerald would be able to claim the defence of infancy to any of these offences charged as he is 13 years old. A child under ten is presumed to be incapable of committing a crime and this presumption is irrebuttable. If a child is over ten but under 14 the same presumption arises but can be rebutted. This presumption may be rebutted by showing that he has 'mischievous discretion'. It must be shown that he knew what he was doing was seriously wrong: *R* v *Gorrie* (1918), *McC* v *Runneckles* (1984). The existence of this presumption was recently confirmed in *C (a minor)* v *DPP* (1995).

When Fitzgerald throws the stone at Dan but hits John the mens rea he has toward Dan is, under the doctrine of transferred malice, transferred to John, provided the actus reus and mens rea are the same: *R* v *Latimer* (1886). Had he intended to hit a car when he threw the stone, his hitting John could not be subject to the doctrine as the actus reus and mens rea would not be the same: *R* v *Pembliton* (1874). Likewise if he had intended to hit Dan but had missed and damaged John's property.

One could have argued that Fitzgerald was reckless in throwing the stone.

Fitzgerald may also have committed the offence of causing danger to a road user contrary to s22A RTA 1988.

3 PARTICIPATION

3.1   Introduction

3.2   Key points

3.3   Recent cases

3.4   Analysis of questions

3.5   Questions

3.1 Introduction

Traditionally, accessorial liability and inchoate offences (incitement, conspiracy and attempt) are dealt with separately. Although a separate chapter is devoted to the law of attempt (chapter 9) incitement and conspiracy will be dealt with here, together with accessories, because of the close relationship between these offences.

3.2 Key points

a) *Incitement*

It was held in *Race Relations Board* v *Applin* [1973] QB 815 that an incitement was not confined to urging another to commit an offence but also included threats, pressure and persuasion.

The incitement must reach the mind of the incitee: *Invicta Plastics* v *Clare* [1976] RTR 251.

The accused must intend that the incitee commits the offence (although it is not necessary that the incitee actually commits the offence): *R* v *Curr* [1968] 2 QB 944.

Impossibility – *R* v *Fitzmaurice* [1983] 1 All ER 189 held that impossibility because of the ineptitude of the methods of committing the crime suggested was no defence but that legal impossibility *was* a defence.

b) *Conspiracy*

A conspiracy is defined in s1 of the Criminal Law Act 1977 as where two or more people agree on a course of conduct which, if carried out, would lead to the commission of an offence.

Note that the actus reus is *agreement* and no steps need actually be taken towards the commission of the offence.

With respect to the mens rea, note the conflict between *R* v *Anderson* [1986] AC 27 and *Yip Chiu Cheung* v *R* [1994] Crim LR 824 on whether the prosecution must prove that the accused actually intended that the agreement be carried out.

Impossibility – under s1(1)b of the 1977 Act impossibility is no defence.

c) *Accessorial liability*

Under s8 of the Accessories and Abettors Act 1861 it is an offence to aid, abet, counsel or procure the commission of an offence.

Note that the person who actually commits the offence (or acts through an innocent agent) is called the 'principal offender' and the person who 'aids', 'abets', 'counsels' or 'procures' the offence is the 'accessory'.

A person aids another to commit an offence where he *assists* in the commission of the offence either at the time the offence is committed or before it is committed.

A person abets another to commit an offence where he *encourages* the commission of the offence at the time the offence is committed.

A person counsels or procures an offence where he encourages its commission before it is committed.

Note that an incitor will become a counsellor or a procuror if the incitee acts on his advice and carries out the offence suggested.

Note that the mere presence at the scene of the crime is insufficient to fix the accused with liability as an accessory: *R* v *Coney* (1882) 8 QBD 534; *R* v *Clarkson* [1971] 1 WLR 1402.

One of the main problem areas in accessorial liability is identifying the accessory's liability where the principal offender has gone beyond the acts or offences contemplated by the accessory:

i) The accessory is liable for all offences commited by the principal offender of a *similar type* to that which he had in his contemplation: *R* v *Bainbridge* (1960) 43 Cr App R 194.

ii) An accessory may be liable for unusual and unforeseen consequences providing they flow from acts by the principal offender which were within his contemplation: *R* v *Carberry* [1994] Crim LR 447.

iii) A person may be convicted as an accessory to murder merely on the basis that he foresaw that the principal offender *might* kill in the course of the crime contemplated: *R* v *Roberts* [1992] NLJ 1503.

Note the problems associated with the accessory's attempts to withdraw from the joint enterprise: see *R* v *Whitefield* (1984) 79 Cr App R 36 and *R* v *Baker* [1994] Crim LR 445.

3.3 Recent cases

Yip Chiu Cheung v *R* [1994] Crim LR 824

R v *Carberry* [1994] Crim LR 447

R v *Baker* [1994] Crim LR 445

3.4 Analysis of questions

Questions concerning participation are usually incorporated into problem questions based on specific offences such as burglary, theft, robbery etc and it is rare for a problem question to include only one actor.

3.5 Questions

QUESTION ONE

Arnold and Benjamin agree to pick the pockets of the person they saw in the distance, standing alone at a 'bus-stop'. Arnold attracted the person's attention whilst Benjamin put his hand in the man's coat pockets. They were empty. In his anger and frustration, Benjamin took out a knife (the existence of which had been unknown to Arnold) and threw it away in the direction of a crowd standing outside a club.

Benjamin realised there was a grave risk that the knife would seriously injure one of the crowd but Benjamin was indifferent as to that risk. In fact the knife hit a boy and injured him. Arnold and Benjamin ran off.

Discuss their criminal liability.

Adapted from University of London LLB Examination
(for External Students) Criminal Law June 1981 Q3

General Comment

The question involves the apportionment of liability between the two actors and their participation in the various offences:

Skeleton Solution

Arnold and)   conspiracy s1 CLA 1977 and common law – ss1 and 1(2) CAA 1981
Benjamin   )   – ss20 and 18 OAP 1861 – s8 A and AA 1861.

Suggested Solution

When Arnold and Benjamin agree to pick-pocket, they may commit an offence contrary to s1(1) of the Criminal Law Act 1977, which provides that 'if a person agrees with any other person or persons that a course of conduct shall be pursued which will necessarily amount to or involve the commission of any offence or offences by one or more of the parties to the agreement, if the agreement is carried out in accordance with their intentions, he is guilty of conspiracy to commit the offence'. From the facts of the question, the most obvious charge would be a conspiracy to steal.

There would still be a possibility of a charge under the old common law. The common law offence of conspiracy has been abolished by the Criminal Law Act 1977 with the exception of conspiracy to defraud and conspiracy to corrupt public morals and outrage public decency. A conspiracy to defraud is an agreement by two or more persons to deprive a person of something which is his: *Scott* v *Metropolitan Police Commissioner* (1975). This would obviously cover the conduct envisaged by Arnold and Benjamin. However in *R* v *Duncalf* (1979), it was stated that if a course of conduct is capable of coming within the s1 of the Criminal Law Act 1977, a charge should be brought under that section in preference to the common law even where retained.

Benjamin is guilty of attempted theft under s1(1) of the Criminal Attempts Act 1981 in that he, with intent to commit an offence – theft – does an act – putting his hands in pockets – which is more than merely preparatory to the commission of the offence whereas prior to the 1981 Act Benjamin might have argued that the pocket being empty made any such attempt impossible and therefore not an offence: *Haughton* v *Smith* (1975). Section 1(2) of the Act states that a person may be guilty of attempting to commit an offence even though the facts are such that the commission of the offence is impossible.

Following *R* v *Shivpuri* (1987) any argument based upon impossibility will not succeed.

Arnold may be liable as aiding and abetting Benjamin and under s8 of the Accessories and Abettors Act 1861 he will be liable to be tried, indicted and punished as a principal offender. By distracting the victim's attention to facilitate the attempted theft, Arnold would seen to be 'aiding' Benjamin in the same way as eg a 'look out' *R* v *Betts and Ridley* (1930) or one who holds another while he is assaulted *R* v *Clarkson* (1971).

Benjamin may be guilty of wounding the boy under s18 or s20 of the Offences Against the Person Act 1861 although he lacks the mens rea ie an intention to wound – for the s18 charge: *R* v *Mowatt* (1968).

He may commit the s20 offences (one of basic intent) of wounding if he is shown to be 'reckless' in the *R* v *Cunningham* (1957) sense (ie consciously takes the risk): *R* v *Savage*; *R* v *Parmenter* (1991). Here we are told that he realises the grave risk of injury and so he would appear to be reckless in the required sense.

Arnold's liability for the injury is less clear. Generally, one who assists a principal offender in his criminal conduct will be liable for the consequences arising therefrom, whether or not those consequences were intended or foreseen, provided the relevant mens rea is present: *R* v *Chan Wing-Siu* (1985); *R* v *Ward* (1987). In order for him to be liable for the violence used by Benjamin, though, there must have been some express or tacit agreement between them that such violence would be used if necessary: *R* v *Slack* (1989). Mere foreseeability that Benjamin might resort to violence is insufficient: *R* v *Wakely and Others* (1990).

However, if the principal goes beyond that which is agreed or contemplated, the other party cannot be held liable for the unauthorised act or its consequences: *R* v *Carberry* (1994). Since Arnold did not know Benjamin was carrying a knife the use of a knife would appear outside his contemplation and it is therefore submitted that Arnold could not be convicted as an accessory to the offence under s20 committed by Benjamin.

As the original plan here was simply to steal, it is unlikely that Arnold, who knows nothing of the knife, would be liable for Benjamin's use of it: *Davies* v *DPP* (1954).

QUESTION TWO

F and G agreed to hit H, a security guard, over the head with a truncheon. They intended to steal the payroll which H delivered on a regular basis to a local factory. G drove F to the factory and remained in the car until H's security van arrived.

The van arrived and F threatened H with violence unless he handed over the bag containing the wages. H handed it over but nevertheless F, who was in an extremely agitated state, hit him three times over the head with the truncheon. H fell to the ground where F started to kick him, giving H a black eye. F was completely out of control. G ran to the scene and dragged F off H. H suffered sleepless nights for three months after the attack and his personality changed so that he became very timid.

Advise F and G of their criminal liability.

University of London LLB Examination
(for External Students) Criminal Law June 1993 Q2

General Comment

A relatively straightforward question dealing mainly with conspiracy, robbery and offences against the person, with the most difficult area being G's accessorial liability for the acts of F.

Skeleton Solution

The agreement – conspiracy – liability of F – assault and theft – robbery – sections 47, 18 and 20 of the OAP 1861 – liability of G – accessorial liability for the theft, robbery and injuries inflicted on H – G's liability for assaulting F.

Suggested Solution

The agreement

Under s1(1) of the Criminal Law Act 1977 a person is guilty of conspiracy if he agrees with another on a course of conduct which will necessarily amount to or involve the commission of an offence. Agreeing to hit the security guard on the head in order to steal the payroll would necessarily involve the commission of assault, assault occasioning actual bodily harm and robbery, and F and G are consequently guilty of conspiring to commit these offences. The more difficult question is whether F and G are guilty of conspiring to commit the more serious offence of causing wounding or grievous bodily harm contrary to s18 of the Offences against the Person Act 1861 as although this may have been committed by F it does not appear to have been part of the original agreed plan. Under s1 of the 1977 Act a person is only guilty of conspiring to commit the offences which will inevitably flow from the agreed course of action, and it is submitted that as grievous bodily harm is a possible but not inevitable consequence of their agreed plan there is no conspiracy to commit grievous bodily harm. It should be noted that the fact that at the time of the agreement it may have been understood between F and G that G would only drive the car and play no direct role in the actual attack, would be no bar to convicting G of conspiracy to commit assault and robbery since s1(1) makes it clear that it is sufficient if the cause of conduct agreed on would amount to an offence by 'one or more of the parties to the agreement'. However, as the offences conspired on have actually been committed the courts discourage the charging of conspiracy (see *R* v *Boulton* (1871)) and it may be more appropriate to charge F with the full offences of assault and robbery and G as an accessory to these offences.

Liability of F

By threatening H with violence F has committed an assault as he has intentionally or recklessly put H in fear of immediate and unlawful personal violence (*Fagan* v *MPC* (1968)) – even though F did not initially use violence, the mere threat of violence is sufficient. When H handed over the money F committed theft contrary to s1 of the Theft Act 1968.

F may also be guilty of robbery contrary to s8 of the 1968 Act which is committed where the accused 'steals and immediately before or at the time of doing so, and in order to do so, he uses force on any person or puts or seeks to put any person in fear of being then and there subjected to force'. Although F only used force on H after he had handed over the money he did threaten to use force before this theft took place and therefore fulfils the requirements of the offence.

By hitting H over the head with a truncheon and kicking him causing him to suffer a black eye F is probably guilty of assault and battery and assault occasioning actual bodily harm – the blows by the truncheon and the black eye almost certainly amount to actual bodily harm which was defined in *R* v *Chan Fook* (1994) as any injury which is more than trivial. Whether or not the sleepless nights and personality change still suffered by H three months after the attack would amount to grievous bodily harm for the purposes of the offences under ss18 and 20 of the Offences Against the Person Act 1861 is less certain. These conditions could not amount to wounding as this requires a breaking of the skin (*JJC (a minor)* v *Eisenhower* (1984)). It would be for the jury to decide whether the conditions suffered by H amounted to grievous bodily harm defined as 'really serious harm' in *R* v *Smith* (1961). If the injuries sustained by H do amount to grievous bodily harm, by hitting H on the head with a truncheon three times and kicking him, it is submitted that the prosecution may well be able to prove that F intended to cause H serious harm and may consequently be guilty of causing grievous bodily harm with intent contrary to s18 of the Offences Against the Person Act 1861. Failing this, it is almost certain that F foresaw that his acts would cause H some harm and may therefore be guilty of recklessly inflicting grievous bodily harm contrary to s20 of the same Act.

G's liability

The extent of G's accessorial liability for the offences committed by F is unclear. A person who assists another before or at the time that other commits an offence may be liable as an aider or abettor contrary to s8 of the Accessories and Abettors Act 1861 provided that the offence committed is the same or a similar offence to that which the aider or abettor intended to assist or participate in, *R* v *Bainbridge* (1960), or was foreseen as a possible incident of the common unlawful enterprise (*Chan Wing-Siu* v *R* (1984)). An accessory will not be liable for offences committed by the principal offender outside the common design as in *R* v *Dunbar* (1988) where a secondary party hired the principal offender to assault a victim but the principal offender killed t he victim. The secondary party was convicted of aiding and abetting manslaughter but acquitted of aiding and abetting murder because the principal offender had gone beyond the common design. It is submitted that in this case although on the one hand it may be said that G only envisaged violence to be used in order to commit the theft and F clearly went beyond this, striking H on the head with a truncheon was part of the plan and it may well be that G foresaw that grievous bodily harm was at least a possible accident of this attack and is consequently an accessory to the grievous bodily harm committed by F.

Liability of G in relation to F

By dragging F off H, G has assaulted F but as F was in the process of attacking H, it is submitted that G would be entitled to raise the defence of self-defence at common law or under s3 of the Criminal Law Act 1967 which allow reasonable force to be used in defence of oneself or another and in the prevention of crime respectively.

QUESTION THREE

A agreed with B that they would sneak into a nearby amusement park in order to enjoy the various rides. A climbed over the perimeter fence in order to avoid paying the £15 entrance fee. A then kept the attendant talking, and while the attendant's attention was elsewhere, B was able to sneak past without paying.

B took several rides on the ghost train and on each occasion he examined handbags belonging to other passengers because he was looking for a special type of perfume which his mother used. None of his fellow passengers had that brand of perfume so he left disappointed.

Advise A and B of their criminal liability if any.

Adapted from University of London LLB Examination
(for External Students) Criminal Law June 1987 Q1

General Comment

Although the question at first sight appears relatively straightforward there are many pitfalls that an unwary student could fall into, particularly in relation to the property offences.

Skeleton Solution

A   Conspiracy – entry to the park as a trespasser but no burglary – s2 Theft Act 1978.

B   Conspiracy – s1 TA 1978, attempted theft – impossibility or conditional intent – s1 CAA 1981.

Suggested Solution

When A and B agree to sneak into the amusement park there may be a conspiracy within the common law or under s1 Criminal Law Act 1977. However a conspiracy under s1 CLA 1977 requires the carrying out of the agreement to necessarily amount to or involve the commission of a substantive offence and therefore it is convenient to consider the conspiracy aspect after the substantive offences have been considered.

When A climbs over the perimeter wall in order to avoid paying the entrance fee he undoubtedly enters the park as a trespasser. This would give rise to possible civil liability but there is nothing in the question to suggest that a crime has been committed at this stage. Section 9 Theft Act 1968 (burglary) does not need consideration as this is only satisfied where there is entry into a building as a trespasser. An amusement park would obviously not amount to a building.

When A keeps the attendant talking thus allowing B to sneak past without paying, he may commit an offence contrary to s2(1)(c) Theft Act 1978. Section 2(1)(c) provides that it will be an offence where a person by a deception dishonestly obtains any exemption from or an abatement of liability to make a payment. 'Obtains' within s2(1)(c) includes obtaining for another or enabling another to obtain.

Undoubtedly there is a deception practised on the attendant by A when he kept the attendant talking. Section 15(4) Theft Act 1968 provides that 'deception' means any deception (whether deliberate or reckless) by words or conduct as to fact or as to law, including deception as to the present intentions of the person using the deception or any other person. However it may be that a prosecution under s2(1)(c) could encounter difficulties on the ground that the term 'exemption' covers more appropriately the type of situation where, for example, an accused by deception dishonestly secures a rate rebate to which he is not entitled.

The only other offence within s2 that might be appropriate is s2(1)(b) which provides that an offence is committed where a person by deception with intent to make permanent default in whole or in part of any existing liability to make a payment, or with intent to let another do so, dishonestly induces the creditor or any person claiming on behalf of a creditor to wait for payment or forgo payment.

This offence, unlike s2(1)(a) may be committed by a unilateral act. Consensus between the creditor or debtor is not required. However it could be argued that at the time of the deception there is no existing liability – this only being created once B has gained entry.

More than one offence under s2 TA 1978 may be satisfied at the same time on the same facts. It is therefore possible that both s2(1)(b) and s2(1)(c) could be established: R v Sibartie (1983).

If A does commit an offence contrary to s2, B could be liable as an accomplice. An aider and abettor is a person; who is present assisting or encouraging the offence: R v Coney (1882); R v Clarkson (1971).

Under s8 Accessories and Abettors Act 1861 persons who are accomplices are to be treated as principal offenders for the purposes of trial and punishment.

When B rides on the ghost train he may commit an offence contrary to s1 Theft Act 1978. Section 1 provides that a person who by any deception dishonestly obtains services from another shall be guilty of an offence.

Section 1(2) provides that it is an obtaining of a service where the other is induced to confer a benefit by doing some act, or causing or permitting some act to be done, on the understanding that the benefit has been or will be paid for.

Certainly it could be that B is representing himself as having paid the entrance fee and this could amount to a deception within s15(4) TA 1968. However it must be shown that the deception operates on a human mind and if there is no one who allows B to ride the ghost train on the basis that he has paid there will not be an operative deception. It has also been argued that B commits the offence of travelling upon a railway without having paid his fare and with intent to avoid payment thereof (s5(3)(a) Regulation of Railways Act 1889), although this scarcely seems to fall within the spirit of that piece of legislation!

When B examines the contents of the handbag looking for a particular perfume he may become liable for attempted theft. Section 1 Theft Act 1968 provides that the offence of theft is established if he dishonestly appropriates property belonging to another with intent to permanently deprive the other of it. An attempted theft would be established if it was shown that there was an act more than merely preparatory towards the full offence with mens rea, s1 Criminal Attempts Act 1981.

There seems little doubt that the actus reus would be satisfied. However there could be difficulties in establishing an intention to permanently deprive. The facts of the question are similar to the facts in *R v Easom* (1971) where the accused was found rummaging through the contents of the handbag. The Court of Appeal quashed a conviction for theft of certain items because there was no intention to permanently deprive but merely a conditional intention, ie an intention to take any items that were worth taking. Their Lordships were of the opinion that an attempt charge would similarly fail if the charge made reference to particular items because unless it could be shown that an accused had mens rea towards those items the elements of theft are not established. This problem would be avoided if a charge of attempted theft were drafted in broad terms alleging that B intended to steal some or all of the contents of the handbag: *Attorney-General's References (Nos 1 and 2 of 1979)* (1979).

The facts in question differ in that B has in mind a particular perfume. It would therefore be necessary to establish that B had mens rea sufficient for theft of the perfume if the indictment alleges that he attempted to steal the particular item of perfume. The perfume is not there and therefore this could be regarded as an example of impossibility where there is no object. Under the CAA 1981 impossibility is no longer to be regarded as defence: s1(2). Under s1(3) in deciding where a person has the necessary intention he must be judged on the facts as he believed them to be. This could be a difficult point on the facts in question. B merely hoped that the handbag would contain the perfume – that is not the same as a belief.

Any difficulties that might arise from this would be avoided if the approach indicated in the *Attorney-General's References* were adopted and an indictment for attempted theft was broadly drafted without reference to the perfume.

B could possibly be liable under s9 Theft Act 1968. Burglary is established where a person enters a building as a trespasser with intent to steal (s9(1)(a)) or where a person having entered a building as a trespasser steals or attempts to steal. Usually a ghost train ride will pass through a tunnel or structure. If this were sufficient to amount to 'a building' s9(1)(a) and s9(1)(b) could be satisfied. B would be a trespasser as he has not paid for his entrance as required. To be a building the structure must have some degree of permanence but beyond that the term may vary considerably in its meaning. On the facts it is impossible to conclude whether s9 is satisfied.

Returning now to the question of liability for conspiracy. A conspiracy contrary to s1(1) Criminal Law Act 1977 would be established if a person agrees with any other person that a course shall be pursued which, if the agreement is carried out in accordance with their intentions:

a)   will *necessarily* amount to or involve the commission of any offence by one or more of the parties to the agreement; or

b) would do but for the existence of facts which render the commission of the offence impossible.

The agreement between A and B appears only to extend to the entry and enjoyment of the amusement park. None of the charges that could arise from that are without difficulty. This means that it may not be possible for the prosecution to establish that their plan will necessarily involve the commission of an offence.

An alternative charge would be a common law conspiracy to defraud which would be established where there is a dishonest agreement which would result in a person suffering economic disadvantage: *Scott* v *Metropolitan Police Commissioner* (1975).

Undoubtedly s1 and the common law do on occasions overlap. Where this occurs s1 must be charged: *R* v *Ayres* (1984). Conspiracy to defraud should only be charged where either there is no substantive offence *necessarily* resulting from agreement or where beyond any agreement to commit a substantive offence there is a separate common law conspiracy: *R* v *Cooke* (1986). However, a prosecution may be brought under either head: s12 CJA 1987.

B may be liable as a co-conspirator providing he has, in addition to the normal mens rea requirement, mischievous discretion.

QUESTION FOUR

A telephoned B and suggested that together they should steal a rare diamond from a local jewellery exhibition. B replied that he would not help. B thought the matter over and decided to steal the diamond for himself. In order to 'case' the exhibition B bought an entry ticket. After inspection B decided it would be too difficult to steal the jewel. On the way out from the exhibition he took a coat from a cloakroom.

On discovering what B had done, A challenged him to a wrestling match. B agreed to the fight but, because he was afraid of A, he later changed his mind and failed to keep his 'appointment'.

Discuss A and B's criminal liability if any.

Adapted from University of London LLB Examination
(for External Students) Criminal Law June 1985 Q1

General Comment

A relatively straightforward question although careful thought and discussion is required on the overlap between counselling and incitement. Another area that would need a very careful approach is the question of whether or not the necessary elements of burglary are satisfied, in particular whether or not there is 'entry as a trespasser'.

Skeleton Solution

Incitement – counselling a crime – attempted theft – burglary under s9(1)(a) Theft Act 1968 – burglary under s9(1)(b) Theft Act 1968 – theft.

Suggested Solution

When A telephones B and suggests that they should steal a rare diamond A commits the common law offence of inciting another to commit an offence. The inciter must

34

spur on or urge on by advice, encouragement, persuasion, threats or pressure: *Race Relations Board* v *Applin* (1973). It is immaterial that the encouragement is unsuccessful provided it has been communicated to the incitee. It could not be argued that A has incited B to conspire because there is no such offence. Section 5(7) Criminal Law Act 1977. A and B do not enter into any agreement, therefore there is no conspiracy either under the common law or under the Criminal Law Act 1977. B proceeds on his own although it may be possible to argue still that A is an accomplice.

When B buys the ticket in order to 'case' the exhibition he may commit an offence contrary to s9(1)(a) of the Theft Act 1968. Under s9(1)(a) the offence of burglary is committed where there is entry by an accused into a building as a trespasser with intent to steal. The entry must be 'effective and substantial' and the accused must have intention or at least recklessness as to the facts which make him a trespasser: *R* v *Collins* (1972). Considering the facts in question there are two main difficulties.

Firstly, B has bought himself a ticket and therefore it could be argued that he has not entered the building as a trespasser. However, B's permission to enter was not given to help plan a theft. B has entered the building for a purpose other than the purpose for which he was given permission and therefore he may have entered 'as a trespasser': *R* v *Jones and Smith* (1976).

Secondly, it seems doubtful that B entered with intent to steal. B's entry was done with the purposes of assisting him in planning the burglary and therefore the requirement of an intention to steal would not appear to be satisfied unless B had a more general intention to steal anything that took his fancy while in the building: *Attorney-General's References (No 1 and 2 of 1979)* (1979).

B could not be liable for an attempt to steal the diamond because he must have done an act which is more than merely preparatory to the full offence with full mens rea, s1 Criminal Attempts Act 1981. This would seem unlikely on the facts here although it is for the jury to decide. If there was an attempt to steal the diamond there may be a further offence under s9(1)(b).

When B removes a coat from the cloakroom he commits the offence of theft contrary to s1 Theft Act 1968. Under s1 a person is guilty of theft if he dishonestly appropriates property belonging to another with the intention of permanently depriving the other of it.

Section 3 provides that an assumption by a person of the rights of an owner will amount to an appropriation. In *R* v *Morris* (1983) the House of Lords held that it was not necessary for the prosecution to prove that an accused assumed all the rights. It is sufficient to prove that he assumed any of the rights.

Furthermore, the concept of appropriation involved an act by way of 'adverse interference with or usurpation of those rights'. The question of dishonesty must be left to the jury: *R* v *Feely* (1973). On the facts given it is unlikely that the jury will require a *Ghosh* direction.

B may also be liable for the offence of burglary under s9(1)(b) of the Theft Act 1968. Under s9(1)(b) a person will be guilty of burglary if he enters a building as a trespasser and steals or attempts to steal. The question of whether or not the entry was a trespassary entry has already been considered.

Returning now to A's possible liability as an accomplice for the offences committed by B. A person who aids, abets, counsels or procures an offence is treated the same as a principal offender. A is not present or constructively present and therefore could not be an aider or abettor.

Possibly he could be said to be a counsellor. However, to establish this it must be shown that the offence he counselled actually took place, and it is fairly doubtful that there was even an attempt to steal the diamond. It could not be argued that he counselled any other of the offences, as they were not within the scope of what he contemplated. A further difficulty with regard to any counselling charge is that while there need not be any causal link there has got to be consensus between the counsellor and the principal offender. Undoubtedly A would contend that this was not present and he had never had in mind that B should proceed as he did.

With regard to the wrestling match, when A challenges B he may again be 'inciting' an offence at common law. He has communicated the encouragement to B and he intends the offence to be committed by B.

The 'offence' to be committed – ie the wrestling match – presents some difficulty. If the match is to take place in public or private it could be an offence under the Public Order Act 1986 or a breach of the peace.

A and B may, in agreeing to fight, be guilty of conspiracy under s1 Criminal Law Act 1977 However, their agreement must be to do an act which would necessarily amount to an offence *R* v *Walker* (1962). Moreover, it will not be a conspiracy here if the only person with whom A agrees in the intended victim of the offence (s2(2)(c)). If it is argued that the match itself is an offence and that B is not the 'intended victim', it would seem that the conspiracy is made out.

QUESTION FIVE

L telephoned M suggesting that they should enter Z's house, 'to do it over.' Z was their teacher. M understood L to be suggesting that they should look over the house and hide one or two of Z's things and leave messages in shaving soap on Z's mirrors. L meant that they should take anything of value and damage the rest of Z's property with paint. M said, 'Alright I'll see you at 8 pm tonight.' In fact, M failed to turn up having thought the matter over. Later, L recruited O to his plan and together they went to Z's house. Unexpectedly, Z returned home and discovered L and O. L hit Z over the head with a poker. Advise the parties of their criminal liability. What difference, if any, would it make to your advice if M was 16 years old?

University of London LLB Examination
(for External Students) Criminal Law June 1991 Q4

General Comment

The question raises a wide range of issues. Particularly trick points to watch for are the possibility of attempted incitement, and the possible absence of any agreement with regard to the conspiracy. The attack upon Z clearly requires reference to the 'Wilson and Jenkins' point on burglary. The point relating to M's age is curious. It would have made more sense if the question had stated that he was under 14, and then asked how his liability would differ.

Skeleton Solution

Incitement – curr point – possible attempt – conspiracy – whether any agreement – conspiracy with O – burglary – section 9(1)(a) – assault on Z – section 9(1)(b) – *R* v *Jenkins* – principal deliberately departs from the common design – the age of M.

Suggested Solution

a) *Incitement and conspiracy*

L suggests the commission of a number of offences to M. He may incur liability for common law incitement. The actus reus of incitement is committed where a defendant suggests the commission of an offence to another person. It has to be shown that the suggestion from the incitor has reached the mind of the incitee, but there is no need to provide evidence that the incitee acted on the suggestion; see comments of Lord Denning MR in *Race Relations Board* v *Applin* (1973). Generally, the incitee must know of the facts that make the conduct incited criminal. Hence a defendant can only be guilty of incitement to handle stolen goods if the incitee knew or believed the good in question to be stolen; see *R* v *Curr* (1968). In that case the defendant ran a loan business whereby he would lend money to women with children in return for their handing over their signed Family Allowance books. He would then use other women to cash the family allowance vouchers. He was convicted of inciting the commission of offences under s9(b) of the Family Allowance Act 1945, which made it an offence for any person to receive any sum by way of Family Allowance knowing it was not properly payable, but appealed successfully to the Court of Appeal, where it was held that the trial judge had erred in not directing the jury to consider whether those women, who were being incited to use the signed allowance books to collect money on behalf of the defendant, had actually known that what they were being asked to do was unlawful. In the present case L may contend that as he and M were at cross purposes, M may not have realised that what was being incited was unlawful. If this were the case, L might be charged with attempted incitement; see *R* v *Ransford* (1874).

It would appear that L did have the mens rea for incitement. In *Invicta Plastics* v *Clare* (1976), the Divisional Court defined it as involving not only an intention to incite, but also an intention that the incitee should act upon the incitement.

L and M may be charged with statutory conspiracy given that they agree to enter Z's house for an unlawful purpose, but there are difficulties here. Section 1(1) of the Criminal Law Act 1977 (as amended) provides that if a person agrees with any other person that a course of conduct shall be pursued which, if the agreement is carried out in accordance with their intentions, either will necessarily amount to or involve the commission of any offence or offences by one or more of the parties to the agreement, he is guilty of conspiracy to commit the offence or offences in question. The problem is that there is no meeting of the minds. Arguably the parties have not even agreed that any offence will be committed. Note that L cannot be charged with attempted conspiracy as the offence was abolished by s5 of the 1977 Act.

From the evidence provided it appears that there is much clearer evidence of a conspiracy between L and O, and that both could be charged with conspiracy to commit burglary contrary to the 1977 Act.

b) *Burglary*

The evidence provided indicates that when M entered the property owned by Z he intended to steal and commit criminal damage. O appears to have been fully aware of this. Under s9(1)(a) of the Theft Act 1968, a person is guilty of burglary if he enters any building or part of a building as a trespasser and with intent, inter alia, to commit the theft of anything in the building, or of with the intent of doing unlawful damage to the building or anything therein. M and O clearly enter a building and have no permission to be there.

c) *Assault on Z*

In striking Z on the head with the poker, L commits an assault, quite probably grievous bodily harm or wounding, depending upon the severity of the injuries. The harm appears to have been inflicted intentionally, thus L may incur liability under s18 or s20 of the Offences Against the Persons Act 1861. A further possibility is that L might be charged under s9(1)(b) of the 1968 Act which provides (inter alia) that a person is guilty of burglary if having entered any building as a trespasser and inflicts on any person therein any grievous bodily harm. Whether or not L entered as a trespasser has already been discussed. Note that L need not have had the intention to steal or inflict grievous bodily harm when he entered the building as a trespasser; such intent can be formed subsequent to entry. The infliction of grievous bodily harm under s9(1)(b) does not have to constitute an offence; it simply requires L to have inflicted grievous bodily harm upon Z. The Court of Appeal in *R v Jenkins* (1983) contemplated that a defendant would be guilty under s9(1)(b) where he entered a house as a trespasser and was observed by an occupant of whose presence he was unaware. Should the occupant suffer a stroke as a result of this shock, the defendant would have inflicted grievous bodily harm regardless of his lack of mens rea. The House of Lords, although allowing the defendant's appeal, in *R v Jenkins*, did not dissent from the above analysis of s9(1)(b).

O will contend that he is not guilty under s9(1)(b) since the attack upon Z was not part of the original agreement. The general rule is that an accomplice will be liable for all the accidental, or unforeseen consequences that flow from the common design being carried out, but where the principal deliberately departs from the common design, an accomplice ceases to be a party to his actions. Thus in *Davies v DPP* (1954), which concerned a gang fight in which the principal offender had killed an opponent with a knife, the defendant accomplice was acquitted of being an accomplice to either murder or manslaughter because the use of a knife during the attack was beyond the scope of what had been contemplated by him. This has been confirmed by *R v Carberry* (1994). Thus the attack upon Z is likely to be seen as something not contemplated by O when he agreed to accompany L.

d) *The age of M*

There is no evidence to suggest that M is not an adult and the suggestions above have been based upon that assumption. If M were below the age of ten he could not incur any criminal liability. Between the ages of 10 and 14, he can only be criminally liable if he is shown to have had 'mischievous discretion', or to have understood that what he was doing was seriously wrong. At the age of 16 he is to be treated as an adult for the purposes of establishing the mental element of criminal liability. The only relevance of his being 16 might relate to whether or not he realised that what was being suggested to him by L was wrong. This matter has already been considered.

4 NON-FATAL OFFENCES AGAINST THE PERSON

4.1   Introduction

4.2   Key points

4.3   Recent cases

4.4   Analysis of questions

4.5   Questions

4.1 Introduction

It is traditional to separate the various offences against the person into those of non-fatal offences against the person, sexual offences and homicide.

The offences ranging from threats to injure, through to grievous bodily harm, form the basis of many examination questions and it is vital that students are familiar with the requirements for each type of 'assault'.

4.2 Key points

a) *Assault and battery*

   i)   Assault

   Fagan v Metropolitan Police Commissioner [1969] 1 QB 439 – 'where the accused intentionally or possibly recklessly causes another person to apprehend immediate and unlawful personal violence'. (See also *R v Lamb* [1967] 2 All ER 1282; *Logden v DPP* [1976] Crim LR 121; *R v Wilson* [1955] 1 All ER 744.) Note that the threat of violence must be immediate: *Tuberville v Savage* (1669) 1 Mod Rep 3.

   ii) Battery

   R v Venna [1975] 3 All ER 788 – 'In our view the element of mens rea in the offence of battery is satisfied by proof that the defendant intentionally applied force to the person of another'. (Note the defence of consent discussed below and that a battery can be inflicted indirectly: *Scott v Shepherd* (1773) Wm Bl 892.)

b) *Defences to assault and battery*

   i)   Consent – *R v Coney* (1882) 8 QBD 534; *R v Donovan* (1934) 25 Cr App R 1 and the importance of public interest: *Attorney-General's Reference (No 6 of 1980)* [1981] QB 715. In *R v Brown* [1992] 2 WLR 441 it was held that whether consent will be a defence to a charge of actual or grievous bodily harm will be determined by considerations of public policy. The infliction of actual or grievous bodily harm during the course of a sado-masochistic act is not in the public interest and the 'victim's' consent will accordingly be no defence.

ii) Chastisement of child by parent, guardian or teachers: *Campbell and Cosans* v *United Kingdom* [1982] 4 EHRR 293 (European Court of Human Rights).

iii) Accident and the *de minimis* rule.

c) *The Offences Against the Person Act 1861*

The offences under this Act must be known thoroughly, especially the differences between the actus reus and mens rea of the main offences.

i) Actual bodily harm (s47)

R v *Chan Fook* [1994] Crim LR 432 held that for the purposes of a charge under s47 of the Offences Against the Person Act 1861 'harm' has the same meaning as injury and 'actual' indicates that the injury must not be so trivial as to be wholly insignificant. The court pointed out that, generally, an injury must be caused and an assault which merely interferes with the victim's health or comfort is *not* sufficient, although the court accepted that psychological illness due to an assault may amount to actual bodily harm providing:

• it amounts to more than mere emotional distress;

• it constitutes an 'identifiable clinical condition'; and

• it is supported by expert evidence.

The House of Lords in *R* v *Savage*; *R* v *Parmenter* [1991] 3 WLR 914 clarified the mens rea of the s47 offence by holding that the accused need have no intention or recklessness as to the injury caused (although of course he must have the mens rea for the assault). Thus a person who only intends to put another in fear of violence but actually caused injury may be convicted of this offence.

ii) Maliciously wounding or inflicting grievous bodily harm (s20)

Note that there are two alternative actus reus to this offence: 'wounding' (*C (a minor)* v *Eisenhower* [1984] QB 331 which is defined as an injury in which both layers of the skin have been broken) and 'grievous bodily harm' (which is a more general term defined as 'really serious harm': *DPP* v *Smith* [1960] 3 All ER 161).

The mens rea of the offence was established in *R* v *Savage*; *R* v *Parmenter* (above) – it being sufficient that the accused *intended* or *foresaw* that his act would cause *some harm* (note that the accused need not intend or foresee serious harm).

iii) Intentionally wounding or causing grievous bodily harm (s18)

The definitions of 'wounding' and 'grievous bodily harm' are the same as that given above for s20. However, one must not assume from this that the actus reus of s20 and s18 are exactly the same. It should be noted that s20 uses the word 'inflict' and s18 'cause' – arguably these have different meanings, the latter being wider than the former: see *R* v *Martin* (1881) 8 QBD 54; *R* v *Halliday* (1896) 61 LT 701; *R* v *Wilson* [1984] AC 242.

Note that for the s18 offence it is not sufficient that the accused intended *some* harm – the prosecution must prove that he intended to wound or cause grievous bodily harm.

d) The provisions of s51 of the Police Act 1964 should be known, together with the question of 'in the execution of his duty'. Also, the defence under s3 of the Criminal Law Act 1967.

e) Students should be aware of the offences of kidnapping and false imprisonment which occasionally feature in OAP questions.

Child destruction under the Infant Life (Preservation) Act 1929 should be known, together with the corresponding provisions of the Abortion Act 1967 and s58 of the Offences Against the Person Act 1861. See *Rance* v *Mid-Downs Health Authority* (1990) 140 NLJ 325.

f) *Administering poison*

Under ss23 and 24 of the 1861 Act it is an offence to administer or cause another person to take a poison, destructive or noxious thing.

Note the wide definition given to 'administer' in *R* v *Gillard* (1988) 87 Cr App R 189 to include spraying someone with a poison or noxious substance.

Note that the meaning of 'poison' or 'noxious thing' may be wider in s24 than in s23. *R* v *Cato* [1976] 1 All ER 260 held that with respect to s23 the substance administered must be *inherently* dangerous. *R* v *Marcus* [1981] 2 All ER 833 indicated that for s24 *any* substance could be 'noxious' if administered with the intention to injure, aggrieve or annoy.

Note that s23 is the more serious offence, subject to a maximum punishment of ten years, because the administration of the poison or noxious substance must actually endanger life or cause grievous bodily harm. Under s24 no effects need actually be caused to the victim, it being sufficient that the substance was administered with the intention to injure, aggrieve or annoy.

4.3 Recent cases

R v *Chan Fook* [1994] Crim LR 432

4.4 Analysis of questions

Students can almost guarantee that they will have at least one question which deals with assaults. The usual format is a problem question with several potential offenders committing various assaults with different mens rea and possible defences. Students will be required to pick their way clearly through quite complex sets of circumstances and to do so they must be able to distinguish the different types of assaults and woundings and to identify the required mens rea for, and defences to each.

4.5 Questions

QUESTION ONE

Andy was of a nervous disposition. He saw three youths walking towards him down a dark street. One of the youths, Basil, was carrying and swinging a bicycle chain. Andy was apprehensive that they were going to attack him. Andy crossed the road. The youths followed. Andy said, 'Not one step further or I'll have to defend myself.' The youths believed that they were being threatened. One ran away. Basil was unable to run because he had a heart illness. His brother Charles stayed with him. Basil, who then began to feel very unwell, stumbled forward and fell on Andy who believed he was being attacked and kicked Basil, inducing a severe heart attack. Charles entered the melee to protect his brother and kicked Andy before a passer-by stopped the fight. The youths had not intended to attack Andy but had been going to retrieve Basil's broken bicycle.

What crimes, if any, have been committed?

University of London LLB Examination
(for External Students) Criminal Law June 1983 Q1

General Comment

This question requires detailed consideration of a range of assaults together with two difficult defences, that of mistake and self-defence. A student should be careful not to confuse all the elements together but should clearly state what type of possible charges the parties may face and then go on to explain how the various defences working in conjunction with each other may operate to relieve any party of responsibility. Unless care is taken to plan the answer to this question it will appear confused.

Skeleton Solution

Andy   Assault – ss47 and 20 OAP Act 1861 – possibly s18 OAP Act – self-defence – s3 CLA 1967: mistake.

Basil   Assault – involuntary battery – recklessness.

Charles Battery – s47 OAP Act.

Suggested Solution

The offences which may have been committed by Andy will be considered first. When Andy, fearing attack informs the youths that if they come any further he will have to defend himself he may commit a common law assault. This is committed where an accused intentionally or recklessly puts a victim in fear of being then and there subjected to harm. There is authority for the proposition that words alone cannot constitute an assault (eg *R v Meade* (1823)). However, this was not supported by Lord Goddard in *R v Wilson* (1955) who was of the opinion that when a thief shouted 'Get out the knives' that would amount to assault.

In *Tuberville* v *Savage* (1669) a declaration by the accused that he would not attack P as it was Assize time was held not to be an assault. Clearly, therefore, words can negative an assault. However, the principle of this case should not be taken too far.

Indeed, in *Read* v *Coker* (1853) a threat by D to break P's neck if he did not leave the premises was held to be an assault.

When Andy kicked Basil, inducing a severe heart attack, he may have committed an offence contrary to s47 or s20 or possibly s18 of the Offences Against the Person Act 1861.

The most likely of those offences is s20 of the 1861 Act which provides that any person who unlawfully and maliciously wounds or inflicts any grievous bodily harm upon any person shall commit an offence. In kicking Basil, Andy has certainly committed an assault (defined in *R* v *Venna* (1976) as where the accused intentionally or recklessly causes the victim to apprehend immediate and unlawful personal violence). Since the resulting heart attack would also amount to actual bodily harm (defined in *R* v *Chan Fook* (1994) as any injury which is more than trivial) it is submitted that Andy has committed the actus reus with the requisite mens rea of the s47 offence. Further, following *R* v *Blaue* (1975) Andy cannot argue that Basil's existing heart condition amounts to a nova causa interveniens.

It is submitted that a heart attack would almost certainly amount to grievous bodily harm and following *R* v *Savage*; *R* v *Parmenter* (1991) Andy could be convicted of inflicting grievous bodily harm upon Basil if it could be shown that he intended or foresaw that he would cause some harm. It is not necessary that Andy intended or foresaw that he would cause wounding or grievous bodily harm.

It seems unlikely that an offence under s18 has been committed, as it would be necessary to show that Andy 'intended to do grievous bodily harm'. Intention requires a desire to bring those consequences about or knowledge of the certainty of them occurring. Recklessness is not sufficient. *R* v *Belfon* (1976).

Andy may wish to raise the defences of self-defence at common law or under s3 of the Criminal Law Act 1967 which allows the use of reasonable force in the prevention of crime. Andy may raise either of these defences, even though he was not under attack because *R* v *Williams (Gladstone)* (1987) established that where an accused made a mistake as to the factual circumstances in which he found himself his liability should be judged according to the facts as he genuinely, albeit mistakenly, believed them to be. Thus on the assumption that the three youths were about to attack Andy, the issue is whether the force used by Andy was reasonable. In *R* v *Shannon* (1980) it was held that an accused would not be using reasonable force where he was acting in retaliation. In *R* v *Whyte* (1987) the court recognised that in deciding whether the force used was reasonable the court must consider the possibility that the accused panicked. Lord Morris said 'a person defending himself cannot weigh to a nicety the exact measure of the necessary defensive action'. In *R* v *Scarlett* (1993) the Court of Appeal held that although the issue of whether the force used was reasonable was an objective question, the accused's subjective belief in the reasonableness of the force used was relevant as a matter of evidence. It was held in *R* v *Bird* (1985) that the fact that the accused retreated (as Andy did in crossing the road) before using force is powerful evidence that the force used was reasonable.

Basil may have committed the offence of common law assault ie putting a person in fear of being then and there subjected to harm by carrying and swinging a bicycle chain. The difficulty in proving that offence on the facts in question would be that he does not appear to have mens rea. The offence may be done intentionally or recklessly. While Basil may not have had any subjective intention to frighten or indeed may not have subjectively seen the risk that he might frighten somebody by swinging the bicycle chain it could be argued that he is still reckless, although it would seem that Cunningham recklessness is to be applied to statutory basic-intent assaults – *R* v *Morrison* (1988) – and such conscious risk-taking is not evident here. Within the *MPC* v *Caldwell* (1982) definition if he did the act which created the obvious risk that the person would be frightened without, however, giving any thought to the possibility of that risk existing, even though a reasonable man would have.

Similar problems arise when he stumbles forward and falls on Andy. This is certainly the actus reus of battery under the common law ie, a direct infliction of force. However, there would be no offence as there is no mens rea and he may be able to show that his actions were involuntary, thereby establishing a defence.

When Charles kicked Andy he may commit the offence of common law battery or an offence contrary to s47 of the Offences Against the Person Act 1861 providing there is some injury, however slight, as a consequence of his assault on Andy. However, he too would wish to claim self-defence under the common law or under s3 of the Criminal Law Act 1967. The right of self defence under the common law extends to immediate family: *R* v *Rose* (1884) and *R* v *Duffy* (1967). Similarly the bystander who intervenes to stop the fight would be able to claim a defence under s3 of the Criminal Law Act 1967 if he used force that was reasonable in the prevention of a crime.

QUESTION TWO

M was a circus performer who as part of his act was fired from a compressed air cannon, landing in a safety net. N and O were watching the performance M landed in the safety net and challenged the audience for a volunteer to do likewise. Usually P, M's assistant, hidden in the crowd, volunteered. However, before P could do so, N came forward while O held P back. M, in order not to lose face, despite considerable doubts allowed N to put on the protective clothing and lowered him into the cannon. N was fired from the cannon but N missed the net and landed on O and P. O was confused and P sustained a broken arm.

Advise the parties of their criminal liability.

University of London LLB Examination
(for External Students) Criminal Law June 1993 Q4

General Comment

A good question to attempt for those students who have revised offences against the person well although the interrelationship between the various offences as well as the individual offences per se needs to be explored.

Skeleton Solution

M's liability for offences against the person to N – whether M can raise the defence of N's consent – M's liability for the injuries sustained by O and P – O's liability for assault and false imprisonment of P.

Suggested Solution

M's liability for N's injuries

The information given does not specify what, if any, injuries were sustained by N being fired out of the cannon and landing on O and P. The fact that a safety net was provided (albeit one that N missed) does indicate that being fired out of the cannon was considered as being potentially dangerous and since N landed on O and P inflicting injuries on them it is likely that N sustained at least some injuries to himself although one can only speculate as to the nature and severity of those injuries.

By firing N out of the cannon M may be liable for battery if he intentionally or recklessly inflicted unlawful and personal violence on N (*R* v *Rolfe* (1952)). The fact that M did not fire N out of the canon out of hostility to him is irrelevant as Lord Lane has said that violence 'in the context of battery includes any unlawful touching of another person even if it is not hostile, rude or aggressive' (*Faulkner* v *Talbot* (1981)). the mens rea of battery is the intentional or reckless infliction of such force (recklessness to be measured in the *Cunningham* (1957) sense – see *R* v *Venna* (1975)) which would appear to be satisfied in this case as M intentionally fired N out of the cannon. M may also have assaulted N if he intentionally or recklessly caused N to apprehend immediate and unlawful personal violence (*Fagan* v *MPC* (1968)). If N sustained any injuries which are 'more than trivial' (*R* v *Chan Fook* (1994)) M may also be guilty of assault occasioning actual bodily harm contrary to s47 of the Offences Against the Person Act 1861. Although M may not have intended to cause any injury to N it has been established in *R* v *Savage*; *R* v *Parmenter* (1991) that this offence is committed once an assault or battery has caused actual bodily harm and that no mens rea is required as to the injury.

If N sustained more serious injuries M may be liable for recklessly inflicting grievous bodily harm contrary to s20 of the 1861 Act, his liability for this offence depending on whether he foresaw that he would cause some harm to N although he need not have foreseen that he would cause serious harm.

Consent

In *R* v *Brown* (1993) it was confirmed by the House of Lords that generally the absence of the victim's consent was an essential ingredient to a charge of an offence against the person, the burden being on the prosecution to prove this absence. However, *Brown* also held that where the accused causes a victim permanent injury or maiming, the consent of the victim is, as a matter of law, irrelevant and in other cases falling short of permanent injury the rule stated in the *Attorney-General's Reference (No 6 of 1980)* (1981) that the court must decide whether the injury was inflicted 'for a good reason' should apply. This rule essentially allows the court to consider as a matter of public policy whether the victim's consent should be allowed as defence in the particular circumstances. If N's injuries were of a permanent nature his consent would be irrelevant but if of a less serious and temporary nature might provide a defence to the charges against M depending on the court's conception of whether firing N out of the cannon was for 'a good reason'. It is submitted that performing the dangerous act of firing someone out of a cannon for the purpose of public entertainment and in order to prevent someone from 'losing face' and thereby causing injury, is not a good reason.

Injuries to P and O

By firing N out of the cannon and causing him to land on P, M may be indirectly responsible for breaking P's arm and may consequently be guilty of recklessly inflicting grievous bodily harm contrary to s20 of the Offences Against the Person Act 1861. A broken arm probably would amount to grievous bodily harm defined as 'really serious harm' in *R v Smith* (1961).

Although *R v Wilson* (1984) laid to rest the rule that the word 'inflict' in s20 requires an assault, it established that the direct application of force was still required. As the injuries to P were caused by N falling on him it could be argued that those injuries were only indirectly caused by M and therefore M should be acquitted of the s20 charge under the principle stated in *Wilson*. However, one could also argue that M was the direct cause of P's injuries if one draws an analogy with N being fired out of the cannon and any other projectile being fired from a weapon such as a bullet – where the accused would be regarded as the direct cause of the injuries sustained by the victim even though the immediate cause of the injuries was the bullet. The House of Lords in *R v Savage*; *R v Parmenter* confirmed that the word 'maliciously' as used in s20 imparts either intention or recklessness (in the *Cunningham* sense) as the mens rea, and that an accused satisfies this mens rea if he foresaw that some harm would result although he need not foresee that serious harm would result. Although it is quite possible that M did foresee that some harm might be caused to N who was fired out of the cannon as he had 'considerable doubts' it is less certain that he would have foreseen that N would land on a spectator causing injury to that spectator. If this is so, M would not be guilty of the s20 offence against P.

Whether M could be liable for assault or battery to O by causing N to fall on him depends on similar arguments to that discussed in relation to M and P above. Since it appears that O suffered no physical injury but was merely confused by N falling on him it is doubtful whether this confusion would amount to actual bodily harm for the purposes of the charge under s47 of the Offences Against the Person Act 1861. Although it was held in *R v Miller* (1954) that actual bodily harm included hysterical and nervous conditions resulting from an assault it was also established in *R v Donovan* (1934) that any harm caused must be more than merely transient or trifling. Arguably, merely being in a confused state may fall into the latter category which would entitle M to an acquittal on the s47 charge.

O's liability towards P

By unlawfully touching P, O is guilty of battery under the definition given above and may also be guilty of an assault by holding P back if he caused P to apprehend violence.

In holding P back O may have committed the offence of false imprisonment defined in *R v Rahman* (1985) as the unlawful and intentional or reckless restraint on a person's freedom of movement from a particular place. It should be noted that although it is not necessary to lock the victim in a confined space (it being sufficient to momentarily detain the victim) some detention is necessary and merely to restrict the victim's movement in one direction while he is free to move in other directions will not be sufficient (*Bird v Jones* (1845)). Therefore if P had merely stood in front of O he would not be guilty of this offence.

I was a plain clothes police officer arresting a violent criminal. J saw the incident and decided to intervene as he knew the man being arrested and wished to help him. J hit I over the head with his bag. I who had a thick skull collapsed from the blow which fractured his skull. I was seriously ill for three months.

Advise I.

Adapted from University of London LLB Examination
(for External Students) Criminal Law June 1984 Q3(b)

General Comment

This part of the question again requires knowledge of serious assaults and also the specific offence relating to assault on police.

Skeleton Solution

I – battery – ss18 and 20 OAP 1861. Assault police – s51 Police Act 1964 obstruction.

Suggested Solution

I should be advised that J has committed a battery which may fall under several headings.

First, under s51 of the Police Act 1964 a person who assaults a constable in the execution of his duty shall be guilty of an offence. It is not necessary that the accused knows that he is a constable provided the constable is acting in the execution of his duty.

Here I would appear to be so acting provided the arrest which he is trying to effect is lawful. His conduct would then fall within the general scope of preventing crime and catching offenders: *R* v *Waterfield* (1964).

Additionally J may be liable for wilfully obstructing a constable in the execution of his duty under s51(2) of the 1964 Act.

These offences are both summary offences and I should be advised to consider charging the following more serious assaults first.

I's injuries are serious enough to amount to grievous bodily harm: *DPP* v *Smith* (1961); *R* v *Saunders* (1985). Section 20 of the Offences Against the Person Act 1861 makes it an offence unlawfully and maliciously to wound or inflict any grievous bodily harm. The 'infliction', requiring direct application of force: *R* v *Wilson* (1984) is undoubtedly satisfied here and whether J is acting 'maliciously' will be determined on the subjective view of whether he foresaw at least the possibility of some harm: *R* v *Mowatt* (1968); *W* v *Dolbey* (1983). In *R* v *Savage*; *R* v *Parmenter* (1991) the House of Lords held that although it need not be proven that the accused intended or foresaw that his acts would cause wounding or grievous bodily harm, it must be established that the accused foresaw that some harm would result from his actions. Thus J would be guilty of the s20 offence in respect of the injuries sustained by I if he intended or foresaw that he would cause I some injury, even if he did not intend or foresee that he would fracture I's skull.

Section 18 of the 1861 Act makes it an offence unlawfully and maliciously to cause grievous bodily harm with intent to do gbh or to prevent the arrest or lawful detainer of any person. Here J's intention appears to be to prevent the arrest in which case, provided that arrest is lawful, the more serious offence under s18 is complete.

QUESTION FOUR

R believed she was pregnant, and asked S, her boyfriend to help her 'to get rid of the baby'. S said he would, though he was only humouring R because in her depressed state S feared R might attempt suicide. S gave R some cough mixture telling her it would 'do the job'. In fact it could not produce a miscarriage. However, R proved allergic to the cough mixture and went blind. R became so depressed she attempted suicide. She failed, but her conduct prematurely induced a miscarriage. The child lived for two hours before dying from premature arrival.

Advise R and S as to their criminal liability.

University of London LLB Examination
(for External Students) Criminal Law June 1985 Q7

General Comment

This was a difficult question and one that only a very competent student who enjoys a challenge should consider. The main difficulty would be to avoid getting bogged down in the technicalities of all the various offences.

Skeleton Solution

Section 58 of the Offences Against the Person Act 1861 – is the substance a 'noxious substance'? – contrast R and S's liability under s58 – S's liability under s59 for procuring the noxious substance – S's liability for the injuries to R – the range of assaults under the Offences Against the Person Act 1861 – s47, s20, s18, s23 and s24 – could R be regarded as the legal cause of the injury to S – Suicide Act 1961 – child destruction contrasted with murder or manslaughter.

Suggested Solution

Section 58 of the Offences Against the Person Act 1861 provides that an offence shall be committed where a woman who is pregnant unlawfully administers to herself any poisonous or other noxious thing, or unlawfully uses any instrument or other means whatsoever with the intention of producing a miscarriage. Section 58 further provides that any person who administers to a woman or causes to be taken by her any poisonous or noxious thing or unlawfully uses any instrument or other means whatsoever with the intention of producing a miscarriage, whether or not the woman is pregnant but merely believes herself to be, shall commit an offence.

The section distinguishes between a 'poison' and a 'noxious thing'. Something other than a recognised poison may still be noxious. A substance that may be harmless when taken in normal quantities can be noxious if it is harmful when taken in excess: *R* v *Marcus* (1981). The fact that the substance may not be an abortifacient is irrelevant.

49

R is pregnant and therefore may be liable under this section if the cough mixture was a noxious substance. S, however, could not be liable as he lacks the necessary intention to produce the miscarriage. Because of his lack of mens rea there would not be an offence of conspiracy contrary to s1 Criminal Law Act 1967 because they are not truly in agreement.

If the substance was not noxious S might be liable for an attempt to commit a s58 offence if she administers a harmless substance believing it to be noxious. Section 1(2) of the Criminal Attempts Act 1981 states that a person may be guilty of attempting to commit an offence even though the facts are such that the commission of the offence is impossible.

Following the House of Lords' decision in *R* v *Shivpuri* (1987), R's belief that taking the cough mixture would procure her abortion is sufficient to make her actions amount to a criminal attempt.

Under s59 an offence of unlawfully and knowingly supplying or procuring a poison or noxious substance may be committed providing that the accused knows that it is intended to be unlawfully used with the intention of procuring the miscarriage of a woman.

In *R* v *Mills* (1963) it was *held* that to procure meant to get possession of something that the accused did not already have. Thus if S already had the mixture this element would not be satisfied.

Furthermore, S would argue that what he did was not unlawful because he thought it would be harmless.

The question of whether or not S can be liable for the injuries sustained by R will depend on whether or not he has sufficient mens rea to satisfy one of the assaults. Furthermore, it must be shown that his conduct is the legal cause of the injuries that resulted. It must be shown that S's conduct was a substantial and operative cause of R's blindness. The fact that R is allergic to cough mixture will not break the causal link because the characteristics of a victim cannot break the chain of causation: *R* v *Blaue* (1975). However, it could be argued that S's conduct was too remote. It is not clear whether S supplied the mixture or actually administered it to R. However, in *R* v *Dalby* (1982) it was *held* that an accused who supplied drugs to a person who administered them to himself was too remote from the death that resulted.

Even if S was *held* to be a substantial and operating cause of the blindness it is difficult to see what offence he may have committed: s47 of the Offences Against the Person Act 1861 (assault occasioning actual bodily harm) and s20 of the Act (wounding or inflicting grievous bodily harm) would not be appropriate as both require an assault against the victim. Furthermore, an accused must have foreseen the possibility of some harm resulting: *R* v *Parmenter* (1991). Similarly s18 of the Act is not appropriate because although S may have 'caused' grievous bodily harm within the section, he did not have the necessary intention to cause grievous bodily harm. Section 23 and 24 of the Offences Against the Person Act 1861 create offences concerning unlawfully administering poisonous or noxious substances. Section 23 provides that it is an offence to unlawfully and maliciously administer a poisonous or noxious substance so as thereby to endanger the life of such person or so as thereby to inflict upon such person any grievous bodily harm. Section 23 may be committed recklessly. In this context recklessness requires a subjective appreciation of the risk involved: *R* v *Cunningham* (1957).

No mens rea at all is required as to the second part of the actus reus. Section 24 requires a specific intent namely 'To injure, aggrieve or annoy such persons'.

On the facts in question S would not have committed any offence under s23 because he was not acting 'maliciously'.

Similarly, s23 is not satisfied because S does not have the necessary specific intent. It should be noted that had S met the necessary requirements under s58 of the Offences Against the Person Act 1861 the fact that the victim consented would be no defence. The consent of the victim would not negative the unlawfulness of his conduct.

When R attempts to commit suicide she commits no offence. The Suicide Act 1961 abolished the offences of suicide and attempted suicide. Furthermore, R will commit no offence under s1(1) of the Infant Life (Preservation) Act 1929 because the section only covers the situation where a child capable of being born alive dies, as a result of a wilful act of any person, before it has an existence independent of its mother. It is not clear on the facts how many weeks old the foetus was. Evidence that a woman was pregnant for a period of 28 weeks is prima facie proof that the child was capable of being born alive: *C* v *S* (1988). Whether or not this is the case s1 would not be appropriate because R's conduct was not done with the intention of destroying the child and furthermore the child did survive independent of its mother, albeit for a very short time.

The question of whether or not R could be liable for murder or involuntary manslaughter of the child must now be considered. In order to be a victim of murder the child must have had an existence independent of its mother. In *R* v *West* (1848) it was *held* that a person who injures a child while that child is in the mother's womb may be liable to murder or involuntary manslaughter. In *R* v *Senior* (1899) it was *held* that an injury inflicted before birth either with mens rea for involuntary manslaughter or by gross negligence a conviction for manslaughter was correct.

While this type of situation would not be one where generally the criminal law would intervene, theoretically R might be liable for murder or manslaughter depending on the mens rea present. Murder would only be satisfied if she intended to kill or intended to do grievous bodily harm. Arguably this is the case on the basis that by killing herself would involve killing the child. Alternatively, liability for manslaughter by gross negligence may be shown if R's conduct was grossly negligent, so much so that it amounted to a crime: *R* v *Adomako* (1994).

QUESTION FIVE

A was engaged in rifle practice on a local firing range. A knew that B was 400 yards away in a trench below the target keeping score. A discharged six rounds at the target and B emerged from the protection of the trench. A decided to frighten him and fired a round over B's head. The round hit a concrete post and ricochetted and hit B who was seriously injured. Advise A of his criminal liability.

Adapted from University of London LLB Examination
(for External Students) Criminal Law June 1986 Q1

General Comment

A question that requires detailed consideration of the assaults. Providing a student does not get bogged down in too much detail on the assaults, good marks could be achieved.

Skeleton Solution

Common law battery – ss47, 20, 18 Offences Against the Person Act 1861.

Suggested Solution

When A fired a round over B's head which ricochetted and hit B, causing a serious injury, he may commit a number of offences both at common law and under the Offences Against the Person Act 1861.

Following *Fagan* v *Metropolitan Police Commissioner* (1969), A may be guilty of assaulting B if he intentionally or recklessly caused B to apprehend immediate personal violence. Although A may argue that firing the last shot was only a joke, since the objective of the joke was to cause B a fright, it is submitted that A has the mens rea for this offence.

When A hit B causing him serious injury he may commit an offence contrary to s47 Offences Against the Person Act 1861. Section 47 provides that it shall be an offence to assault occasioning actual bodily harm. In *R* v *Chan Fook* (1994) it was held that actual bodily harm was defined as an injury which is more than trivial. It must be proven that A intentionally or recklessly put B in fear of personal violence, a condition which would appear to be met as we are told that A 'decided to frighten' B. Following *R* v *Savage*; *R* v *Parmenter* (1991) no mens rea is required as to the actual bodily harm caused and it is thus irrelevant that A did not intend or foresee that the bullet would ricochet off a concrete post and injure B.

The injuries B sustains are serious. It may therefore be appropriate to charge A under s20 Offences Against the Person Act 1861. Section 20 provides that it is an offence to unlawfully and maliciously wound or inflict any grievous bodily harm. Grievous bodily harm means 'really serious bodily harm': *DPP* v *Smith* (1961).

The 'wounding' requires a break in the external skin, and not just bruising: *JJC* v *Eisenhower* (1984).

R v *Wilson* (1984) held that although the use of the word 'inflict' in s20 did not imply the requirement of an assault, the direct application of force was required. It is debatable whether the fact that B's injuries were caused by a ricochet would mean that the force was not directly applied.

In *R* v *Savage*; *R* v *Parmenter* (1991) it was held that although it need not be proven that the accused intended or foresee that his acts may wound or cause grievous bodily harm, it must be established that the accused intended or foresaw some harm. It is possible that A did not intend or foresaw that the bullet would ricochet and actually hit B, and accordingly A may be acquitted of the charge under s20.

Section 18 Offences Against the Person Act 1861 provides that it will be an offence to unlawfully and maliciously wound or cause any grievous bodily harm by any means whatsoever with intent to do grievous or bodily harm. While the actus reus of s18 may be satisfied the necessary intention to do grievous bodily harm is not shown. In *R* v *Belfon* (1976) it was held that recklessness as to the grievous bodily harm was not sufficient.

In addition, A would commit various offences under the Firearms Act 1968.

QUESTION SIX

L laced M's orange juice with a drug. M felt strange but was not sure that he had been drugged. He was travelling home on the underground train when he started to have hallucinations.

Advise L of his criminal liability.

> Adapted from University of London LLB Examination
> (for External Students) Criminal Law June 1986 Q5

General Comment

The question is a straightforward examination of knowledge of the relevant parts of the Offences Against the Person Act 1861.

Skeleton Solution

Battery – ss23 and 24 OAP 1861 – 'noxious substance'.

Suggested Solution

When L laced M's orange juice with a drug it will not amount to a battery as there must be some amount of force applied to the victim's body in order to constitute a battery, *R* v *Hanson* (1849). He may however be liable under ss23 or 24 Offences Against the Person Act 1861.

Section 23 provides that it is an offence to unlawfully and maliciously administer or cause to be administered any poisonous or noxious substance so as thereby to endanger the life of such person or to inflict upon him any grievous bodily harm. Section 24 provides that it is an offence to administer or cause to be administered any poisonous or noxious substance with intent to injure, aggrieve or annoy.

In *R* v *Marcus* (1981) the term noxious was broadly interpreted to include substances taken in small quantities if that quantity is administered with intent to injure, aggrieve or annoy. It was necessary to take into account quantity, quality and all circumstances to decide if a substance is noxious.

M suffers hallucinations. This may amount to an infliction of grievous bodily harm. Under s23 there is no need to show either a direct or an indirect assault for there to be an infliction of grievous bodily harm unlike s20 OAP 1861. The only mens rea required under s23 is intention or recklessness as to the administration of the noxious substance. No mens rea is required as to the consequence *R* v *Cato* (1976). For s24 there must be an ulterior intent to injure aggrieve or annoy.

QUESTION SEVEN

A, a religious zealot, seized B's son. He telephoned B telling him to collect and post a parcel to a leading churchman if he did not wish to see his son hurt. B posted the

53

parcel as directed. B thought the parcel contained a bomb but he knew that the churchman's mail was being intercepted and therefore expected that no injury would occur. In fact, the postman handling the parcel was injured when it exploded in the sorting office where it had been delayed. Advise the parties of their criminal liability.

Adapted from University of London LLB Examination
(for External Students) Criminal Law June 1988 Q1

General Comment

In order to decide which non-fatal offence against the person to consider first, assess the level of injury the facts indicate. One would expect more than slight harm to be caused, so start with the more serious offences, not the least serious offences. Obviously, a key issue here is the mens rea (or lack of it) of B.

Also, remember to consider A's criminal liability, as a secondary party to B's offence and as a principal offender, ie kidnapping and incitement.

Skeleton Solution

Postman injured – non-fatal offences against the person – degree of injury – actus reus of s18 and s20 Offences Against the Person Act 1861 – definition of 'wound' – definition of 'grievous bodily harm' – mens rea – intention – *Cunningham* recklessness – s47 Offences Against the Person Act 1861 – actus reus – mens rea.

Defence of duress – was threat sufficiently serious – was it immediate – not directed at defendant – was it reasonable for B to give in to the threat.

Liability of A – secondary party to B's offences – principal offender – kidnapping – incitement.

Suggested Solution

What offences has B committed in sending the parcel bomb and thereby causing injury to a postman?

It appears that the postman has suffered a non-fatal injury to the person.

Section 18 Offences Against the Person Act 1861 makes it an offence to wound or cause any grievous bodily harm.

To wound, the continuity of the whole skin must be broken: *Moriarty* v *Brooks* (1834); *JJC (a minor)* v *Eisenhower* (1984). It is not enough that the cuticle or outer skin be broken if the inner skin remains intact: *R* v *M'Loughlin* (1838); *R* v *Wood* (1830); *R* v *Waltham* (1849); *R* v *Jones* (1987). It is probably sufficient that the wound is directly inflicted whether by a battery or not: *R* v *Wilson* (1983); *R* v *Taylor* (1869); *R* v *Austin* (1973).

'Grievous bodily harm' must be given its ordinary natural meaning. 'Grievous' means 'really serious' and the word 'really' probably adds nothing but emphasis to the fact that the harm caused must be actually or really serious: *DPP* v *Smith* (1961); *R* v *Saunders* (1985).

'Cause' requires proof of a positive act: *Price* v *Cromack* (1975).

4 NON-FATAL OFFENCES AGAINST THE PERSON

On the facts, it is not possible to decide whether the postman was wounded or suffered grievous bodily harm or both.

If the charge is causing grievous bodily harm with intend to cause grievous bodily harm, then only intention will be sufficient mens rea. Smith and Hogan argue (in 'Criminal Law', 6th edition, p400) that if the charge is wounding with intent to do grievous bodily harm, then a defendant may intend to do grievous bodily harm *without* intending to wound so that if he in fact wounds, it must be proved that he intended to cause grievous bodily harm and that he foresaw that he might wound.

On the facts, as B knew that the mail was being intercepted and therefore expected no injury to occur, he cannot be said to have intended the injury or subjectively foreseen the consequences of his act. He would therefore appear to lack mens rea.

Section 20 Offences Against the Person Act 1861 makes it an offence to wound or inflict any grievous bodily harm.

'Wound' and 'grievous bodily harm' have the same meaning as in s18 Offences Against the Person Act 1861. 'Inflict' does not imply an assault but does imply the direct application of force: *R* v *Wilson* (1983).

The mens rea is either intention or *Cunningham* recklessness: *R* v *Parmenter* (1991).

Again, for the same reasons, whereas B may have caused the actus reus of the s20 offence, he would appear to lack the required mens rea.

Section 47 Offences Against the Person Act 1861 makes it an offence to commit an assault occasioning actual bodily harm. Actual bodily harm need not be really serious but must be an injury which is more than trivial: *R* v *Chan Fook* (1994).

On the facts, the injuries suffered by the postman whatever their nature would appear to come within the actus reus of this offence.

Following *R* v *Savage*; *R* v *Parmenter* (1991) the mens rea of the s47 offence is that required for the assault only and no mens rea is required as to the actual bodily harm caused.

Again, B may well have caused the actus reus of this offence but would appear to lack the required mens rea.

However, if B was to be found liable for any of these offences, he may be able to plead the defence of duress.

The threat must be sufficiently serious to constitute duress. The threat must be one of death or serious personal injury to the person of the defendant or to a third person, ie the defendant's family, others to whom he owes a duty and even a complete stranger in some circumstances, eg a stranger held as a hostage to force the defendant to do a criminal act: *R* v *Steane* (1947); *R* v *Hudson* (1971). The gravity of the threat must be assessed against the enormity of the crime: *Abbott* v *R* (1977). The threat must be immediate or imminent: *R* v *M'Growther* (1746). There is now no longer any rule of law that the defendant must resort to the protection of the law if he is able to and is physically out of the range of his oppressors: *R* v *Hurley* (1967); *R* v *Hudson*.

The law applies an objective standard when considering the defendant's action. The defendant must have done what he did as a result of having reasonably believed what his oppressor had said or done, he had good cause to fear that he (or a person to whom he owed a duty) would suffer death or serious personal injury, and a sober person of reasonable firmness, sharing the characteristics of the defendant, would have also so responded: *R* v *Howe* (1987); *R* v *Graham* (1982). A person is expected to display the steadfastness reasonably to be expected of an ordinary citizen in the same situation.

Although B's son and, therefore, someone to whom he owed a duty, was seized it is not at all clear what the nature of the threats against the boy was, or whether it was reasonable for B not to seek police protection as he was not under the direct control of A.

A is liable for the false imprisonment of B's son and if the detention was accompanied with a taking away, force or fraud, it will also amount to kidnapping: *R* v *Brown* (1985).

A is also liable as a secondary party to any offence B may have committed with respect to the postman. Although A did not directly and must immediately cause the actus reus of the crimes, anyone who aids, abets, counsels or procures the commission of any offence is liable to be tried, indicated and punished as a principal offender: s8 Accessories and Abettors Act 1861, as amended by s1 Criminal Law Act 1967.

He also appears to have committed the offence of incitement in that by his threats he sought to reach and influence the mind of A to commit an act which, when done, would be a crime by the person incited: *R* v *Nkosiyana* (1966); *Race Relations Board* v *Applin* (1973); *R* v *Whitehouse* (1977).

QUESTION EIGHT

A disliked B, a well known local councillor. A believed that B was a rogue who had made secret profits from his office. A threw paint at B's car intending to frighten B as B was being driven past. A shouted, 'It is necessary to teach you a severe lesson and draw your behaviour to public notice.' The paint damaged the car and obscured B's driver's view and as a result the car crashed into a bus queue injuring a mother and her three children. B was slightly injured in the collision and B's driver suffered severe nervous shock.

Advise A of his criminal liability.

Adapted from University of London LLB Examination
(for External Students) Criminal Law June 1990 Q1

General Comment

A complicated and lengthy question combining non-fatal assaults, criminal damage, and homicide. Note that both types of criminal damage require consideration. The nature of the injuries suffered by the children is not specified. It is suggested that they are merely discussed in general terms.

Skeleton Solution

Common law assault – words as an assault – simple and aggravated criminal damage – homicide, causation, disregard murder – unlawful act manslaughter, whether unlawful act is dangerous – non-fatal assaults.

Suggested Solution

A may have committed common law assault in throwing the paint at the car. The actus reus of the offence requires proof that the victim apprehended immediate physical violence; see *Logden v DPP* (1976). The determining factor will be the perception of the victim. The reasonable bystander would realise that the paint would not make physical contact with the victim, and that there was in fact no threat of direct physical violence. The victim, however, might have momentarily thought that the paint was going to hit him.

The mens rea for common assault is intention or recklessness; see *R v Venna* (1976). In *Venna* the court took recklessness to mean subjective recklessness, basing this decision on the earlier case of *R v Cunningham* (1957). Subjective recklessness requires proof that the defendant was aware of the risk that the victim would apprehend immediate physical violence. It would appear that the application of this form of recklessness to assault remains unaffected by developments in cases such as *MPC v Caldwell* (1982). *R v Spratt* (1990) and *R v Parmenter* (1991) both of which confirm that, as far as assault occasioning actual bodily harm contrary to s47 of the Offences Against the Persons Act 1861 is concerned, *Cunningham* type recklessness applies. It is submitted that the same reasoning should apply to the offence of assault at common law. On the facts it may be that A will say that, as he was throwing the paint at the windscreen of the car, he could not have foreseen any risk that the victim would apprehend physical contact, but it is submitted that he may have some difficulty in persuading any court to believe this.

A's act of shouting at B cannot of itself constitute the offence of common law assault. Words alone cannot constitute an assault; see *R v Meade and Belt* (1823) 'no words or singing could constitute an assault'.

It would appear that A has committed the offence of 'simple' criminal damage contrary to s1(1) of the Criminal Damage Act 1971. The car is clearly property belonging to another as against A. The paint has caused damage to the bodywork of the car. Damage can occur even where the effects can be rectified relatively easily; see *Hardman v Chief Constable of Avon* (1986). A appears to have had the necessary mens rea for the offence, either intention or recklessness.

A more difficult question is that of whether or not A could be convicted of the more serious offence of 'aggravated' criminal damage contrary to s1(2) of the 1971 Act. The aggravating factor lies in the mens rea. A must be proved to have had either an intention to endanger life, or at least to have been reckless as to whether life would be endangered. Following the House of Lords' decision in *R v Steer* (1988), the prosecution must establish that the defendant intended the criminal damage itself to endanger life, or that he was reckless as to whether it would endanger life. It is not sufficient, for example, merely to show that he was reckless as to whether the act causing the criminal damage might endanger life. On the facts of the problem, the minimum that the prosecution would have to establish in relation to the mens rea for the aggravated offence would be that A gave no thought to an obvious risk that obscuring the driver's view, by covering the car windscreen with paint would endanger the lives of others. The test for recklessness here is that laid down by the House of Lords in *MPC* v *Caldwell* (above). It is submitted that on the facts, the prosecution might be able to establish the necessary mens rea.

A has caused injuries to the woman's children. If causation is established in relation to the homicide it is submitted that it will be established in relation to these unspecified non-fatal offences. The precise charge brought against A will depend to a large extent on the nature of the harm done to the children. In any event it is unlikely that A will be convicted of anything more serious than malicious wounding, or maliciously inflicting grievous bodily harm contrary to s20 of the Offences Against the Persons Act 1861, since he appears not to have intended to cause any such harm.

The injuries to B and his driver are likely to constitute actual bodily harm contrary to s47 of the 1861 Act, in that they are injuries which interfere with the health and comfort of the victim: see *R* v *Miller* (1954). The mens rea for this offence is intention or recklessness as described above. The prosecution would have to prove that A was at least aware of a risk of the victims being frightened by his actions, which on the facts, seems likely.

5 HOMICIDE

5.1   Introduction

5.2   Key points

5.3   Recent cases

5.4   Analysis of questions

5.5   Questions

5.1 Introduction

Homicide, which covers the killing of one human being by another, forms a complex, fascinating and very important part of the criminal law syllabus. It is very important therefore that students are familiar with the varying types of homicide, both lawful and unlawful, together with the available defences.

5.2 Key points

a) *Homicides*

   i) Homicides involve the killing – that is, the acceleration of the death of – a person under the Queen's peace within a year and a day of the accused's act which brought about that death: *R* v *Dyson* [1908] 2 KB 454.

   ii) Murder is homicide with malice aforethought. Such malice aforethought, the mens rea, is an intention to cause the death, or a grievous bodily harm to another: *R* v *Moloney* [1985] AC 905. The apparent dual states of mind involving foresight expanded in *Hyam* v *DPP* [1975] AC 55 are no longer good law.

   Students **must** know the cases of *R* v *Hancock and Shankland* [1986] AC 455 and *R* v *Nedrick* [1986] 1 WLR 1025.

   iii) A jury might infer an intention to kill or cause grievous bodily harm only if it appears to them that the accused foresaw such death/gbh as an 'overwhelming probability' (*R* v *Hancock and Shankland*) or, where those consequences were 'virtually certain' to occur and that they are satisfied that the accused knew that to be the case (*R* v *Nedrick*).

   The decisions in *R* v *Hancock and Shankland* and in *R* v *Nedrick* do not contradict *R* v *Moloney*: they uphold the rule that foresight is something from which intention **might** be inferred but restrict the scope of the *R* v *Moloney* direction.

b) *Voluntary manslaughter*

   Voluntary manslaughter is where the accused commits murder but in circumstances in which what would otherwise be a conviction for murder will be

59

mitigatged down to manslaughter on the grounds of provocation or diminished responsibility.

i) Provocation

The definition of this defence is a combination of statements in *R* v *Duffy* [1949] 1 All ER 932 and s3 Homicide Act 1957.

The first stage of the defence is to establish whether or not the accused lost his self-control (a subjective test). This is a question of fact for the jury.

The second stage is to establish that the loss of self-control was 'sudden'. Note that the cases which establish that any time delay between the act or words of provocation and the killing will prevent the successful raising of the defence (such as *R* v *Hayward* (1833) 6 C & P 157 and *R* v *Thornton* [1992] 1 All ER 306) must now be read in the light of dicta in *R* v *Ahluwalia* [1993] Crim LR 63 to the effect that such a delay will not necessarily be fatal to the defence.

The third stage in the defence is to establish that a reasonable man in similar circumstances would also have lost his self-control. Although this is an objective text it has a subjective element, ie whether the reasonable man sharing the same *characteristics as the accused* would have lost his self-control: *DPP* v *Camplin* [1978] AC 705. For restrictions on what type of characteristics can be imputed see: *DPP* v *Camplin* (above); *R* v *Newell* (1980) 71 Cr App R 331.

The final stage of the defence is to investigate whether the reasonable man who has lost his self-control might have reacted as the accused did. This is a question of fact for the jury.

ii) Diminished responsibility

The first stage of this defence under s2 of the Homicide Act 1957 is to investigate whether the accused was suffering from an abnormality of mind due to retarded development, inherent causes or disease or injury. Note that an abnormality of mind due to external causes, such as the consumption of drink or drugs, is excluded (see *R* v *Gittens* [1984] QB 698, although the exceptions to this rule stated in *R* v *Tandy* [1989] 1 WLR 350 when alcoholism may sustain the defence should be noted).

The second stage (often omitted in candidates' examination scripts) is to investigate whether the abnormality is so great that it has substantially impaired the accused's responsibility.

Note that the burden of proof is on the accused to prove this defence on balance of probabilities.

Note that the following have been held to amount to diminished responsibility: abnormal urges (*R* v *Byrne* [1960] 3 All ER 1); epileptic upset (*R* v *Bailey* (1977) 66 Cr App R 31); morbid jealousy (*R* v *Vinagre* (1979) 69 Cr App R 104); depression (*R* v *Gittens* [1984] QB 698); and the effects of alcoholism (*R* v *Tandy* [1989] 1 WLR 350).

c) *Causation*

When discussing any charge of homicide a candidate should begin the discussion by investigating whether the accused's act or omission is a factual and legal cause of death. The rules of causation and circumstances in which the different rules should be used must be known.

Negligent medical treatment will not necessarily break the chain of causation – the question is whether the accused's act is still 'an operating and substantial cause' (*R v Smith* [1959] 2 QB 35) or 'a significant contributory factor' (*R v Cheshire* [1991] Crim LR 709).

Note that the above cases also establish that the accused's act need not be the sole or even the main cause of death.

Following *R v Roberts* (1971) 115 Sol Jo 809 an accused may be responsible for the injuries sustained by the victim in the course of escaping from an attack providing the victim's response is 'reasonable and not daft'.

The accused will be responsible for the consequences he causes even though they are exacerbated by the victim's existing medical or psychological condition, or where the victim's religious beliefs forbid certain treatment: *R v Blaue* [1975] 3 All ER 446.

d) *Involuntary manslaughter*

This is where the accused kills without the mens rea of murder.

i) Manslaughter by gross negligence

In *R v Adomako* [1994] 1 WLR 15 the House of Lords in a landmark decision effectively abolished the offence of reckless manslaughter as defined in *R v Lawrence* [1982] AC 510 and replaced it with a newly defined offence of manslaughter by gross negligence. To secure a conviction for this offence the prosecution must prove:

• that the accused owed the victim a duty of care;
• that the duty was breached causing death;
• that the accused's act or omission is 'grossly negligent' which is defined as 'supremely a question for the jury to decide whether the risk of death was so great as to amount to a criminal act or omission'.

Note that this is purely an objective test and manslaughter by gross negligence has now effectively become an offence of strict liabililty.

ii) Causing death by dangerous driving

The offence of causing death by dangerous driving under s1 Road Traffic Act 1988 has replaced the offence of causing death by reckless driving under s1 Road Traffic Act 1972. The new offence will be committed when the accused's driving 'falls far below the standard expected of the competent and careful driver', and it would be obvious to such a driver that driving in that way would be dangerous. Note that the offence is essentially one of strict liability and there is no longer any room for the 'lacuna' argument.

iii) Unlawful act/constructive manslaughter

R v *Church* [1966] 1 QB 59 – 'the unlawful act must be such as all sober and reasonable people would inevitably recognise must subject the other person to, at least, the risk of some harm resulting therefrom, albeit not serious harm'.

Note that the unlawful act need not be directed at the victim: *R* v *Goodfellow* (1986) 83 Cr App R 23 and *R* v *Mitchell* [1983] 2 WLR 938.

Note that the 'dangerousness' of the act is measured in an objective sense: *R* v *Ball* [1989] Crim LR 730.

See also *R* v *Lamb* [1967] 2 QB 981 and *DPP* v *Newbury* [1977] AC 500.

5.3 Recent cases

R v *Ahluwalia* [1993] Crim LR 63

R v *Adomako* [1994] 1 WLR 15

5.4 Analysis of questions

It is a safe bet that at least one question on the paper will be concerned with homicide in its various forms. There are usually several such questions, aimed particularly at one essential element eg causation or intention.

It cannot be stressed too much that a sound knowledge of this topic is vital to examination success and good overall marks can be attained by a student who has a strong grasp of the principles in this chapter.

5.5 Questions

QUESTION ONE

J had visited K, his hypnotherapist for treatment of relief of pain. After treatment J was still under the influence of hypnosis though he gave no signs of this. Whilst driving home J ran down and killed L, a child aged six years who had run out in front of J's car. Unaware of the accident, J walked away to his home nearby. J then went for a walk and met M who called him a 'thick idiot'. J lost his temper and hit M over the head with his walking stick. M had a thin skull and died from the blow.

Advise J and K as to their criminal liability.

> Adapted from University of London LLB Examination
> (for External Students) Criminal Law June 1985 Q4

General Comment

A difficult question. The range of the question is wide, covering a number of fairly difficult aspects of the syllabus including recklessness. Furthermore, the difficulties are aggravated because of the need to consider the defence of automatism.

A student should take great care to ensure that his answer is clear and well planned. Although there is no one correct approach a student would probably find that the best approach would be to explain all the possible offences committed by J first and only then go on to consider and apply the defence of automatism.

Skeleton Solution

Causing death by dangerous driving – s1 Road Traffic Act 1988 – overlap with involuntary manslaughter – murder and the defence of provocation – alternative charge of constructive manslaughter – the defence of non-insane automatism – limits on such a defence – *R* v *Bailey* (1983) whether K could be the legal cause of the deaths – liability of K for manslaughter by gross negligence – doctrine of innocent agency.

Suggested Solution

J may be guilty of causing death by dangerous driving contrary to s1 of the Road Traffic Act 1988 (as amended by the Road Traffic Act 1991) which abolished and replaced the offence of causing death by reckless driving contrary to s1 of the Road Traffic Act 1972. J may be guilty of this offence if the way he drove fell far below what would be expected of a competent and careful driver. Although J ran down L and killed him there is no information as to the manner in which he was driving and therefore whether the 'accident' was due to J's poor driving or L's own carelessness in running across the road. If J's driving did fall below this standard it must also be proven that it would have been obvious to a competent and careful driver that driving in that way would be dangerous.

In *R* v *Seymour* (1983) the House of Lords held that the offence of causing death by reckless driving contrary to s1 Road Traffic Act 1972 coexisted with manslaughter at common law.

J could also be charged with manslaughter by gross negligence as defined in *R* v *Adomako* (1994). As a driver he clearly owes other road users (including pedestrians) a duty of care; this duty is likely to have been broken by driving in a hypnotic state. It will be for a jury to decide whether this conduct is so negligent that it amounts to a criminal act.

J may be liable for either murder or manslaughter when he strikes and kills M. He will not be able to claim that he did not cause the death because an accused must take his victim as he finds him and a characteristic like a thin skull will not break the chain of causation: *R* v *Blaue* (1975).

J will be liable for murder if he kills while intending to kill or intending to do grievous bodily harm. If he did the act foreseeing that it was highly probable that he would kill or do grievous bodily harm that may be evidence that he had the necessary mens rea but no more than that: *R* v *Moloney* (1985). If the judge considers it appropriate he may leave it to the jury to infer intention from J's foresight but they must only do so if J foresaw death or grievous bodily harm as 'virtually certain' per *R* v *Nedrick* (1986) or as being 'highly probable' per *R* v *Hancock and Shankland* (1986); *R* v *Barr, Kenyon and Heacock* (1989).

The jury is not bound to infer foresight of consequences by reason only of there being a natural and probable consequence of those actions – s8 Criminal Justice Act 1967.

If J had the necessary mens rea for murder but was provoked by M he may be able to claim the defence of provocation which would reduce murder to voluntary manslaughter. Provocation may be established if an accused can show that he lost his self control as a result of actions or words of the victim or a third party.

Furthermore, it must be shown that a reasonable man would also have lost his self control and done as the accused did. In deciding the reasonable man test the jury must give a reasonable man the age, sex and other characteristics of the accused that affect the provocation: *DPP* v *Camplin* (1978), also *R* v *Doughty* (1986). In *R* v *Newell* (1980) the Court of Appeal found that an accused's characteristics had to be permanent and directly relate to the provocation. Thus drunkenness and a hypnotic would obviously not be characteristics that could be imputed to the reasonable man.

An alternative charge to murder is that of constructive manslaughter. The prosecution must establish that J intended to do an unlawful act which was likely to subject the victim to at least the risk of some harm, albeit not necessarily serious harm: *R* v *Church* (1965). The unlawful act, which J must have intended, would be the striking of M on the head with a stick. It would not be necessary, however, to show that J foresaw the possibility of harm. It is sufficient if a reasonable man would have seen the risk involved.

It is now necessary to consider whether J can claim a defence resulting from his hypnotized state. Whatever offence under criminal law is being alleged it must be shown that an accused acted 'voluntarily' ie that his mind was in control of his body. If this is not the case he will be acting as an automaton. On the facts in question the automatism does not arise from a disease of the mind (insane automatism) and therefore non-insane automatism may be pleaded as a defence. It should, however, be noted that where the automaton state arose as a result of the accused's own recklessness he will be unable to claim it as a defence to a crime where recklessness is sufficient mens rea: *R* v *Bailey* (1983); *R* v *Hardie* (1985). The defence of automatism would therefore only be available to J if he can show that he has not acted 'voluntarily' through no fault of his own. While this might possibly be the case where L is killed it is not as easy to apply the principles where M's death is considered. Intoxication and automatism are acting in conjunction with each other. The need to protect the public would probably result in the principles relating to voluntary intoxication being applied.

K's liability would depend on whether or not his conduct rather than J's could be regarded as the legal cause of the deaths that occurred. If it could be established that K's conduct was a substantial and operating cause of death he might possibly be liable for manslaughter by gross negligence in respect of each victim. The type of conduct sufficient for such a charge has been detailed above: *R* v *Bateman* (1925); *R* v *Seymour* (1983).

It would not be appropriate to apply the doctrine of innocent agency because it does not appear that K had been acting intentionally. Had K been acting with the intention that J should perform such acts while under hypnosis K would be the principal offender while J would have been his innocent agent.

QUESTION TWO

P, an anti-hunt demonstrator, hid behind a fence in Q's field intending to startle horses and riders. In pursuit of a fox Q was galloping across his field preparing to jump a wall. P jumped out from his concealed position and startled Q's horse. Q was thrown to the ground. He was a haemophiliac and died as a result of the fall. P had foreseen that there was a possibility of a rider being dismounted but he had not desired death. Other hunt members, X and Y, picked P up, carried him out of the field and threw him into a lake.

Advise P, X and Y as to their criminal liability.

Adapted from University of London LLB Examination
(for External Students) Criminal Law June 1985 Q6

General Comment

A rather difficult question and one that requires careful consideration in order to recognize all the possible offences that may have been committed. A student must examine in detail the mens rea of murder and contrast it with involuntary manslaughter. A full range of assaults may have been committed against P and detailed consideration of those will be required.

Skeleton Solution

Murder and involuntary manslaughter contrasted – ss47, 20 and 18 Offences Against the Person Act 1861 – defence contained in s3 Criminal Law Act 1967.

Suggested Solution

The first point to consider in relation to Q's death is whether or not P can be regarded as the legal cause of the death ie 'a substantial and operating cause' of what occurs. There seems little doubt that this would be the case and it should be noted that the fact that Q was a haemophiliac will not break the chain of causation: *R v Blaue* (1975). P will be responsible for Q's death if it can be shown that he had the necessary mens rea for murder or came within involuntary manslaughter either constructive manslaughter or manslaughter by gross negligence.

The mens rea for murder is intention to kill or intention to do grievous bodily harm. It is not sufficient mens rea for murder to show that the accused foresaw that death or grievous bodily harm was highly probably going to occur, although such foresight *may* be evidence to show that an accused had the necessary mens rea: *R v Moloney* (1985). However, the jury must believe that P foresaw death or grievous bodily harm as being a 'virtually certain' consequence of his actions and virtually certain to occur: *R v Nedrick* (1986), or as being 'overwhelmingly probable': *R v Hancock and Shankland* (1986).

Applying these principles to the facts in question, P may not desire to kill Q but he could still have mens rea if he knew that death or grievous bodily harm was 'virtually certain' or 'overwhelmingly probable' but the jury must be sure that such an inference of intention is right. A conviction for murder carries with it a mandatory life sentence. Alternative charges to murder would be constructive manslaughter and manslaughter by gross negligence. A conviction for manslaughter carries a maximum life sentence.

Constructive manslaughter would be satisfied if it could be shown that Q died as a consequence of P's actions and that P had an intention to do an unlawful act which was likely to cause at least a little harm. The 'unlawful act' that an accused must intend must be more than a civil wrong. In *R v Franklin* (1883) the accused threw a box belonging to X into the sea killing P. It was held that such a civil wrong was not sufficient for constructive manslaughter. Applying this to the facts of the case undoubtedly P is committing the tort of trespass but this could not be relied on for constructive manslaughter. If it could be established that P intended to frighten Q and not just the horse when he jumped out he would have committed a common law assault in that he intended to put Q in fear of being then and there subjected to harm.

Terrifying an animal, contrary to s1(1) Animals Act 1911 would also amount to an 'unlawful act' here. The second limb of the test for constructive manslaughter requires that a reasonable man would have foreseen the possibility of at least a little harm, albeit not the serious harm that actually occurred *R v Church* (1965) and it could be argued that a reasonable man would foresee harm being caused to the rider of an animal which was deliberately terrorised. The 'act' need not be directed at the victim, *R v Pagett* (1983), provided there is no new intervening act – *R v Goodfellow* (1986). Once both limbs for constructive manslaughter have been established, the question of whether the act was dangerous will be judged against the appreciation of a reasonable and sober man and not that of P: *R v Ball* (1989).

P could also be charge with manslaughter by gross negligence as defined in *R v Adomako* (1994). It should be noted that this offence has now replaced reckless manslaughter. P will be liable if he owed Q a duty of care (which it is submitted he did), if this duty was breached causing death (which it was), and if the jury considers P's negligence to be so great as to amount to a crime.

When X and Y pick P up they could possibly be liable for false imprisonment or kidnap. False imprisonment is committed where a victim is detained against his will and without lawful excuse. Kidnap is committed where the victim is detained and carried away from the place he wishes to be without lawful excuse.

Undoubtedly X and Y would claim that they were entitled to detain P in view of what had just occurred and therefore they were acting with lawful excuse. They were not, however, entitled to throw him into the lake. Insufficient detail is given to establish exactly what offences X and Y have committed. They seem to be equally involved and would therefore be regarded as joint principals to whatever offences are shown.

The common law offence of assault and battery is committed if a victim is put in fear of immediate force being used against him (assault) and there is a direct infliction of force (battery). It must be shown that an accused acted intentionally or recklessly in his actions: *R v Venna* (1975).

If some injury is sustained by P an offence under s47 of the Offences Against the Person Act 1861 may have been committed. Section 47 contains the offence of assault occasioning actual bodily harm, which was defined in *R v Chan Fook* (1994) as any injury which is more than trivial. Section 47 requires the same mens rea as for s20 (below), ie intention or *Cunningham* (1957) recklessness as to the assault and the harm caused: *R v Spratt* (1990); *R v Parmenter* (1991).

Section 20 of the Offences Against the Person Act 1861 provides that it is an offence to wound or inflict grievous bodily harm. Grievous bodily harm is 'really serious' bodily harm: *DPP v Smith* (1960). The mens rea for s20 requires that the accused foresaw at least the possibility of some harm: *W v Dolbey* (1983). Section 18 of the Act contains the offence of wounding or causing grievous bodily harm with intention to cause grievous bodily harm. It is not sufficient to show recklessness as to causing grievous bodily harm: *R v Belfon* (1976).

The most serious charge of all would be attempted murder if it could be shown that X and Y had done an act more than merely preparatory to the full offence with intention to kill: s1 Criminal Attempts Act 1981; *R* v *Whybrow* (1951).

Depending on the state of mind of X and Y and the injuries, if any, that P sustained they could be liable for one or more of these offences.

X and Y would not be able to claim that they used reasonable force in the prevention of a crime within s3 of the Criminal Law Act 1967 because the crime (if any) has already occurred and in any event it would appear that they are acting aggressively and not defensively: *R* v *Palmer* (1971).

They have also gone beyond the use of reasonable force to make a citizen's arrest of P for an arrestable offence (under s24 Police and Criminal Evidence Act 1984) which might otherwise come under the s3 CLA defence.

QUESTION THREE

E while driving along a road, saw a policeman step out in front of him and signal for him to stop. E, wishing to avoid apprehension drove at the policeman who was knocked down and killed. A pregnant woman who was crossing the road was also knocked down and, although uninjured herself, the woman lost her baby as a result.

Advise E of his criminal liabilities.

Adapted from University of London LLB Examination
(for External Students) Criminal Law June 1986 Q3

General Comment

A straightforward question on homicide and the mens rea to support murder/ manslaughter charges. Also a consideration of 'killing a person'.

Skeleton Solution

Murder/involuntary manslaughter, can foetus be victim? – death by reckless driving: s1 RTA 1988 – overlap with common law.

Suggested Solution

Taking the case of the foetus first.

Whether E can be regarded as criminally responsible for the death of the child will depend on whether the child died in the womb or lived independent of the mother before it died. Only if the child has lived independent of the mother, for however short a time, can the child be a victim of unlawful homicide. The facts of the question would seem to indicate that the child had died in the womb in which case E has no criminal responsibility. If the child was born alive and then died it could be murder or manslaughter. Murder would be established by operating the doctrine of transferred malice whereby the mens rea that he had towards one victim transfers to the actus victim: *R* v *Pembliton* (1874). The mens rea for murder is intention to kill or intention to cause grievous bodily harm. As stated previously, 'intention' in criminal law includes not just desiring a consequence but knowing that it is certain to occur (oblique intent). Indeed if E is liable under s18 OAP Act 1861 the mens rea required

67

for s18 – intention to cause grievous bodily harm, will be sufficient for murder if a death results, *R* v *Vickers* (1957). However, it must be shown that the child had been born alive before this would be appropriate. Furthermore, following the recent decisions of *R* v *Moloney* (1985) and *R* v *Hancock and Shankland* (1986), *R* v *Nedrick* (1986), it is not sufficient to show that he foresaw death or grievous bodily harm as a natural and probable consequence of what he did. While such foresight may be useful as evidence of intention it is not to be equated with intention.

Alternatively charges of constructive manslaughter or manslaughter by reckless conduct would be appropriate. Constructive manslaughter is shown where there is an intention to do an unlawful act which a reasonable person would foresee is likely to cause a little harm, albeit not the serious harm which actually results: *DPP* v *Newbury* (1976). The unlawful act must be a crime and cannot be sufficient for constructive manslaughter unless the act is invariably unlawful, not merely unlawful when it is badly done: *Andrews* v *DPP* (1937). It would not therefore be appropriate to allege that the unlawful act was for example reckless driving, because this would be an example of an act which became unlawful only when it was badly done. It would be sufficient to rely on one of the assaults.

E is most likely to be charged with causing death by dangerous driving contrary to s1 RTA 1988; his standard of driving clearly falls far below that expected of a competent and careful driver who would clearly be of the opinion that driving in such a manner was dangerous.

E may also be charged with manslaughter by gross negligence as defined in *R* v *Adomako* (1994); it is submitted that E's driving is so negligent that a jury is likely to regard it as amounting to a crime.

In the Scottish case of *McCluskey* v *HM Advocate* (1988) it was held that, in circumstances such as these where a foetus is destroyed by reckless driving, that would be sufficient to support a conviction for 'causing death by reckless driving' if the child was born alive. It did not matter that the child had not been born at the time of the recklessness.

The less serious offence of driving recklessly under s2 RTA 1988 (as amended) may also be established. In *R* v *Lawrence* (1981) it was stated that reckless driving was shown where the accused drove in such a manner that it created an obvious and serious risk of causing physical injury to any other road user or substantial damage to property, without giving any thought to the risk or, having recognised that it existed, decided to take it.

In respect of the policeman, E could face charges of murder or manslaughter as previously outlined. On the facts it is quite possible that murder would be alleged as intention to kill or do grievous bodily harm may well be satisfied if E knew that death or grievous bodily harm was certain or virtually certain to occur as a result of what he did.

QUESTION FOUR

X kissed Y, his girlfriend, good night. He kissed her so vigorously that she had a bleeding lip. The lip became infected but Y refused medical treatment because of her irrational fear of doctors. Eventually she became unconscious and her parents called a doctor. He mistakenly administered an anti-viral drug. Y died from the drug.

Advise X and the doctor about their criminal liability.

University of London LLB Examination
(for External Students) Criminal Law June 1986 Q9

General Comment

A good question to do as it involves a progression through the assaults and the homicides without too many diversions to lead a student astray.

Skeleton Solution

CL battery – s47 Offences Against the Person Act 1861 consent as a defence – s20 Offences Against the Person Act 1861 – s18 Offences Against the Person Act 1861 causation – murder/involuntary manslaughter – constructive manslaughter – manslaughter by reckless conduct.

Suggested Solution

When X kissed his girlfriend so vigorously that he caused her lip to bleed he may commit an assault occasioning actual bodily harm within s47 Offences Against the Person Act 1861 and common law battery.

A common law battery is an unlawful infliction of force against the victim committed intentionally or recklessly. Recklessness in this context requires the accused to have appreciated the risk of force against the victim but nonetheless gone on to take the risk ie – *Cunningham* (1957) recklessness as opposed to *Caldwell* (1982) recklessness, *R* v *Morrison* (1988).

Section 47 of the Offences Against the Person Act 1861 provides that it shall be an offence to assault occasioning actual bodily harm. 'Actual bodily harm' is defined as any injury which is more than trivial: *R* v *Chan Fook* (1994).

Following *R* v *Savage*; *R* v *Parmenter* (1991) for a charge under s47 the accused need only have the mens rea for the assault or battery – no mens rea is required as to the actual bodily harm caused.

For both common law battery and s47 there will only be an offence if the act was unlawful ie without consent. The onus of proving lack of consent is on the Crown: *R* v *Donovan* (1934).

Following *R* v *Brown* (1993) the victim's consent may be a defence to an offence which has caused no injury but may not be a defence where injury has been caused. Therefore X may raise his girlfriend's consent as a defence to a charge of battery but not under s47 of the 1861 Act.

When the lip became infected arguably that could be regarded as grievous bodily harm, grievous bodily harm being really serious bodily harm: *DPP* v *Smith* (1961). However s20 Offences Against the Person Act 1861 would not be appropriate on the facts because X has not acted 'maliciously' in the sense of foreseeing a little harm, *W* v *Dolbey* (1983), and there would not be an 'infliction' of grievous bodily harm as there is no assault either direct or indirect because there is consent.

Similarly for s18 of Offences Against the Person Act 1861 although he may have 'caused' grievous bodily harm he does not have the necessary intention to do grievous bodily harm: *R* v *Belfon* (1976).

In order to decide whether X or the doctor can be liable for Y's death it must first be shown that one or other of them was the legal cause of the death. Causation is a question of fact and law. The act must be a sine qua non of the event (in this case the death). This is a question of fact for the jury to decide. However certain acts which are the sine qua non of the event cannot be regarded as the legal cause of the event.

It is not necessary to show that an accused is the sole or even the main cause of death. It is sufficient that the accused is a substantial and generating cause of the death without any subsequent act breaking the chain of causation between what the accused did and the death that resulted.

Applying these principles to the facts of the question only if X can be regarded as a substantial and operating cause of the death will he regarded as the legal cause of death. Y's refusal to obtain treatment will not break the chain of causation: *R* v *Holland* (1841) and *R* v *Blaue* (1975). X must take his victim as he finds him and the neglect of the victim will not break the chain. Less easy to deal with is the question of whether the medical treatment breaks the chain of causation. Medical evidence may be introduced to show that the medical treatment of the injury was the cause of death and not the injury itself: *R* v *Jordan* (1956). If the original injury can only be regarded as the setting in which another cause generates can it be said that the death does not result from the injury: *R* v *Smith* (1959). The doctor administered the wrong drug from which Y died – if this can be regarded as wrong and abnormal treatment ie treatment that no competent doctor would give, then it may break the chain of causation. However, the fact that such treatment fell below that which a competent doctor might be expected to provide will not of itself break the chain of causation: *R* v *Cheshire* (1991). If however the treatment was treatment that a competent doctor would have given then it will not break the chain of causation: *R* v *Malcherek and Steel* (1981).

If X is found by the jury to be the cause of the death then it is necessary to consider what crime he may have committed. On the facts there is nothing to indicate the mens rea for murder ie intention to kill or to do grievous bodily harm. Preferable charges to murder would be constructive manslaughter or manslaughter by reckless conduct.

Constructive manslaughter is only established where it can be shown that there was an intention to do an unlawful act which a reasonable person would foresee as likely to cause at least a little harm: *DPP* v *Newbury* (1976). On the facts this does not appear to be satisfied because it is doubtful that it is an unlawful act. Furthermore it is not an act that a reasonable man would foresee as likely to cause a little harm: *R* v *Church* (1965).

X may be charged with manslaughter by gross negligence as defined in *R* v *Adomako* (1994). It is submitted that X owes his girlfriend a duty. However it is arguable whether kissing her so hard amounts to a breach of this duty; even if it does, it is unlikely that jury would regard it as being sufficiently 'criminal' to justify a conviction for manslaughter.

The doctor could also be charged with manslaughter by gross negligence if the jury thought that his negligence in administering the drug was so great as to amount to a crime.

QUESTION FIVE

During a wrestling match between E and F, E bit F's ear infecting him with AIDS. Subsequently E threw F out of the ring onto Miss G's lap. Both F and G died from their injuries.

Advise E of his liability in respect of the deaths.

Adapted from University of London LLB Examination
(for External Students) Criminal Law June 1987 Q2

General Comment

The question of AIDS and causation is a topical one and provides a useful vehicle for testing a number of concepts in homicide cases.

Skeleton Solution

Murder/involuntary manslaughter – causation – recklessness – ss47, 20, 18 OAP 1861.

Suggested Solution

In respect of F, it is necessary to consider E's possible liability for unlawful homicide. However this would only be necessary if F died within a year and a day of being infected by E. If F died after this period of time then as a matter of law E will not be regarded as the legal cause of F's death: *R* v *Dyson* (1908). If F dies within a year and a day E could be liable for murder or one of the involuntary manslaughters. Murder is established if E kills F intending to kill or intending to do grievous bodily harm. This is a very high mens rea and on the facts would be difficult to establish unless for example E knew he had AIDS and he knew that by biting he was certain or virtually certain to cause grievous bodily harm or kill. It was not sufficient that E foresaw that grievous bodily harm was high probable: *R* v *Moloney* (1985); *R* v *Hancock and Shankland* (1986); *R* v *Barr, Kenyon and Heacock* (1989). It must be established that E either desired to kill or do grievous bodily harm or knew that it was certain or virtually certain to occur. Furthermore a jury should be directed that they are not entitled to infer the necessary intention unless they feel sure that death or grievous bodily harm was virtually certain as a result of E's actions and that E knew this to be the case: *R* v *Nedrick* (1986).

Even if E did know that he had AIDS, it would be difficult to show that E knew of the 'virtual certainty' of F's dying or suffering grievous bodily harm from the bite.

On the facts it seems unlikely E would be liable for murder. Constructive manslaughter would be established if there is an unlawful act that kills and E had intention to do an unlawful act which a reasonable man would foresee is likely to cause at least a little harm: *DPP* v *Newbury* (1976); *R* v *Church* (1965).

Only if E's acts against F were held to amount to a crime would there be the necessary intention to do the unlawful act.

71

CRIMINAL LAW

Assuming the wrestling match itself is not unlawful as otherwise any assault during the match would be 'unlawful' (*R* v *Coney* (1882)), an assault likely to occasion actual bodily harm or more serious harm will be unlawful: *R* v *Donovan* (1934).

Moreover, F's 'consent' to the wrestling will not negative the 'assault' by E as E has gone outside the bounds of the game.

E could also be charged with manslaughter by gross negligence as defined in *R* v *Adomako* (1994). This would depend primarily on whether a jury thought that throwing F out of the ring was sufficiently negligent to amount to a crime. The problem here is that such acts are a common feature of wrestling matches and may not therefore be sufficiently negligent.

Similar considerations would apply to E's liability for the constructive manslaughter of Miss G. In relation to the 'unlawful act', when E threw F out of the ring there would be a common law battery – a use of force intentionally or recklessly applied. When F lands on Miss G causing her serious injury it seems very unlikely that F could have any criminal responsibility for her injuries as he lacks mens rea and at this time he is not acting voluntarily. Indeed F would be regarded as simply the means whereby the actus reus is achieved against Miss G. E could be liable under s47, s20 or even s18 but only if the doctrine of transferred malice is applied, so that the mens rea E has towards F transfers to Miss G: *R* v *Latimer* (1886). Mens rea may be transferred providing the mens rea coincides with the actus reus of the same type of crime. Alternatively, E could be charged with the manslaughter by gross negligence of Miss G, without the need to use the doctrine of transferred malice.

It does not appear that there is evidence of the high degree of mens rea required to prove murder of Miss G.

QUESTION SIX

K was attacked in a street by a group of youths. L, who was the leader caused K to be thrown to the ground where several of the gang kicked him until he became unconscious. They then left the scene. Whilst K was on the ground M passed by and removed K's wallet to see if there was anything worth stealing. M took five pounds from the wallet and kicked K twice before leaving causing severe bruising. N who was next to pass the scene saw that K was seriously ill but did nothing, deciding that he did not want to become involved. O, a doctor, also passed by without rendering assistance. P finally came over to K's aid but because of his inexperience in such matters, he moved K which in turn caused K's internal injuries to become severe.

K subsequently died within a few days.

Advise the parties of their criminal liability in relation to the death of K.

Adapted from University of London LLB Examination (for External Students) Criminal Law June 1987 Q4

General Comment

Although there are numerous offences disclosed in the question – indeed it is used elsewhere in the book to illustrate other aspects of the subject – the primary concern here is with causation, omission and duty of care in homicide.

72

Skeleton Solution

Murder/involuntary manslaughter – recklessness – omission and duty to act – causation – mens rea.

Suggested Solution

It is necessary to consider who was the legal cause of the death of K in order to assess the culpability of each of the actors.

It is most likely that the youths who killed K unconscious would be the legal cause of his death. They would only be liable for murder if they had a very high mens rea – intention to kill or intention to do grievous bodily harm. Intention means desiring a result or knowledge that it is certain or virtually certain to occur: *R v Moloney* (1985). In *R v Hancock and Shankland* (1986) the House of Lords emphasised again that foresight of a consequence is not the same as intending that consequence. It may be useful as evidence but only if it can be established that the accused foresaw the consequence as at least highly probable. Even then it is not conclusive evidence.

In *R v Nedrick* (1986) it was stated that a jury are only entitled to infer the necessary intention if they are sure that death or grievous bodily harm was virtually certain as a result of the defendant's actions and the defendant appreciated this.

Constructive manslaughter is established where a person kills as a result of an unlawful act. The unlawful act must be a crime (*R v Franklin* (1883)) and a positive act (*R v Lowe* (1973)). Furthermore it must be one that a reasonable man would foresee is likely to cause at least a little harm: *DPP v Newbury* (1976).

This would appear to be appropriate on the facts as the assaults already outlined would constitute the unlawful act.

All the youths could be liable for manslaughter if it were shown that their acts were within the common design. Liability for murder would be more difficult with a number of joint principals. It is the cumulative acts and circumstances that lead to the death. It is not possible to show one particular act that kills therefore the parties are equally involved and best regarded as joint principals. Therefore individually there would have to be established mens rea for murder. If this were only present in one or some but not others those that lacked such mens rea would be liable for manslaughter.

L who may be an accomplice to the assaults could not be an accomplice to murder unless he had contemplated one of his gang was going to inflict grievous bodily harm: *Chan Wing-Siu v R* (1984); *R v Slack* (1989).

M's kicking caused severe bruising but it is not clear whether this attack had any contributory effect upon K's death. In *R v Grundy* (1989) it was held, in relation to grievous bodily harm, that a jury should look at all the injuries together to decide if they amount collectively to grievous bodily harm.

N would appear to have no liability in this matter. Undoubtedly certain crimes may be committed by omission. But there can be no liability by this means unless there is a duty to act in law. In these circumstances N has no duty to act in law and therefore would have no liability. It should be noted in relation to matters already discussed that an assault cannot be performed by omission. It must invariably take place by means of a positive act: *Fagan* v *MPC* (1969).

It is arguable that O, being a doctor, has a duty by virtue of his office to preserve and sustain life and that his omission to act makes him liable in the same way that a police officer would be: *R* v *Dytham* (1979).

When P moves K causing his internal injuries to become severe, he would not become liable in criminal law for as a matter of law he would not be regarded as the *legal* cause of the injuries. The chain of causation will not be broken in these circumstances – P would be regarded as an innocent or non-responsible intervener. Where such a person intevenes by an act instinctively done to assist someone he would not break the chain of causation and the harm resulting would not be in law attributable to him but rather to those who started the chain of causation.

However, it may be argued that, having apparently undertaken to care for K he thereby attracts a duty of care towards him per *R* v *Stone and Dobinson* (1977).

QUESTION SEVEN

U, who was 22 years but with a mental age of ten years, had a terrible temper, which he did his best to control. Also, because of a motoring accident he had only one leg. He was in the playground when a fellow pupil, V, abusively called him, 'Peg-leg'. U lost his temper and pushed V to the ground. V, who had a thin skull, was concussed by the fall. X, who was U's best friend, tried to pull U away from V whom U was trying to kick. Released U ran and kicked V on the ground.

Advise the parties of their criminal liability on the basis that V had died as a result of concussion and internal injuries.

Adapted from University of London LLB Examination
(for External Students) Criminal Law June 1987 Q7

General Comment

A good question to tackle. Core elements of the syllabus were examined and all the main aspects were easily recognisable on the facts.

Skeleton Solution

U assault – s47, s20 OAP 1861 – causation – murder; diminished responsibility; constructive manslaughter.

X battery – lack of MR – accomplice role – s3 CLA 1967.

Suggested Solution

When U, having lost his temper, pushes V to the ground he may commit a number of assaults contrary to the Offences Against the Person Act 1861.

Section 47 OAP 1861 provides that it will be an offence to assault occasioning actual bodily harm. 'Actual bodily harm' was defined in *R* v *Chan Fook* (1994) as 'any injury which is more than trivial'. Following *R* v *Savage*; *R* v *Parmenter* (1991) it need only be proven that the accused had the mens rea for the assault or battery, there being no mens rea necessary as to the actual bodily harm.

Section 20 OAP 1861 provides that it is an offence to unlawfully wound or inflict grievous bodily harm. 'Grievous bodily harm' means really serious bodily harm. The term 'inflict' requires an assault either direct or possibly indirect: R v Martin (1881); R v Wilson (1984). Undoubtedly this is satisfied in the facts in question as U uses direct force on V. The mens rea for s20 is intention or recklessness as to circumstances (as for s47). Furthermore the accused must foresee the possibility of at least a little harm: W v Dolbey (1983).

Both s47 and s20 are 'result crimes', that is crimes where a consequence must be shown as part of the actus reus.

V who had a thin skull was concussed by the fall. In order to establish the actus reus of either s47 or 20 it must be shown that U is the legal cause of the injury sustained by V. However U must take his victim as he finds him R v Blaue (1975), and therefore the chain of causation will not be broken because of the victim's special characteristic of a thin skull.

When U later returns to kicking V he will commit further assaults within s47 or s20 depending on his state of mind. If he has the necessary foresight he may be liable under s20. If he lacks this he will be liable under s47.

The victim dies as a result of concussion and internal injuries. V's possible liability for murder must be considered. In order to established this very serious offence it must be shown that U is the legal cause of V's death. Furthermore it must be shown that U had the necessary mens rea for murder at the time of the actus reus. The mens rea for murder is very high. The prosecution would have to establish that U killed V intending to kill or intending to do grievous bodily harm. 'Intention' includes both desiring to kill or do grievous bodily harm (direct intent) or knowing that death or grievous bodily harm is certain or virtually certain to occur (oblique intent). Where the prosecution rely on oblique intent it is not sufficient to establish the accused foresaw the result as highly probable. While this may be useful as evidence it is no more than that: R v Barr, Kenyon and Heacock (1989). Foresight is not to be equated with intention. A jury should be directed that they are not entitled to infer the necessary intention unless they are satisfied that death or grievous bodily harm was virtually certain as a result of the defendant's actions and the defendant appreciated that this was the case: R v Moloney (1985); R v Hancock and Shankland (1986); R v Nedrick (1986).

On the facts in question there seems little doubt that U is the legal cause of death. If he has intention to kill or intention to do grievous bodily harm at any time when the actus reus is continuing he may be liable for murder.

The offence of murder carries a mandatory life sentence. Provocation is a limited defence available to murder which, if successful, will reduce murder to voluntary manslaughter thus avoiding the mandatory life sentence. Provocation is a common law defence available to a charge of murder where by words or acts an accused is so provoked by the victim or a third party that he suffers a sudden and temporary loss of self-control, which would have caused a reasonable man to lose his self-control and so act as the accused did, ie kill R v Duffy (1949), as amended by s3 Homicide Act 1957. Section 3 also provides that the question of whether a reasonable man would have lost control and killed must be left to the jury. Also *R* v *Gilbert* (1977).

The jury must attribute to the reasonable man the power of self control to be expected of an ordinary person of the same age and sex of the accused and also sharing such of the accused's characteristics as would affect the provocation: *DPP* v *Camplin* (1978).

Moreover, the judge must bring any peculiarities of U to the jury's attention, provided those peculiarities are relevant: *R* v *Burke* (1987).

In *R* v *Newell* (1980) it was stated that, in addition to age and sex, only permanent characteristics where there was some real connection between the nature of the provocation and the particular characteristic of the offender could be attributed to the reasonable man.

Applying these cases to the facts in question U's bad temper could not be attributed to the reasonable man as it is a temporary state that came from time to time, furthermore the provocation does not relate to it. However his disabilities could be attributed to the reasonable man as that is permanent and the provocation does relate to it. U has a physical age of 22 but a mental age of ten. Applying *R* v *Raven* (1982), the jury should be directed to consider the reasonable man test on the basis of a person aged 22 but with retarded development and a mental age of ten.

The fact that shouting abuse may not of itself be unlawful does not prevent it amounting to provocation provided it would have provoked a reasonable person with U's characteristics to lose self-control: *R* v *Doughty* (1986).

There was a time lapse between the provocation and the ultimate killing of V. The longer the time lapse the more difficult it is to establish provocation because the accused will have had opportunity to recover control: *R* v *Ibrams and Gregory* (1982). However on the facts the period of time involved is not sufficient to discount provocation as a defence.

In addition to the defence of provocation, the statutory defence of diminished responsibility under s2 Homicide Act 1957 may be available. Section 2 provides that where a person kills he shall not be convicted of murder if he was suffering from such abnormality of mind (whether arising from arrested or retarded development or any inherent causes or induced by disease or injury) as substantially impaired his responsibility. Thus murder will be reduced to voluntary manslaughter. On the facts in question this may well be available.

If U lacked mens rea for murder he could be liable for constructive manslaughter. This is established where a person kills as a result of an unlawful act – in this case one of the assaults. Furthermore in addition to an intention to do the unlawful act it must be shown that a reasonable man would foresee the possibility of at least a little harm from the act: *DPP* v *Newbury* (1976).

X has no criminal responsibility on the facts as given. Undoubtedly he uses force against U when pulling him away and this could amount to a common law battery – a direct use of force, intentionally or recklessly committed. However, under s3 Criminal Law Act 1967, a person may use reasonable force in the prevention of a crime. It must be established that X was acting defensively and not aggressively: *R* v *Shannon* (1980). The question of whether the force used was reasonable must be considered by reference to the circumstances the accused found himself in *R* v *Palmer* (1971); *R* v *Whyte* (1987). There seems little doubt on the facts that this would be available to X as a defence.

QUESTION EIGHT

'Infecting another when one knows one has AIDS is murder.'

Discuss.

Adapted from University of London LLB Examination
(for External Students) Criminal Law June 1988 Q6

General Comment

This question is more of an essay type question than a problem question and requires a thorough knowledge of the offence of murder. You must be systematic and carefully identify the actus reus and mens rea of this offence. It is not as easy as it looks. Furthermore, remember that you are asked by the question *only* to consider murder, not any other form of homicide.

Skeleton Solution

Homicide – murder.

Murder – actus reus – mens rea.

Suggested Solution

The actus reus of homicide is committed when a person of sound mind and discretion unlawfully kills any reasonable creature in being and under the Queen's peace, the death following within a year and a day: Coke, 3 Inst 47.

A person is 'of sound mind and discretion' if he is not insane within the meaning of the M'Naghten Rules: 10 Cl & F 200, or under ten years of age at the time the act was committed.

'Unlawfully' means without legal justification or excuse.

The defendant must 'kill' the victim, ie he must be the factual and legal cause of the death of the victim. A defendant's act cannot be held to be the cause of death if death would have occurred without his act. The defendant's act must be a sine qua non of the death and whether it is so is a question of fact. However, even if an act is the sine qua non of homicide, it may not be the cause of the homicide in law. Whether a particular act which is a sine qua non of an alleged actus reus is also the cause of it is a question of law.

'Any reasonable creature in being' means a person who has had an existence independent of its mother: *R* v *Poulton* (1832).

The person killed must be 'under the Queen's peace'. The killing of any person, even an alien, not in the actual heat and excise of war would be murder: *R* v *Page* (1954).

Death must occur within a year and a day of the date when the defendant inflicted his

77

injury upon the deceased. If a victim dies more than a year and a day from that time, the law conclusively presumes that death was *not* caused by the defendant's act: *R* v *Dyson* (1908).

Therefore, in so far as the actus reus of homicide is concerned, the difficult issue in an AIDS case may well be that death does *not* occur within a year and a day of a defendant infecting his victim. Secondly, as the AIDS virus can be transmitted to a foetus, the issue would be whether the foetus had an independent existence *before* its death (from AIDS) and whether death occurred within a year and a day of it being infected.

Homicide can take one of three forms: murder, voluntary manslaughter and involuntary manslaughter.

Homicide is murder when the defendant has the mens rea of an intention to kill or an intention to cause grievous bodily harm. 'Grievous bodily harm' means injury which is serious but not necessarily dangerous to life: *R* v *Cunningham* (1982); *R* v *Vickers* (1957).

'Intention' in the crime of murder must be distinguished from motive or desire. Foresight by the accused of death or causing grievous bodily harm as a probable consequence of his voluntary act, where that probability can be defined as exceeding a certain degree, cannot be equated or considered to be an alternative to the mens rea required for murder, ie an intention to kill or an intention to cause grievous bodily harm. A man is *not* to be *presumed* to *intend* the natural and probable consequences of his acts: s8 Criminal Justice Act 1967 and a jury is to have regard to all the circumstances in deciding whether an accused intended those consequences or not: *DPP* v *Smith* (1961); *R* v *Steane* (1947).

In cases where the defendant's motive or purpose was *not* primarily to kill or seriously injure then it must be shown that the defendant did the act which caused death knowing that he was doing and intending to do it, and if he did, then the defendant's act must be of a kind which was highly likely to cause death or serious bodily injury. If it was, then the defendant must have appreciated that what he did was highly likely to cause death or serious bodily injury. The fact that he may not have desired the result will be irrelevant for 'desire' and 'intent' are two different things: *R* v *Hancock and Shankland* (1986); *R* v *Moloney* (1985).

The decision of the House of Lords in *R* v *Hancock and Shankland* emphasised that *R* v *Moloney* clarified the law with respect to the mens rea of murder in three respects.

It restated that the mental element in murder is a specific intent – an intention to kill or an intention to cause grievous bodily harm. Nothing less will suffice.

Secondly, foresight of consequences is no more than evidence of the existence of intention; it must be considered and its weight assessed together with all the evidence of the case: *R* v *Barr, Kenyon and Heacock* (1989). Foresight does not necessarily imply the existence of intention, though it may be a fact from which, when considered with all the other evidence, it may be right to infer the necessary intent.

Thirdly, the probability of the rest is an important matter and can be critical in determining whether the result was intended. Where foresight of consequences is an issue, the greater the probability of a consequence the more likely it was that the consequence was foreseen and that if it was foreseen the greater the probability that it was also intended.

In *R v Nedrick* (1986), the Court of Appeal endeavoured to crystallise the effect of the speeches in *R v Moloney* and *R v Hancock and Shankland.*

A jury should be told that a defendant might intend to achieve a certain result while at the same time not desiring it to come about. Because the greater the probability of a consequence, the more likely that it is that the consequence was foreseen and the greater the probability is that that consequence was also intended, the jury could helpfully ask themselves how probable was the consequence which resulted from the defendant's voluntary act.

Then, they should ask themselves whether the defendant foresaw that consequence.

If he did *not* appreciate that death or grievous bodily harm was likely to result from his act, he could *not* have intended to bring it about.

If he *did* appreciate that death or grievous bodily harm was likely to result from his voluntary act *but* thought that the risk to which he was exposing the person killed was only *slight*, it is open to a jury to conclude that he did *not* intend to bring about that result.

If however, the jury are sure beyond reasonable doubted that at the material time the defendant recognised that death or grievous bodily harm was virtually certain (barring some unforeseen intervention) to result from his voluntary act, then it would be open to a jury to infer that the defendant intended to kill or cause grievous bodily harm, *even* thought he might not have had the desire to achieve that result.

A jury would *not* be entitled to infer intention *unless* they feel sure that death or grievous bodily harm was a virtual certainty as a result of the defendant's actions *and* that the defendant appreciated that such was the case.

Therefore, it is not possible to say that knowingly infecting a person with AIDS is the equivalent to the mens rea of murder or that a jury would, in every case, infer such mens rea.

QUESTION NINE

O entered P's circus tent to release animals which O believed were being ill-treated. O let out a lion and a tiger. The lion attacked and killed a person nearby.

Advise O of her criminal liability in relation to the death of the passer-by.

Adapted from University of London LLB Examination (for External Students) Criminal Law June 1988 Q8

General Comment

A brief examination of causation and mens rea for homicide.

Skeleton Solution

Murder/involuntary manslaughter – causation; remoteness – mens rea.

Suggested Solution

The possible offences arising from the killing of the passer-by are murder or involuntary manslaughter. O requires a high degree of mens rea to satisfy murder – ie an intention to kill or an intention to cause grievous bodily harm to any person *R* v *Moloney* (1985). O's intention here appears to be simply to release the animals for their own welfare.

Intention *may* be inferred from O's foresight of the consequences of her actions but only if the judge considers it appropriate to leave the matter before the jury who may only make the inference of intention if they believe that O foresaw death or gbh as 'highly probable' or 'virtually certain' per *R* v *Hancock and Shankland* (1986) and *R* v *Nedrick* (1986).

The fact that releasing a lion may have serious harm or death as a natural and probable consequence does not allow a jury to infer that O intended those consequences and they must look at all the circumstances in determining the question of O's intention s8 Criminal Justice Act 1967.

Grievous bodily harm here would be serious bodily harm: *R* v *Saunders* (1985).

When the lion attacked and killed a man, the possible offences are either murder or involuntary manslaughter.

On the facts, O does not appear to have the mens rea of murder, ie an intention to kill any person or an intention to cause grievous bodily harm to any person: *R* v *Moloney*; *R* v *Hancock*; *R* v *Nedrick*. 'Grievous bodily harm' means serious bodily harm: *DPP* v *Smith* (1961); *R* v *Saunders*.

If O does not have the mens rea for murder she cannot, a fortiori, be guilty of voluntary manslaughter which requires the *same* mens rea as for murder.

O appears to have committed an unlawful act of involuntary manslaughter which consists of an intention to do an act which, whether O knows it or not, is unlawful and dangerous in the sense that it is likely to cause direct personal injury, though not necessarily serious injury.

There must be an intention to do an act which is in fact unlawful and dangerous. If the defendant knows all the relevant facts, it will be irrelevant that he did not know that the act was unlawful or dangerous. The defendant's ignorance that the act was unlawful will be irrelevant for ignorance of the criminal law is no defence *Grant* v *Borg* (1982).

A material mistake of fact or of civil law might, if reasonable, be a defence. The test of dangerousness is objective not subjective, ie irrespective of whether the defendant knew that his act was dangerous, would all sober and reasonable people have recognised its danger: *DPP* v *Newbury* (1976).

There must be an unlawful act which was unlawful for some reason other than the negligent manner of its performance: *Andrews* v *DPP* (1937).

The act must also be one which all sober and reasonable men would realise was likely to cause harm, which need not be serious but must involve some degree of pain or injury. The harm caused need not be directed at the victim: *R v Goodfellow* (1986).

Therefore, on the facts, O appears to be guilty of involuntary manslaughter with respect to the person killed. Her act was unlawful and dangerous; it was unlawful other than because of its negligent performance and was one which was likely to cause harm. Her unlawful and dangerous act appears *not* to have been directed at any specific person but this, on present case law, would not prevent her from being liable.

O may also be charged with manslaughter by gross negligence as defined in *R v Adomako* (1994). The House of Lords in *Adomako* held that everyone is under a duty not to do acts endangering the lives of others. Following this wide definition it is likely that O did owe all passers-by a duty. Releasing the lion would almost certainly constitute a breach of this duty which caused death. It is submitted that a jury would regard such an act as being so negligent as to amount to a crime.

QUESTION TEN

H, who had been drinking, had forgotten his front door key. He climbed into the back bedroom of what he took to be his house. In fact, it was an identical house belonging to a neighbour, I. He climbed into what he thought was his bed and failed to recognise that the occupant was not his girlfriend but I's wife, J, who had taken a sleeping pill. I returned to find the two asleep in bed and was so angry that he threw the two of them out of the bedroom window. J was killed by the fall.

Advise the parties of their criminal liability.

University of London LLB Examination
(for External Students) Criminal Law June 1992 Q3

General Comment

This question involves some speculation about the possible commission of a number of crimes. From the information provided the only crimes that have clearly been committed stem from the assault on H and the death of J. Possible crimes arise from H's intoxication, his entry into a house belonging to another and his climbing into bed with J.

Skeleton Solution

Drunk and disorderly – s91 Criminal Justice Act 1967 – Public order offences, no evidence.

Criminal damage – honest belief his own property: *R v Smith* – relevance of intoxication: *Jaggard v Dickinson*.

Burglary – Theft Act 1968 s9 – trespass alone not enough: *R v Collins*.

Indecent assault – ingredients: *R v Court* – right minded people – intoxication: *R v Culyer* – unambiguous assault – unaware of external facts – J unaware of indecency: *R v Johnson*.

Grievous bodily harm/homicide – attempted murder: *R* v *Nedrick* – intent to cause grievous bodily harm equals murder – grievous bodily harm on H if intent or virtual certainty – H lesser intent lesser offences against the person – J murder intent: *R* v *Moloney* and *Frankland and Moore* v *R* – provocation – mistake as to facts: *R* v *Brown* – lesser intent manslaughter.

Suggested Solution

a) *Drunk and disorderly*

From the evidence provided it is not possible to tell if H has committed any offence as a consequence of his drinking before he arrives at what turns out to be the wrong house. H may have been drunk and disorderly contrary to s91 of the Criminal Justice Act 1967 if he was intoxicated and acting in a disorderly manner in a public place. Other bad behaviour by H while on the public highway may have amounted to one or other of the public order offences in the Public Order Act 1986. However, from the information provided no offence by H is disclosed.

b) *Criminal damage*

If H, when climbing into the wrong house, caused any damage he will not have committed the offence of criminal damage under s1(1) of the Criminal Damage Act 1971. Although it is not clear whether or not H causes damage to the property on entering, his criminal liability should be considered. No offence is committed under this section if a person destroys or causes damage to property belonging to another if he does it in the mistaken belief that the property is his own. Provided that the belief is honestly held it is irrelevant to consider whether or not it is a justifiable belief: see *R* v *Smith* (1974). As long as the mistake negatives the mens rea, however egregious the error may have been, no offence is committed: see also *R* v *Langford* (1842). H will be able to rely on his level of intoxication as evidence, simply that it made his honest mistake more credible. A denial which might be incredible in the case of a sober man may be readily accepted where there is evidence that H was drunk and the fact that the belief was only honestly held because of intoxication is not relevant: see *Jaggard* v *Dickinson* (1981). The situation will of course be different where H is merely the tenant of his own house and he is aware that he is damaging the property of his landlord, who would not consent to damage being caused, rather than damaging his own property.

c) *Burglary*

When H enters the property he has potentially committed a burglary contrary to s9 of the Theft Act 1968, as he has entered another's property as a trespasser. However, H does not have the necessary intent for the offence to have been committed and trespass alone is not sufficient to amount to a criminal offence, per Edmund Davies LJ in *R* v *Collins* (1973). For H to have committed a burglary he must have entered the property as a trespasser with intent to rape, cause grievous bodily harm, to steal anything in the property, or cause unlawful damage to the building or anything therein. According to the evidence provided H has no such intent before entering the building. Having entered the building as a trespasser H will only be guilty of burglary if he steals or attempts to steal anything, or inflicts or attempts to inflict on any person therein grievous bodily harm (under s9(1)(b) of the Theft Act 1968). He has therefore not committed the offence of burglary.

d) *Indecent assault*

When H climbs into bed with J, I's wife, he has potentially committed an indecent assault on her contrary to s14 of the Sexual Offences Act 1956 (as amended by the Sexual Offences Act 1985). 'The offence of indecent assault includes both a battery or touching and psychic assault without touching. If there was no touching, then to constitute an indecent assault the victim must be shown to have been aware of the assault and of the circumstances of indecency': see *R v Court* (1987). J has taken a sleeping pill and is asleep, therefore she cannot be subjected to a psychic assault. According to the information H clearly has not done any more than touch J; there is no question of intercourse taking place. If H touches J in a manner that right-minded people would consider to be indecent and he knows or is reckless as to whether she consents, he is guilty; as in *R v Culyer* (1992) where indecent assault was found to be a crime of basic intent where the assault was unambiguously indecent. H's climbing into bed with J who is presumably dressed only in night attire would, it is submitted, amount to an unambiguous indecent assault, whether H has an indecent purpose or not, provided only that he is aware of the external circumstances. In the present case H is not aware that the woman in the bed is not his girlfriend, which is part of the external circumstances of the alleged offence. In any event H will not have committed an indecent assault on J if he did not handle her indecently, even if his behaviour was indecent (for example if he were naked) as J did not see and was unaware of H's indecency: see *R v Johnson* (1968).

e) *Grievous bodily harm/homicide*

When I arrives back and throws H and J out of the window he has committed a homicide of some description. If, as seems likely, I intended to cause H grievous bodily harm he will be guilty of grievous bodily harm, contrary to s18 of the Offences Against the Person Act 1861 against H (if H is in fact seriously injured, or attempted grievous bodily harm if he was not). I may have committed the offence of attempted murder against H. His actions in throwing H and J out of the window were clearly more than merely preparatory. If he intended to kill H, or death as a result of his actions was a virtual certainty, then I will have committed the offence of attempted murder: see *R v Nedrick* (1986). With regard to J's death, if I intended to cause her grievous bodily harm, then unless I can raise a defence, he is guilty of the murder of J provided she died within a year and a day of the incident. If I did not intend to cause grievous bodily harm he will be guilty of H's grievous bodily harm if there was a virtual certainty that H would be seriously injured, as that amounts to evidence from which the jury may infer that he had the necessary intent. If the fall from the bedroom window is insufficient to lead to the conclusion that serious injury was a virtual certainty then, in the absence of intent, I will be guilty of one of the lesser offences against the person. It is suggested that a fall from a first floor window is likely to provide a virtual certainty that serious injury will result.

The position regarding intent is the same for the offence of murder as it is for grievous bodily harm with intent: see *R v Moloney* (1985) and *Frankland and*

Moore v *R* (1987). I can, however, raise the defence of provocation to the murder of J. It is a long accepted principle that if I has acted in a sudden and temporary loss of self-control against what he perceives to be his adulterous wife and her lover he will be guilty of voluntary manslaughter and not murder. A jury will have to be satisfied that a reasonable man with the defendant's characteristics would have been provoked by the events as he perceived them. The fact that I is provoked by a mistake of fact makes no difference, he is entitled to be treated as if the facts were as he mistakenly supposed them to be: see *R* v *Brown* (1776). If I's intent was anything less than an intent to cause J grievous bodily harm he likewise will have committed the offence of manslaughter.

6 THEFT, BURGLARY AND DECEPTION

6.1   Introduction

6.2   Key points

6.3   Recent cases

6.4   Analysis of questions

6.5   Questions

6.1 Introduction

These areas are of crucial importance in understanding the criminal law and make up a large part of the syllabus.

Students will be examined closely on the different elements of the Theft Acts of 1968 and 1978 and a clear understanding of each individual offence and its relationship to other and crimes of 'dishonesty' is required.

6.2 Key points

a) *Theft*

   i) Property

   Note that under the definition in s4(1) of the 1968 Act although intangible property is included, information is not: *Oxford* v *Moss* [1979] Crim LR 119. Note also the circumstances in which plants and animals may fall within the definition.

   ii) Appropriation

   Property can be appropriated even if the accused is acting with the owner's consent: *Lawrence* v *Metropolitan Police Commissioner* [1972] 2 All ER 1253; *R* v *Morris* [1983] 3 All ER 288; *R* v *Gomez* [1993] 1 All ER 1 HL.

   iii) Belonging to another (s5(1) Theft Act 1968)

   The property must belong to someone: *R* v *Woodman* [1974] 2 All ER 955; *Williams* v *Phillips* (1957) 41 Cr App R 5. Ownership may not pass to the receiver if it is given for a particular purpose: s5(3); *DPP* v *Huskinson* [1988] Crim LR 620; *R* v *Hall* [1973] 3 WLR 381. Ownership may not pass to the receiver where it was given by mistake and the recipient is under an obligation to make restoration: s5(4); *Attorney-General's Reference (No 1 of 1983)* [1984] 3 All ER 369.

   iv) Dishonesty

   Students should always consider dishonesty as a two-part test: the three statutory circumstances under s2(1)(a), (b) and (c) Theft Act 1968 in which the accused cannot be dishonest and the main definition contained in *R* v *Ghosh* [1982] Crim LR 608.

Note that the dishonest intent must be formed while the goods still belong to another: *R* v *Stewart* (1982) The Times 14 December; *Edwards* v *Ddin* [1976] 1 WLR 942.

v) Intention to permanently deprive

On borrowing money see: *R* v *Velumyl* [1989] Crim LR 299. On borrowing generally see: s6(1) Theft Act 1968; *R* v *Lloyd and Ali* [1985] 3 WLR 30. Note that in *DPP* v *Lavender* [1994] Crim LR 297 it was held that an accused may have an intention equivalent to an intention to permanently deprive under s6(1) of the 1968 Act if it is 'his intention to treat the thing as his own regardless of the other's rights' even if this is *not* equivalent to an outright taking or disposal.

b) *Obtaining property by deception*

i) Deception

Section 15(4) of the 1968 Act states that a deception may be as to fact, law or intention, by conduct or words and must be made deliberately or recklessly. On conduct and intention see: *DPP* v *Ray* [1974] AC 370.

ii) Obtaining (s15(2) Theft Act 1968)

The deception must precede and cause the obtaining (*R* v *Collis-Smith* [1971] Crim LR 716) and influence the victim (*R* v *Hensler* (1870) 22 LT 691; *R* v *Rashid* [1977] 1 WLR 298).

The presentation of a cheque or credit card carries with it an implied representation that the user has authority to use the card or cheque and is therefore within their overdraft or credit limit: *Charles* v *Metropolitan Police Commissioner* [1977] Crim LR 615; *R* v *Lambie* [1981] 1 All ER 332.

iii) Following *R* v *Gomez* (above) a charge under s15 may also give rise to a charge of theft under s1.

iv) With respect to obtaining services by deception contrary to s1 of the Theft Act 1978 deception has the same meaning as described above.

v) The definition of dishonesty laid down in *R* v *Ghosh* (above) applies to all the deception offences but the s2(1) excluded categories do not.

c) *Obtaining a pecuniary advantage by deception (s16 Theft Act 1968)*

This offence can only be committed in one of five specified ways and a student should always point out which of these applies when answering a question. The five ways are where the accused obtains (or obtains better terms for) an overdraft insurance policy, annuity contract, employment or bet.

Note that the use of a cheque where there is insufficient funds in the account to meet the cheque may cause the account to go into overdraft and therefore constitute this offence (*R* v *Waites* [1982] Crim LR 369), although this is of course subject to a dishonest intention not to repay the overdraft.

d) *Evasion of liability by deception*

There are three separate offences under s2(1) of the Theft Act 1978:

i) Section 2(1)(a)

Securing the remission of a debt by deception (ie where a debtor deceives a creditor into letting the latter off the debt). Note that in *R* v *Jackson* [1983] Crim LR 617 it was held that the use of a stolen credit card would constitute this offence since the creditor (eg a shop) would look to the credit card company for payment rather than the user of the card.

ii) Section 2(1)(b)

By deception, persuading a creditor to wait for payment – however it is important to note that the accused will not be guilty despite a deception unless he intends to permanently avoid payment. Note that inducing someone to accept a cheque may also create this offence: s2(3) Theft Act 1978; *R* v *Andrews and Hedges* [1981] Crim LR 106.

iii) Section 2(1)(c)

The dishonest obtaining of an exemption from liability: see *R* v *Sibartie* [1983] Crim LR 470.

e) *Making off without payment (s3 1978 Act)*

This offence is especially useful where the accused has formed a dishonest intent after obtaining goods and therefore cannot be charged with theft or deception.

'Make off' – the accused must have left the premises (*R* v *McDavitt* [1981] Crim LR 843); 'without having paid' – payment with an invalid cheque does not constitute this offence as it amounts to conditional payment (*R* v *Hammond* [1982] Crim LR 611); the accused must know that payment is expected of him (*R* v *Brooks and Brooks* [1983] Crim LR 188); payment must be contractually due (*Troughton* v *Metropolitan Police Commissioner* [1987] Crim LR 138); the accused must intend to permanently avoid payment (*R* v *Allen* [1985] 3 WLR 107).

f) *Burglary*

Note that there are two distinct types of burglary and a good student should always specify which is being referred to: s9(1)(a) Theft Act 1968 – where the accused has entered with the intention of stealing, raping or committing criminal damage; and s9(1)(b) Theft Act 1968 – where the accused has entered without any of these intents, but once inside commits theft or grievous bodily harm or attempts to do either.

The accused must be a trespasser at the time the burglary takes place. This would apparently prevent anyone who is in a building lawfully but commits one of the above-mentioned prohibited acts from being convicted for burglary. However, note that a dishonest intent may exceed the scope of the accused's permission to enter the premises and therefore make him a trespasser: *R* v *Jones and Smith* [1976] 3 All ER 54. Also, a person may have permission to enter part of a building but become a trespasser when he enters another part: *R* v *Walkington* [1979] 2 All ER 716.

Note that the entry must be 'effective' (*R* v *Brown* [1985] Crim LR 212) but need not be substantial and effective (*R* v *Collins* [1972] 2 All ER 1105). Consequently, an accused who puts his arm through a window in order to steal may be guilty of burglary.

Note that for a charge of aggravated burglary under s10 the accused must have the weapon of offence with him at the time of the burglary. Thus a person who arms himself after entering a building cannot be said to have committed an aggravated s9(1)(a) burglary. However, an aggravated burglary may still occur if such a person subsequently commits a s9(1)(b) burglary while having the weapon with him: *R* v *O'Leary* (1986) 82 Cr App R 341.

Note also that any item may be converted to a weapon of offence if it is adapted or the *moment* it is intended to be used as a weapon: *R* v *Kelly* [1993] Crim LR 763.

6.3 Recent cases

R v *Gomez* [1993] 1 All ER 1

DPP v *Lavender* [1994] Crim LR 297

R v *Kelly* [1993] Crim LR 763

6.4 Analysis of questions

As with the chapter on homicide, this forms an essential part of the syllabus and one can expect several property – based questions in the examination. Occasionally there will be questions which are purely based on offences against property, some of which have recently appeared in three parts (as at Q10). More commonly, questions will include other theft related offences (see Chapter 7) and/or elements of criminal damage (see Chapter 8).

6.5 Questions

QUESTION ONE

X put the appropriate coins in a car park barrier machine but it did not rise. X hit the machine with his fist. It disgorged a large quantity of coins from the change slot and did not work at all for the rest of the evening because of the blow. X put the coins in his pocket and removed his car from the car park. Later he used some of the coins in a vending machine to buy drinks. X then went to Y's shop where he used a stolen building society cheque to pay for a £50 coat which he had agreed to buy. X sold the coat to a market trader for £25. He returned to his car and noticed some groceries on the back seat of a neighbouring car. He forced open the car door, put the items in the boot of his car and was arrested by a policeman who had been keeping watch.

Advise X of his criminal liability.

University of London LLB Examination
(for External Students) Criminal Law June 1993 Q6

General Comment

The only question which concentrates on offences against property on a paper which otherwise concentrates heavily on offences against the person. The question does not raise any awkward academic points although it does require a discussion of a wide variety of offences involving dishonesty as well as criminal damage.

Skeleton Solution

Criminal damage to the machine – theft of the coins – making off without payment – possession of stolen property – obtaining property by deception – criminal damage to the car and theft of the items inside.

Suggested Solution

Criminal damage to the machine

By striking the barrier machine and causing it not to work for the rest of the day X may be guilty of criminal damage contrary to s1 of the Criminal Damage Act 1971. Although X may not have damaged any individual parts of the machine it has been held in *Morphitis* v *Salmon* (1990) that damage includes not only physical harm but also the permanent or temporary impairment of value or usefulness. As the machine did not work for the rest of the evening its usefulness has been temporarily impaired. Although X may not have intended to damage the machine it is sufficient that he created an obvious risk that such damage might occur and it is irrelevant whether he was aware of the risk but went ahead regardless or he never thought about the risk (*MPC* v *Caldwell* (1982)). Whether or not banging on the machine would create an obvious risk of damaging it would depend on how hard he hit it, where he hit it and how sturdy the machine appeared to be.

Theft

X may be guilty of theft of the coins from the machine contrary to s1 of the Theft Act 1968. It must be established that the coins belonged to another and although some of the coins may have been the ones X originally put in the machine, by analogy with the case of *Edwards* v *Ddin* (1976) which held that property in petrol passes the moment it flows from the petrol pump into the petrol tank, it is submitted that ownership of the coins passed to the garage the moment they were put into the machine and accordingly, X would be appropriating coins belonging to another.

The prosecution must also establish that X has acted dishonestly according to the standards of ordinary and reasonable people (*R* v *Ghosh* (1982)). As X has already spent some of the money on a drink and does not intend to return it he has probably acted dishonestly with this money. With respect to the remaining unspent money, whether X is dishonest may well depend on what he intends to do with it – spend it, or perhaps he was merely safeguarding it until he could return it to the garage, although this would seem unlikely.

Making off without payment

As X appears to have removed his car from the car park without paying the parking fee he may be guilty of making off without payment contrary to s3 of the Theft Act 1978. To be convicted of this offence the accused must know that payment on the spot is expected of him and make off without making such payment – both requirements would appear to be met in this case. The accused must also have acted dishonestly within the meaning of *Ghosh* mentioned above and it is submitted that unless X intended to return to the garage at a later date and pay for the parking he would have acted dishonestly. The case of *R* v *Allen* (1985) requires the prosecution to prove an intention to permanently avoid payment and X will be entitled to an acquittal in the unlikely event that he had such an intention to return and pay at a later date.

Possession of stolen property and obtaining property by deception

As X is in possession of a stolen building society cheque he may have committed the offence of possessing stolen goods contrary to s22 of the Theft Act 1968 which would require that X knew or believed the cheque to be stolen. Since he bought the coat for £50 using the stolen cheque and later sold it for only half this amount it is likely that he knew that the cheque was stolen.

In purchasing the coat by using the stolen cheque X may also be guilty of obtaining property by deception contrary to s15 of the 1968 Act. In *Charles* v *MPC* (1977) it was held that the presentation of a cheque carries an implied representation that the shop will be paid. If the cheque is stolen the shop will not be paid and this false representation if coupled with the appropriate mens rea will constitute a deception. However if X used a cheque guarantee card the building society would honour the cheque and this representation would no longer be false in which case the prosecution must look elsewhere to locate a deception. *Charles* appears to have solved this problem by holding that when a cheque is presented for payment not only is the presenter representing that the shop will be paid but also that he has authority to use the cheque. If the cheque is stolen this authority is lacking and once again if the accused has knowledge of this, a deception has occurred. It has been held that the deception must cause the obtaining (*R* v *Clucas* (1949)) in consequence of which one may argue that if X used a cheque guarantee card the shop's only concern would have been that they would get paid and therefore the fact that X did not have authority to use the cheque would not have been a factor in the minds of the shop staff which induced them to accept the cheque and consequently did not cause the obtaining as required by s15. However, the House of Lords in *R* v *Lambie* (1981) did not regard a similar argument as a bar to the conviction of the accused who had used her credit card in excess of the stipulated credit limit and therefore without authority.

The groceries

If, in forcing open the car door X caused any damage to the car, he may be guilty of criminal damage contrary to s1 of the Criminal Damage Act 1971. By removing the groceries and placing them in the boot of his car X has committed theft contrary to s1 of the 1968 Act.

QUESTION TWO

Peter was a house painter. He was contracted to paint a house for a particular fee and was given £50 with which to buy materials. Believing he had £50 at his home, Peter spent the £50 he was given on a suit. However, he discovered that his wife had spent the £50 at his home. Furious, he took his wife's favourite ring and threw it into a nearby river.

Peter visited his bank manager and told him that his wife was expecting their first baby, and he requested an overdraft facility of £50 to purchase some garments for the baby. The story was entirely untrue. His bank manager, however, readily agreed to the overdraft and added that there was no need for any explanation as to why it was required when the amount was so small. Peter cashed a cheque for £50 and bought the materials.

Peter met a friend, Brian, and told Brian that he was painting a house for charity and wondered whether Brian would like to assist him although, being a charitable work, there was no payment. Brian agreed to help and did do half the painting. Unknown to Peter, when the work was finished, Brian saw Peter being paid by the householder.

Brian kept silent but went around to Peter's house that evening, intent upon taking goods to the value of half what Peter had been paid. Peter's wife, Anne, let Brian in. Peter was out. Anne poured Brian a brandy and left the drawing room to make some sandwiches for Brian. Whilst she was out of the room Brian finished off the bottle of brandy.

Discuss the criminal liability of Peter and Brian.

Adapted from University of London LLB Examination
(for External Students) Criminal Law June 1981 Q7

General Comment

A straightforward examination of knowledge of the various elements of theft and burglary, and also deception.

Skeleton Solution

Theft, 'appropriates', 'belonging to another', 'dishonestly': ss1–7 TA 68 – burglary, enters as trespasser: s9 TA 68 – deception, obtaining property/services: 15 TA 68; s1 TA 78 – obtaining pecuniary advantage: s16 TA 68.

Suggested Solution

Peter may have committed offences contrary to the Theft Act 1968 and the Theft Act 1978.

When Peter used the £50 given to him to buy materials in purchasing a suit he may have committed an offence contrary to s1 of the Theft Act 1968 which states that it will be an offence to dishonestly appropriate property belonging to another with the intention of permanently depriving the other of it. However, on the facts of the question, there may be difficulty in showing first of all that Peter was dishonest and secondly, that the property did belong to another. Section 5(3) states that where a person receives property from or on account of another and is under an obligation to the other to retain and deal with that property in a particular way, the property shall be regarded as belonging to the other. Therefore, s5(3) will be useful in showing that prima facie, there is the actus reus of theft. To come within the section it would have to be shown that there was an obligation to deal with that particular property in a certain way. If Peter received the payment as a straightforward advance of remuneration, it would be unlikely that he would come within the scope of the section. However, the money has been received to buy materials and it is therefore submitted that this will bring his act within the scope of the actus reus of theft. However, it should be noted that in *R* v *Hall* (1972) it was stated that the obligation had to be a legal obligation, although this appears to be satisfied on the facts in question. The requirement for a legal obligation was reiterated in *DPP* v *Huskinson* (1988).

As to the question of dishonesty, it would be open to Peter to claim the benefit of s2 of the Theft Act 1968 on the basis that he believed that he would have had the owner's consent if the owner knew of the appropriation and the circumstances of it. However, it has to be shown subjectively that Peter did have such a belief. If this cannot be shown then the usual rule will apply. In *R* v *Feely* (1973), it was stated that the question of dishonesty was one always to be left to the jury and the jury would apply the standard of the ordinary decent person. However if Peter raises his own subjective belief in the honesty of what he was doing the *R* v *Ghosh* (1982) direction must be given (*R* v *Price* (1990)), ie did Peter regard himself as dishonest by his own standards and are those standards shared by the community, or has he been dishonest by the standards of the ordinary man and is he aware of that standard?

At the time when he spent the £50 on the new suit, he may have committed a further offence contrary to s15 of the Theft Act 1968 in that he dishonestly obtained the property (the suit) by deception with intention to permanently deprive the other of it. The same test for dishonesty would apply as for s1 of the Theft Act except that in relation to an offence other than theft, he would not be able to claim the benefit of s2. To come within s15, it would have to be shown that he intentionally or recklessly deceived the vendor of the suit. The deception may be by words or conduct as to fact or as to law including his deception as to the present intention of the person using the deception or any other person s15(4). Furthermore, it is not just enough to show that there was a deception as to the ownership of the money, it has to be shown that the deception was the operative factor in him obtaining the goods: *R* v *Kovacs* (1974) The question of whether it was the operative cause is one of fact to be left to the jury: *R* v *King and Stockwell* (1987). Therefore, on the facts of the question, it would have to be shown that Peter intentionally or recklessly deceived by implying that the money was his and that the deception enabled him to obtain the suit ie, that the vendor would not have sold the suit to him if he had known that the money was not Peter's to use in this particular way.

Peter may have committed a further offence of theft when he threw his wife's favourite ring into a river. By virtue of s30(1) of the Theft Act 1968 husband and wife can steal or indeed, do any other offence within the Theft Act 1968 and 1978 in relation to the property of the other. The proceedings may be instituted by the injury spouse and therefore, on this basis, Peter's wife may prosecute him for stealing her property. Furthermore, she may give evidence for the prosecution at every stage of the proceedings. The elements necessary to show theft of the ring appear to be satisfied. There is an appropriation when he takes the ring and throws it into the river in that he will have assumed the right of an owner at that stage. The property belongs to another and therefore the actus reus is complete. Once again, the question of dishonesty is to be left to the jury: *R* v *Feely*. Furthermore, his conduct evidences an intention to permanently deprive in that he treats the ring as his own to dispose of regardless of the other's rights: s6(1).

Peter may commit an offence contrary to s16 of the Theft Act 1968 when he asks his bank manager for an overdraft facility. Section 16(1) provides that a person who by any deception dishonestly obtains for himself or another any pecuniary advantage shall commit an offence. A pecuniary advantage obtained by Peter is that within s16(2)(b) in that he was allowed to borrow by way of overdraft. However, once again there may be problems in showing that there was a complete offence. Certainly there is a deception within s15(4) made intentionally by Peter. Furthermore, he does obtain a pecuniary advantage within s16. However, there may be problems in showing that Peter does indeed obtain an overdraft by deception. It has to be shown that there is a causal link between the deception and the obtaining of the overdraft: *R v Kovacs* (1974) and *R v Collis-Smith* (1971). If he would have obtained the overdraft without the deception, then there cannot be an offence within s16 although there may be an attempt under the Criminal Attempts Act 1981 s1(3).

When Peter persuades Brian to assist in the painting of the house for charity, there is prima facie an offence within s1 of the Theft Act 1978 which states that a person who by any deception dishonestly obtains services from another, shall be guilty of an offence. However, there would be problems within s1(2) because it provides that there will only be an obtaining of services within s1(1), where the other is induced to confer a benefit by doing some act or causing or submitting some act to be done on the understanding that the benefit has been or will be paid. Because Brian has agreed to receive no renumeration, there will be no offence within the section.

Brian may be liable for attempted theft when he enters Peter's house intending to take property to the value of half what Peter had been paid. However, once again, there would be a number of problems in showing such an offence. First of all, it would have to be shown that Brian had mens rea within s1 of the Theft Act 1968, which defines theft as dishonestly appropriating property belonging to another with intention of permanently depriving that other. There is certainly an intention to permanently deprive but it would not be so easy to show that Brian was dishonest.

It may be that he could claim the benefit of s2 of the Theft Act 1968 in that he believed that he had the right in law to the property. If he cannot claim the benefit of s2, then the question of dishonesty is one to be left to the jury *R v Feely* (1973) and the *R v Ghosh* (1982) direction given. In *R v Woolven* (1983) it was held that such a direction should cover all occasions where a claim of a right in law was made although in *R v Wootton and Peake* (1990) the sufficiency of a *Ghosh* direction in such cases was questioned. It is the honesty of Brian's belief in such a case by which his 'dishonesty' will be determined and not the reasonableness of such a belief: *R v Holden* (1991).

As to the actus reus of theft, it would have to be shown that Brian had done an act which was more than simply an act of preparation and was so proximate to the commission of the offence that it would amount to an attempt. The question of whether an act is or is not proximate, is one always to be left to the jury: *DPP v Stonehouse* (1978). However, as Brian has not got in mind to steal particular items, but simply stating that Brian attempted to steal from the contents of the house, the charge should be successful: *R v Easom* (1971); *Attorney-General's References (Nos 1 and 2 of 1979)* (1979).

It is necessary to consider whether s9 of the Theft Act 1968, is applicable. Section 9 of the Theft Act 1968, provides that a person is guilty of burglary, if:

1) he enters the building or part of the building as a trespasser with intent to steal, causing grievous bodily harm, rape or do criminal damage; or

2) having entered any building or part of a building as a trespasser, he steals or attempts to steal anything in the building or inflict or attempt to inflict on any person therein any grievous bodily harm.

The most obvious problem here would be whether Brian had entered as a trespasser or as an invitee. It could be argued that because Brian had the intention of taking property when he came into the building, he did indeed enter as a trespasser. If this view is correct, then providing what he intended to do would have amounted to theft, then he would commit an offence within s9(1)(a) in that he entered, as a trespasser, with intent to steal: *R v Jones and Smith* (1976).

If the entry were established as trespassary then, having so entered, Brian may commit a further offence of theft by drinking the contents of the bottle of brandy while Anne was out of the room. Certainly, he has appropriated property belonging to another with intention to permanently deprive. However, once again, it would have to be shown that there was dishonesty and Brian may be able to invoke s2 again, based on the fact that Anne has already given him some of the brandy.

QUESTION THREE

Lionel was blind. He drew his old age pension from the post office and Nina, the village postmistress, by mistake gave him £1 too much. Lionel was unaware of this fact till later when shopping he discovered the additional note. He used it to buy extra meat.

Lionel purchased groceries from Morgan's market stall. The bill came to £4 and Lionel presented a £10 note saying, 'This is a fiver. Don't forget my change.' Morgan gave Lionel £1 change.

When talking home Lionel stopped for a rest in the park. He put his basket on the park bench beside him. Orlando, aged 13 years, who was sitting on the seat removed one of Lionel's apples and threw it to his friend Paul, who was playing nearby. Lionel suspected that something had happened when he heard Orlando laugh.

Advise Lionel, Orlando and Paul.

Adapted from University of London LLB Examination (for External Students) Criminal Law June 1982 Q6

General Comment

Although the question requires the student to 'advise Lionel, Orlando and Paul' it is necessary to include in the answer the possible liability of Morgan as this would be included as part of the advice to Lionel.

The issues involved are fairly straightforward and primarily concern offences against property. In view of the case law on the point a student should be able to give a very detailed explanation of the controversy surrounding the test to be applied in ascertaining 'dishonesty'.

Skeleton Solution

Theft: ss1–7 TA 1968 – 'dishonestly', 'appropriates', obtaining property by deception: s15 TA 1968.

Suggested Solution

When Lionel uses the £1 given to him by mistake he may commit an offence contrary to s1 of the Theft Act 1968. Section 1 states that 'a person is guilty of theft if he dishonestly appropriates property belonging to another with the intention of permanently depriving the other of it'. The two elements of theft which require particular consideration in this instance are: 'belonging to another' and 'dishonesty'.

Under s5(4) where a person gets property by another's mistake, and is under an obligation to make restoration of the property, then to the extent of that obligation the property shall be regarded as belonging to the person entitled to restoration, and an intention not to make restoration shall be regarded as an intention to deprive that person of the property. In *R v Gilks* (1972) it was stated that the word 'obligation' in s5(4) means a legal obligation. it is not sufficient simply to show a moral or social obligation. However, on the facts of the question it would seem that the £1 paid in error still belonging to Nina, and at the time when he used the money to purchase extra meat, he 'appropriated property belonging to another'. If this were so there would be no need to rely on s5(4).

The question of 'dishonesty' is one to be left to the jury unless Lionel can claim to have held one of the beliefs contained in s2. Section 2 outlines three situations where an accused would not be dishonest. However, it does not give any positive guidance as to what will amount to dishonesty. In *R v Feely* (1973) the Court of Appeal held that it was for the jury to decide in each case what the accused's state of mind was and whether or not that amounted to a dishonest state of mind. However, there has been much debate as to whether a jury, in making that decision, should apply an objective standard, ie that of the ordinary, decent person, or whether they should take into account the subjective views of the accused as to whether or not he is dishonest. In *R v McIvor* (1982) the Court of Appeal stated that dishonesty could be established independently of the knowledge or belief of the defendant, ie they supported an objective test although the jury could consider the defendant's evidence as to his state of mind at the time of the alleged offence in making their decision.

The question of dishonesty was again considered by the Court of Appeal a few weeks after *R v McIvor* in the case of *R v Ghosh* (1982). Judgment in this case was given by the Lord Chief Justice who took a rather different approach from that in *R v McIvor*. The Lord Chief Justice considered that by seeking to reconcile an objective and a subjective approach, *R v McIvor* was seeking to reconcile the irreconcilable. It was, therefore, necessary to choose between the two alternative views, and the test to be applied was subjective.

'In determining whether the prosecution had proved the person charged was acting dishonestly, a jury had first of all to decide whether, according to the ordinary standards of reasonable and honest people, what was done was dishonest. If it was not dishonest by those standards, that was the end of the matter and the prosecution failed.

If it was dishonest by those standards then the jury had to consider whether the person charged himself must have realised that what he was doing was by those standards dishonest. In most cases, where the actions were obviously dishonest by ordinary standards there would be no doubt about it. It would be obvious that the person charged himself knew that he was acting dishonestly.' However the Court of Appeal has stated that the *Ghosh* direction need not be given in every case where dishonesty is in issue: *R* v *Spencer and Turner* (1989), and that in some cases it may even be misleading to do so: *R* v *Price* (1990). It is only necessary where D is saying in his defence 'I thought that what I was doing was honest but other people and the majority of people might think that it was not honest' (per Lord Lane CJ in *Price*).

It could be argued that there is a further offence under s15 of the Theft Act 1968 when by deception Lionel dishonestly obtains property belonging to another with the intention of permanently depriving that other of the property. Section 15(4) defines 'deception' to include any deception (whether deliberate or reckless) by words or conduct, as to fact or as to law. The question to be considered here was whether Lionel impliedly deceived by using the money which was not his to use to purchase meat. Furthermore, it must be shown that the deception was 'operative', ie that he would not have obtained the property had it not been for the deception: *R* v *Clucas* (1949); *R* v *Rashid* (1977).

Lionel should be advised that when Morgan keeps the extra £5 change which belonged to Lionel, he has committed an offence contrary to s1 of the Theft Act 1968 providing that the jury are satisfied that the taking was a dishonest appropriation. Certainly, there is a mistake on Lionel's part, and it will be possible to argue that s5(4) is applicable in this situation also. However, it may be unnecessary in this case to apply s5(4) as it could be argued that property in the £5 never passed to Morgan at all, and therefore, irrespective of s5(4), he was appropriating property belonging to another.

It is unlikely that Morgan's silence will amount to a 'deception' and his moral duty to tell Lionel that the note is actually a ten pound note will probably not be translated into a legal duty, although it is arguable on the principles of *DPP* v *Ray* (1974) that his actions in giving Lionel change for a £5 note may well support a charge of deception.

When Orlando removes the apple from Lionel's basket he is committing the actus reus of theft, in that he is appropriating property belonging to another. 'Appropriation' is defined in s3 of the Theft Act 1968 and requires an assumption of the rights of an owner. Certainly this has been satisfied in this situation, although it is possible that Orlando was not dishonest and/or did not have an intention to permanently deprive. It is unclear from the question whether Orlando and Paul are taking part in a prank. Obviously, this would be important in deciding whether or not they were dishonest. If the jury were satisfied that Orlando did have the necessary dishonest intention to permanently deprive, then the elements of theft are satisfied. It could be argued that Paul was also involved in the theft in that he aided and abetted the offence committed by Orlando who was the principal offender. To be an aider and abettor, he has to be present, assisting or encouraging at the scene of the offence: *R* v *Coney* (1882). Furthermore, he must have full knowledge of all the circumstances of the offence: *Johnson* v *Youden* (1950).

It could be argued that Paul was not involved in the initial theft. However, he may still commit an offence contrary to s22 of the Theft Act 1968 if he dishonestly receives stolen goods for his own benefit, knowing or believing them to be stolen. Providing that Orlando has satisfied all the necessary elements of theft, then the apple that he removed will be within the definition of 'stolen goods' which includes goods taken contrary to s1 of the Theft Act 1968. However, before there could be any liability under s22, it must be shown that the original theft is complete.

Orlando is 13 years old, and therefore, before he may be liable for any criminal offence the jury must be satisfied that as well as having the ordinary mens rea necessary for the particular offence involved, that he has the extra element of 'mischievous discretion'. Indeed, children over ten and under 14 years of age are exempt from criminal responsibility unless it is proved that they have this additional element of mischievous discretion which involves a comprehension of right and wrong. There is no information given as to Paul's age. However if he were to be between ten and 14, the same principles would apply. If he were under ten years old, then in no circumstances could he be liable for a criminal offence. If he was 14 years or more, then he would be liable as an adult although the sentences in respect of juvenile offences may be different.

QUESTION FOUR

K was employed in a bank. One of his tasks was to take deposits from customers. K joined a religious sect which believed that money was tainted. K began to give customers excess payments and to strike out debits on customers' statements. K used the computer to add sums to customers' accounts and then wiped out the computer records which would have made it possible to trace these alterations. All the customers failed to report the additional credits to their account and some of them spent the excess. Also, K filled in credit application forms which K knew to be false. The advances which K received K gave to various charities who refused to return the proceeds.

Advise K and the charities.

University of London LLB Examination
(for External Students) Criminal Law June 1992 Q4

General Comment

This question requires consideration of the Theft Acts 1968 and 1978 and also the Computer Misuse Act 1990. Note that the latter Act came into force on 29 August 1990 and that no offence can be committed under this Act unless all the elements of the offence are made out after that date. It is a pity that the part of the question which mentions K's giving of excess payments and striking out of debits is not clearer as to the precise nature of the excess payments and the debits. That is, were the excess payments actual bank notes or were they credits on the statements, and were the debits records of completed transactions or records of transactions which had yet to take place?

CRIMINAL LAW

Skeleton Solution

Theft Act 1968 sl(1) – property 'belonging to another' – theft from the bank rather than account holders – dishonesty: *R* v *Ghosh* test – *R* v *Bernhard*, *R* v *Turner (No 2)*.

Computer Misuse Act 1990 – Theft Act 1968 s17(1)(a): *R* v *Kohn*.

Obtaining property by deception, contrary to s15 Theft Act 1968.

Obtaining services by deception, contrary to sl(1) Theft Act 1978.

Restitution orders under s28 Theft Act 1968: *R* v *Ferguson*; *R* v *Calcutt and Varty*.

Suggested Solution

a) *Theft*

When K gave the customers excess payments he committed the offence of theft contrary to sl(1) Theft Act 1968. This offence consists of the dishonest obtaining of property belonging to another with the intention of permanently depriving that other of the property. When K gave the customers excess payments it is submitted that he was stealing the property – the money – from the bank. Money can be 'property' for the purposes of the Act (s4(1) Theft Act 1968) and, although the money in all probability came from customers of the bank in the first place, the Act provides that property shall be regarded as belonging to that person who has possession or control of it or has a proprietary right or interest in it (s5(1)). Accordingly, it is submitted that the bank is the 'owner' of the money. When K gave this money to the customers it is averred that this amounted to a dishonest course of conduct by him within the definition propounded by Lord Lane in *R* v *Ghosh* (1982), because his course of conduct would be considered to be dishonest by ordinary decent people and he must have realised this. The fact that K was a member of a sect which believed money was tainted does not absolve him from the second (subjective) limb of the Ghosh test for although his sect believed thus, there is no information in the question which points to them knowing that ordinary decent people (as opposed to members of their sect) would not consider it dishonest to give bank customers excess payments. Holding a belief that money is tainted does not amount to holding a belief that it is right and proper to give people more money; indeed quite the reverse. It may be that K would try to show that he believed he had a right in law to deprive the bank of the money under s2(1)(a) Theft Act 1968: see *R* v *Bernhard* (1938). However, it is averred that K would not be able to succeed on this basis as a belief that one has a moral right to deprive the owner of the property is no defence: *R* v *Turner (No 2)* (1971). When K wipes out debits on customers' statements his course of conduct becomes more complicated.

b) *Computer misuse*

The debits on the statements are, it is averred, mere records of a transaction which has taken place and it is therefore submitted that this activity amounts only to computer misuse within the terms of s2 Computer Misuse Act 1990, or to false accounting within the terms of s17(1)(a) Theft Act 1968. If, on the other hand, the debits were records of transactions by customers which had yet to be fully completed (for example, a record showing that a customer had written a cheque which K then wiped before the cheque was cleared) then K could still only be properly charged under the Computer Misuse Act or s17 of the Theft Act because no property (money) would have been appropriated by this action, as the bank would still have the value of the money expressed on the cheque. If, however, the debit was a record of a transaction (for example, a cheque written by a customer) which had yet to be fully completed and the cheque did clear once the record of the cheque having been written by the customer had been wiped, then it is submitted that this also amounts to theft from the bank by K for by his actions he would have stolen a *chose in action*, namely a debt owed to the bank by the customer who wrote the cheque which cleared: *R* v *Kohn* (1979).

c) *Obtaining by deception*

It is submitted that when K filled in the credit application forms and when he received the advances he committed two offences, namely, obtaining services by deception and obtaining property by deception, contrary to s1(1) Theft Act 1978 and s15(1) Theft Act 1968 respectively. The former offence consists of dishonestly inducing another to confer a benefit (in this case, credit) on one on the understanding that the benefit will be paid for. The latter offence consists of dishonestly obtaining property belonging to another with the intention of permanently depriving the other of it. As K knew the applications to be false and as he gave the monies which he received to the charities, it is submitted that he had the necessary mens rea for each offence. However, K is not guilty of the offence of obtaining a pecuniary advantage by deception, contrary to s16(1) Theft Act 1968 because his actions do not come within the ambit of the offence as exclusively defined in s16(2).

d) *The position of the charities*

If it could be shown that the charities or an employee or agent of the charities received the money from K knowing or believing it to be dishonestly obtained or stolen, then this may amount to the offence of handling stolen goods, contrary to s22(1) Theft Act 1968. However, this would only be so if dishonesty could be proved by the test outlined in *R* v *Ghosh*. Even if dishonesty could not be proved, it is submitted that the charities are at risk of being ordered to restore the money they received by virtue of s28 Theft Act 1968 which empowers a court to make an order that whoever has possession of the stolen goods shall restore those goods to the owner (ie the bank) but only provided that it could be shown plainly that the money they received came from the bank and the bank alone: *R* v *Ferguson* (1970); *R* v *Calcutt and Varty* (1985). If the court which convicted K did not consider that the origins of the money which the charities received was sufficiently plain then the bank would have to pursue its claim for the return of the money via the civil courts. Pending this action, the charities would be well advised to keep money to the value of that claimed by the bank in a separate interest-bearing account.

QUESTION FIVE

Xeres took a spear from Zepher's house. Zepher was not at home when Xeres removed it. Whilst using the spear, Xeres broke it. Till then Xeres had intended to return it.

Xeres went to a public baths where he was bathed by slaves. He left without paying as was the usual custom. From Berclay, Xeres borrowed £100 intending never to repay it.

Advise Xeres. Would your advice differ if he had decided not to repay Berclay after receiving the money?

Adapted from University of London LLB Examination
(for External Students) Criminal Law June 1982 Q9

General Comment

This question involves a number of offences under the Theft Act 1968 and the Theft Act 1978. It is quite a straightforward question but it does require detailed knowledge and explanation of the definitions of the various offences together with supporting case law.

Skeleton Solution

Burglary: s9(1)(a) and (b) TA 1968 – theft: ss1–7 TA 1968 'appropriates' – making off without payment: s3 TA 1978 – obtaining a service by deception: s1 TA 1978 – obtaining property by deception: s15 TA 1968.

Suggested Solution

When Xeres removes a spear from Zepher's house he may commit offences contrary to s9(1)(a) and s9(1)(b) of the Theft Act 1968.

Under s9 a person is guilty of burglary if:

a) he enters any building or part of a building as a trespasser with intent to steal, or inflict grievous bodily harm, or rape any woman therein, or do criminal damage; or

b) having entered any building or part of a building as a trespasser he steals or attempts to steal anything in the building or part of it or inflicts or attempts to inflict grievous bodily harm on any person therein.

There are two aspects of burglary which would have to be particularly considered in relation to the facts in the question. Firstly, was Xeres a trespasser and did he have the necessary intention or recklessness as to the facts which made him a trespasser? R v Collins (1973). If he believed on reasonable grounds that Zepher would have consented to him entering to remove the article, then he may not have the necessary mens rea as to the trespass which is required for an offence contrary to s9.

Secondly, for an offence under s9(1)(a) it must be shown that Xeres had intention to steal as he entered and s9(1)(b) it must be shown that the taking of the spear amounted to theft or attempted theft.

Section 1 of the Theft Act 1968 states the person is guilty of theft if he dishonestly appropriates property belonging to another with the intention of permanently depriving the other of it. Certainly, Xeres had appropriated property belonging to another in that he has assumed the rights of an owner over that property. There may be more difficulty in showing that he has the necessary mens rea. 'Dishonesty' is not defined for the purposes of the Theft Acts although s2 states that a person's appropriation of property belonging to another is not to be regarded as dishonest if he appropriates the property in a belief that he would have the owner's consent if the other knew of the appropriation and the circumstances of it. This is a subjective test and providing Xeres honestly held that view it is immaterial that it turned out to be incorrect. In the event of s2 not applying, then it is for the jury to decide whether or not the taking was dishonest: *R* v *Feely* (1973). In the case of *R* v *Ghosh* (1982) the Court of Appeal stated that a subjective test was to be applied by the jury in deciding dishonesty, nevertheless a person should be regarded as being dishonest if that person subjectively appreciated that the ordinary person would find the conduct dishonest even though he himself did not believe it as such. The element of theft which appears not to be satisfied is that of 'intention to permanently deprive'. As with dishonesty, there is no definition of an intention to permanently deprive under the Theft Acts. It is for the jury to decide whether an accused has the necessary intention. Section 6 of the Theft Act 1968 gives two examples of what can amount to an intention to permanently deprive. Under s6(1) a person appropriating property belonging to another without meaning the other permanently to lose the thing itself is nevertheless to be regarded as having an intention to permanently deprive the other of it if his intention is to keep the thing as his own to dispose of regardless of the other's rights, and the borrowing or lending of it may amount to so using, if, but only if, the borrowing or lending is for a period and in circumstances making it equivalent to an outright taking or disposal. On the facts of the question it seems unlikely that Xeres had the necessary intention to treat it as his own when he removed the spear because at that time he intended to return it. When Xeres decided not to return it, it could be argued that there is no offence because the mens rea and actus reus do not coincide. However, by s3(1) Theft Act 1968 a later assumption of rights after an initial innocent taking may amount to theft.

The next situation to be considered is when Xeres goes to the public bath and leaves without paying. It is unclear whether the usual custom was to pay or to leave without paying. Obviously, if the usual custom was to leave without paying then Xeres will perform no offence by following what was the usual custom. However, if the usual custom was to pay on leaving then Xeres may commit an offence contrary to s3 of the Theft Act 1978 when he dishonestly makes off without having paid knowing that payment on the spot for goods supplied or services done is required or expected of him, intending not to pay.

Xeres must know that such payment is required and he must be shown to be dishonest and also shown to have intended permanently to avoid paying: *R* v *Allen* (1985).

Furthermore, if Xeres had decided not to pay before he went into the baths then he may commit an offence contrary to s1 of the Theft Act 1978 in that he dishonestly obtained services by deception. Section 1(2) states that there will only be an obtaining of services where the other is induced to confer a benefit by doing some act on the understanding that the benefit has been or will be paid for. If Xeres had decided not to pay before he went into the public baths then he will be impliedly deceiving by conduct within the definition of deception contained in s15(4) of the Theft Act 1968: *DPP* v *Ray* (1974).

However, it must be shown that the deception was operative, ie that he would not have been provided with the service had it not been for the deception: *R* v *Clucas* (1949).

Both ss1 and 3 of the Theft Act 1978 require the action of the accused to be 'dishonest'. The test to be applied has been previously outlined. However, s2 of the Theft Act 1968 is not applicable to offences other than theft, and therefore, the question of dishonesty is to be left entirely to the jury in all circumstances.

When Xeres borrows money from Berclay intending never to repay it, he may commit an offence contrary to s15 of the Theft Act 1968 in that he has by deception dishonestly obtained property belonging to another for the intention of permanently depriving the other of it.

Under s15(4) the term 'deception' means any deception (whether deliberate or reckless) by words or conduct as to fact or as to law. There is an intentional implied deception on the part of Xeres as he clearly had no intention of carrying out his promise at the time he made it. Furthermore, it seems that there is no doubt that deception was the operative factor in obtaining the property. The fact that the property is money creates no problem under s15 as the definition of 'property' contained in s4 of the Theft Act 1968 includes money.

It is necessary to consider the overlap between s15 and s1 of the Theft Act 1968. In *Lawrence* v *Metropolitan Police Commissioner* (1971) the Court of Appeal stated that whenever the defence contained in s15 was shown there was automatically an offence contrary to s1 of the Theft Act at the same time. This view was not altogether reflected in the House of Lords judgment in *Lawrence* v *MPC* where it was stated that in certain circumstances there would be an overlap between s15 and s1 but it would not occur in all situations. It has been suggested that the overlap between s15 and s1 would only occur where ownership remained in the original party and that it would not be a direct overlap where by deception the accused claimed ownership, possession and control. On the facts of the question it seems that ownership of that money had passed to Xeres there being no intention that that particular £100 be repaid to Berclay. If this were the case then s15 would apply on its own, although if the Court of Appeal judgment were to be applied literally then a s1 offence would also be shown.

If Xeres decided not to pay Berclay until after receiving the money then there would be no offence contrary to s15 at the time when the money was borrowed. However, an existing liability had been created and if Xeres used any deception to avoid repaying the liability, then he may commit an offence contrary to s2 of the Theft Act 1978.

Section 2(1) states that a person commits an offence when by deception he:

a) dishonestly secures the remission of the whole or part of any existing liability; or

b) with intent to make permanent default in whole or in part of any existing liability to make payment dishonestly induces the creditor to wait for the payment or to forego the payment.

Section 2(1)(a) requires the deception to induce Berclay to consent to the remission of the whole or part of the existing liability, ie it requires the consensus.

Section 2(1)(b) can be satisfied where a party does an unilateral act which does amount to a deception for example, where he gives a cheque which he knows is not going to be met.

Until there is a further deception after Xeres has decided not to repay the money there will be no offence on the facts as given.

QUESTION SIX

Russell went to his local self-service garage and filled his car with ten gallons of petrol. On the pump was a notice that property in the garage was not to pass till the petrol was paid for. Russell who had only limited cash with him, saw that the forecourt attendant's attention was elsewhere, so he started to drive off to avoid payment. Before leaving the forecourt he changed his mind, stopped the car and went to the attendant. He explained the position and the attendant reluctantly agreed to accept a cheque without a banker's card in full settlement. The cheque was dishonoured because of insufficiency of funds due to the fact that Russell's wife had drawn out a lot of money from their joint account without telling Russell.

Russell decided to purchase some oil and offered the attendant a £1 note. The attendant gave Russell change for a £5 note. Russell realised this but because of the assistant's unhelpful attitude he decided to say nothing. He resolved not to spend the excess change and left in his car. Had he been asked for it, he would have given it up.

Advise Russell about his criminal liability.

University of London LLB Examination
(for External Students) Criminal Law June 1983 Q9

General Comment

A detailed but straightforward question on the Theft Acts in which a well-prepared student could obtain very good marks.

Skeleton Solution

Making off without payment: s3 TA 1978 – obtaining property by deception: s15 TA 1968 – deception, evasion of liability: s2 TA 1978 – Theft ss1–7 TA 1968.

Suggested Solution

Russell should be advised that by starting to drive off from the garage without having paid for the petrol he may have committed an offence contrary to s3 of the Theft Act 1978. Under s3 a person who knowing that payment on the spot for any goods supplied or service done is required or expected from him dishonestly makes off without having paid as required or expected and with intent to avoid payment of the amount due shall be guilty of an offence.

Under s3 there is no requirement that any party be deceived in order to enable an accused to make off, but it must be shown that the accused acted dishonestly and intended to avoid payment, not simply to delay it: *R* v *Allen* (1985).

The question of dishonesty is always for the jury to decide: *R* v *Feely* (1973). In *R* v *Ghosh* (1982) the Court of Appeal considered the various cases concerning dishonesty

103

and concluded that the test to be applied in all cases was subjective. However, it was not subjective in the sense that if an accused felt he was not dishonest he would not be liable. The test was whether firstly the jury was satisfied that according to the standards of the ordinary man, what was done was dishonest. If it was not dishonest by those standards that was the end of the matter and the prosecution failed. If, however, it was dishonest by those standards then the jury had to consider whether the person charged must himself have realised that what he was doing by those standards was dishonest. Furthermore, it is dishonest for a person to act in a way which he knows ordinary people consider to be dishonest, even if he genuinely believes that he is morally justified in acting as he does.

Applying those cases to the facts in question it would seem that the mens rea required under s3 may well be satisfied. However, the actus reus of the offence may not be made out because it could be argued that Russell had not 'made off' but merely attempted to make off. In *R* v *McDavitt* (1981) it was held that as the accused had not actually left the spot he had not 'made off' although the jury could return a verdict of attempt.

The need to show a 'making off' was reiterated in *R* v *Allen* (1985). In *R* v *Brooks and Brooks* (1982) the Court of Appeal considered that the words 'dishonesty makes off' were easily understandable by any jury and therefore in the majority of cases required no elaboration in summing up. However, in a case where an accused was stopped before passing the spot where payment was required a jury should be directed that that might constitute an attempt.

On the facts in question, although Russell was not stopped but rather had a change of heart, it could be argued that until he had left the premises he had not 'made off' but had merely attempted the offence. Under s1 of the Criminal Attempts Act 1981 there will be an attempt to commit an offence provided an accused has done an act 'more than merely preparatory' to the full offence accompanied by the necessary full mens rea for the offence. It is for the jury to decide whether the accused's conduct has satisfied the test contained in s1: *DPP* v *Stonehouse* (1977). Furthermore, the fact that Russell has a change of heart will in no way negative his liability providing the attempt elements were satisfied.

Although s3 of the Theft Act 1978 is the most likely offence to be shown on the facts in question Russell may commit other offences under the Theft Act. If he intended not to pay before he went into the garage he may have committed an offence contrary to s15 of the Theft Act 1968. Under s15 it is an offence dishonestly by any deception to obtain property belonging to another intending to permanently deprive. The deception may be intentional or reckless by words or by conduct, express or implied, s15(4). However, it must be shown that the deception was the operative factor (in obtaining the property here) and that the deception operated on a human mind. Therefore unless the attendant saw Russell coming into the self-service garage to take petrol and therefore assumed that he was going to pay, there would be no operative deception.

The fact that on the pump there was a notice saying that property was not to pass until the petrol was paid for means that Russell should be advised that he may face a charge of theft contrary to s1 of the Theft Act 1968. The general rule in relation to self-service garages is that property in the petrol passes to the customer on delivery: *Edwards* v *Ddin* (1976).

If Russell had the necessary dishonest intention permanently to deprive the garage at that stage, the offence of theft may be complete. The fact that Russell was doing something he was authorised by the garage to do would not relieve him of responsibility: *Lawrence* v *Metropolitan Police Commissioner* (1971) and *R* v *Morris* (1984). However, it would have to be shown that he had the necessary mens rea at the time of putting the petrol in the car. If he formed the mens rea after the petrol was put into the car and if the notice were effective, then it could be argued that at the time he drove off there was an appropriation of property belonging to another with a dishonest intention permanently to deprive. Under s3(1) of the Theft Act 1968 there is an appropriation where there is any assumption by the person of the rights of an owner and this includes a later assumption where that person had originally come by the property (innocently or not) without stealing it. In *R* v *Morris* the court considered that it was unnecessary for the prosecution to prove that the defendant had assumed all the rights of the owner.

When Russell gives a cheque to the attendant which later is dishonoured it seems probable that he commits no offence under s15. At the time when he gives the cheque he is impliedly warranting that the cheque will be met on presentation: *Metropolitan Police Commissioner* v *Charles* (1977). However, on the facts in question it seems that Russell believes that it would be met. Under s2(1)(b) of the Theft Act 1978 it is an offence dishonestly by deception to induce a creditor to wait for payment or forego payment of an existing liability with intent to make permanent default. On the facts this offence is not shown as there is no intention to default. Under s15(4) Theft Act 1968 'deception' means any deception (whether deliberate or reckless) by words or conduct as to fact or as to law including the deception as to the present intentions of the person using the deception.

It is arguable that Russell does not obtain the petrol by his presentation of the cheque and that any deception in relation thereto would more appropriately fall under s2 of the 1978 Theft Act as the deception comes after the liability to pay has been incurred.

Certainly it appears that Russell is not intentional in his deception. However, it could be argued that perhaps he was reckless as to whether or not the cheque would be met. Recklessness would be shown if he knew there would be a risk, or closed his eyes to what would to the ordinary man be an obvious risk that the cheque might not be met. However, even if this element to the offence were found to be satisfied, it seems very unlikely on the facts in question that he would have satisfied the necessary 'dishonest' state of mind.

When Russell keeps the excess change given to him by the garage assistant he may commit a further offence of theft contrary to s1 of the Theft Act 1968. As already stated the actus reus of the theft is an 'appropriation of the property belonging to another'. The problem here is whether the property belongs to another or whether ownership has passed to Russell. If the mistake were 'fundamental' then it could be argued that there had been no intention to pass ownership to Russell. However, it would appear more likely that the attendant had intended to give that amount of money to Russell acting on a mistake of fact. If this is the case then ownership will have passed to Russell.

A charge of theft may still be satisfied if it is possible to apply s5(4) of the Theft Act 1968. This subsection provides 'where a person gets property by another's mistake and is under an obligation to make restoration (in whole or in part) of the property then to the extent of that obligation the property or proceeds shall be regarded (as against him) as belonging to the person entitled to restoration, and the intention not to make restoration shall be regarded accordingly as an intention to permanently deprive that person of the property or proceeds'.

A most difficult point to decide is when there is 'an obligation to make restoration of the property'. This is decided according to principles of civil law, although an important aspect of quasi-contractual liability is that of repaying money where it is received as a result of the payer's mistake of facts and therefore it could be argued that there is an obligation to make restoration on the facts in question. It would seem that in order to amount to an obligation under s5(4) it must be a legal obligation to make restoration not simply a moral obligation: *R* v *Gilks* (1972).

It seems therefore that Russell, simply by keeping the excess change given to him, which indeed may belong to him in law, may commit the actus reus of theft by appropriation of property which because of the application of s5(4) belongs to another. It must now be considered whether he has the necessary mens rea to satisfy s1. The test for dishonesty has already been outlined, see *R* v *Feely* (1973) and *R* v *Ghosh* (1982). However, it should be remembered that in certain circumstances where there is a charge of theft, the jury must find that an accused is not dishonest. These circumstances are outlined in s2 of the Theft Act 1968 and include a situation where an accused believes he has the right in law to deprive the other of the property. If Russell believed he had a right to keep the property then he will not be dishonest and must be acquitted of any charge of theft. Such a belief must be honestly held and the reasonableness or otherwise of that belief is irrelevant to the issue of 'dishonesty': *R* v *Holden* (1991). However, if that belief is not present it is for the jury to decide in accordance with the case law already outlined and the jury must be directed on the specific provisions of s2: *R* v *Wootton and Peake* (1990).

There is no definition of 'an intention permanently to deprive' under the Theft Act. Under s6 of the Theft Act 1968 there are two examples of circumstances which would amount to an intention permanently to deprive. However, it would seem likely that on the facts in question even though Russell had no intention to spend the excess change and indeed would have given it up had he been asked for it, simply by keeping it when he could have returned it he is in effect treating it as his own and so long as he intends to keep it over a period then he may well have satisfied this element of theft. Ultimately, however, it would be for a jury to decide on this point.

QUESTION SEVEN

A who was 15 years old represented he was 14 years old and as a result obtained half-price admission to a local cinema. The ticket seller knew that A was 15 years old but despite instructions from her employer did not insist on full payment.

In the cinema, B an ice-cream vendor, gave A incorrect change. A had presented a £1 note but B believed that A had given a £5 note for his ice-cream. A thrust the change – which was all in coins – into his pocket without looking at them. It was only later he realised he had excess change.

A found a sealed box on the floor of the cinema. He put it in his pocket and forgot about it.

Advise A of his criminal liability.

Adapted from University of London LLB Examination
(for External Students) Criminal Law June 1984 Q8

General Comment

A more general question and one from which a reasonably well prepared student should be able to pick up good marks. The scope of the question includes the Theft Act 1968 s1 and s9, the Theft Act 1978 s1 and s2.

Skeleton Solution

Deception: obtaining services s1 TA 1978 – evading liability: s2 TA 1978 – attempted deception: Criminal Attempts Act 1981 – burglary: s9 TA 1968.

Suggested Solution

When A aged 15 represents that he is 14 years old in order to gain half-price admission to the local cinema there is a deception for the purposes of s1 and s2 of the Theft Act 1978. Under s15(4) of the Theft Act 1968 'deception' means any deception (whether deliberate or reckless) by words or conduct as to fact or as to law including a deception as to the present intention of the person using the deception or any other person. On the facts in question there is a deliberate deception by words as to facts. Section 1 of the Theft Act 1978 provides that where a person by any deception dishonestly obtains services from another he shall be guilty of an offence. Under s1(2) of the Theft Act 1978 it is an obtaining of services where the other is induced to confer a benefit by doing some act or causing or permitting some act to be done on the understanding that the benefit has been or will be paid for.

Under s2(1)(c) of the Theft Act 1978 a person commits an offence where by any deception he dishonestly obtains any exemption from or abatement of liability to make a payment.

On the facts in question the ticket seller is not deceived and therefore the full offence will not be shown. However, it seems that A will have satisfied the requirements for an attempt to commit a s1 and a s2(1)(c) offence under the Theft Act 1978. In *R* v *Hensler* (1870) the accused wrote a begging letter to P containing a number of lies. P was not deceived but nevertheless sent some money. The accused was convicted of an attempt to obtain the money by false pretences.

Under the Criminal Attempts Act 1981 the jury must be satisfied that A has done an act 'more than merely preparatory': *DPP* v *Stonehouse* (1977). The mens rea for an attempt is generally the same as for the full offence. However, to result in crime it is necessary to show that the accused intended the consequences contained within the actus reus of any particular offence. Therefore on the facts in question it would have to be shown that as well as having the necessary mens rea towards the deception he intended to obtain the service by deception or to evade liability by deception. Also it is necessary to show that he was acting dishonestly.

It is for the jury to decide whether or not the accused is acting dishonestly *R* v *Feely* (1973) and the test to be applied is that stated in *R* v *Ghosh* (1982). The jury has first of all to decide whether according to the ordinary standards of reasonable, honest people what was done was dishonest. If it was not dishonest by those standards that is the end of the matter and the accused must be acquitted. If it was dishonest by those standards then the jury has to go on to consider whether the person charged must have realised that what he was doing was by those standards dishonest. Furthermore, a person will still be dishonest if he knew the ordinary person would consider his conduct to be dishonest even if he asserted or genuinely believed that he was morally justified in acting as he did.

When A gained entry into the cinema it is necessary to consider in the light of what happens later whether or not he enters as a trespasser. In order to be a trespasser for the purposes of s9 of the Theft Act 1968 it is insufficient to show that the accused is a trespasser in civil law; it is also necessary to show that he knew or was reckless as to the facts which made him a trespasser. The point is not clear on the facts in this question as theoretically the ticket seller has permitted A to enter the building even though he has not paid the proper ticket price. However, as the ticket seller was acting contrary to her employer's instructions it may be that her permission would be insufficient and that A still entered as a trespasser for the purposes of s9: *R* v *Collins* (1973).

When A realises he has excess change he may commit an offence under s1 of the Theft Act 1968. The actus reus of theft provides that there must be an appropriation of property belonging to another. Under s3 of the Theft Act 1968 any assumption by a person of the rights of the owner amounts to an appropriation and this includes where he has come by the property (innocently or not) without stealing it and makes any later assumption of a right to it by keeping or dealing with it as the owner, as this would amount to an innocent taking. However, there would be a later assumption of a right by keeping it when he realises he has the excess change.

Section 5(1) and s5(4) of the Theft Act 1968 should be examined when considering whether or not the property 'belongs' to another. Under s5(1) property shall be regarded as belonging to any person having possession or control of it or having any proprietary right or interest to or in it. If the ice cream vendor retained ownership of the money then s5(1) would be the appropriate section to consider in relation to property 'belonging to another'. However, on the facts it would seem that ownership of the money has passed to A and therefore the appropriate section to consider is s5(4) which provides that where a person gets property by another's mistake and is under an obligation to make restoration (in whole or in part) of the property then to the extent of that obligation the property or proceeds shall be regarded (as against him) as belonging to the person entitled to restoration, and an intention not to make restoration shall be regarded accordingly as an intention permanently to deprive that person of the property or proceeds. 'Obligation' means a legally enforceable obligation: *R* v *Gilks* (1972). This would seem to be the appropriate section in relation to the facts of the question. It would therefore seem that at the time of keeping the excess change he would have satisfied the necessary actus reus of theft and have an intention permanently to deprive. The question of 'dishonesty' will be left to the jury in the absence of A having a belief within s2 of the Theft Act 1968. The test for dishonesty as stated in *R* v *Ghosh* (1982) has been outlined above.

If A has entered the building as a trespasser and stolen it should be noted that he has committed an offence under s9(1)(b) of the Theft Act 1968.

Where A finds the sealed box on the floor of the cinema, picked it up and puts it in his pocket, he may commit an offence of theft contrary to s1 of the Theft Act 1968 in that he appropriated property belonging to another with an intention permanently to deprive the other of it. The question of dishonesty is the aspect that may create difficulties in that it is possible that A would claim he believed the owner could not be found taking reasonable steps. This is one of the defences contained with s2 of the Theft Act 1968.

In the absence of the application of s2 the question of dishonesty is left to the jury applying the test as stated in *R* v *Ghosh*.

QUESTION EIGHT

D, a doctor engaged in medical research, used to remove organs from dead bodies as part of his transplant experiments.

He removed the liver from E's dead body even though E before his death had said that neither he nor his family wanted his body to be so used.

D removed the left lung from E's dead body and transferred it to G. When F's executor discovered this he demanded the return of the lung because F and his executor belonged to a religious sect which believed that spiritual peace was not obtainable unless the whole body was buried. G would not return the lung.

What is D's criminal liability?

Adapted from University of London LLB Examination
(for External Students) Criminal Law June 1984 Q9

General Comment

This question is a very difficult one as it covers an area where the criminal law is as yet unclear. A student could very easily get bogged down in an area where lack of any clear rules would lead him to generalise too greatly.

Skeleton Solution

Theft – ss1–7 TA 1968 – 'property' – 'belonging to another'.

Suggested Solution

A person commits theft contrary to s1 of the Theft Act 1968 where he dishonestly appropriates property belonging to another with an intention permanently to deprive that other of it. Section 4(1) gives a basic definition of 'property' as including money and all other property real or personal including things in action and other intangible property. However, this is by no means an all-embracing definition and on occasions substances have been held not be property for the purposes of the Theft Act: *Low* v *Blease* (1975) where electricity was held not to be property.

This problem concerns whether or not E's dead body is 'property belonging to another' for the purposes of the Theft Act so that removal of the liver from it would

109

amount to theft. The traditional rule at common law is that there is no property in a corpse and therefore it was not larceny to remove a corpse. It is generally thought that this same rule applies to theft. Indeed, evidence of the rule in areas other than criminal law can be seen by the fact that a person's body, not being regarded as property, is not part of his estate passing to his personal representatives on death.

It should be noted that in certain circumstances a proprietary interest in a corpse could be acquired by one who expended work and skill on the corpse with a view to its preservation. In *Doodeward* v *Spence* (1908) such a right existed where embalmers had spent time mummifying a corpse.

It can be argued that, under s5(1) of the 1968 Act which states that property shall be regarded as belonging to any person having (inter alia) possession or control of it, D may be the owner of the body. Alternatively, it could belong to the hospital or undertakers when argued along the same lines.

In recent years there has been some case law to support the contention that certain products of the human body are capable of being the subject matter of theft. In *R* v *Welsh* (1974) the accused was convicted of theft when he disposed of a urine sample he had given in compliance with s9 of the Road Traffic Act 1972. In *R* v *Rothery* (1976) a driver who had provided a blood specimen was convicted of stealing the capsule and its container although he was not charged with theft of the contents. However it would seem logical that had he been so charged he would have been liable. None of the decided cases have actually involved the removal of organs from a corpse and it would seem that the common law rule in this area would still prevail.

However, it could also be argued that D has received the 'property' (if property it be) under an obligation (that is, a legal one *R* v *Hall* (1973) to retain and deal with it in a particular way, in which case the property will be treated as belonging to another (s5(3)).

Undoubtedly by removing a liver in these circumstances from E's body D would have committed offences contrary to the Human Tissue Act 1961 and other pieces of legislation concerning the removal of organs from a corpse.

The same considerations apply to removal of the left lung from F's dead body. However, D should be advised as to the difficulties involved when G refuses to return the lung. In that event any action by D to recover the lung would amount to an assault. Indeed, in view of the nature of the operation that would have to be performed and the resulting condition that G would be left in, it would seem quite possible that D would be laying himself open to a charge of causing grievous bodily harm with intent to cause grievous bodily harm contrary to s18 of the Offences Against the Person Act 1861. It should be recalled that under s18 intention as to the consequence is required: *R* v *Belfon* (1976). 'Intention' includes not just desiring that a consequence be brought about but knowing that it is certain to occur. In the event of the jury not being satisfied that D had the necessary mens rea required under s18 then a verdict for the lesser offence contained in s20 could be returned providing the jury is satisfied that he inflicted grievous bodily harm. The term 'inflict' requires an assault of some kind although not a direct assault as originally stated in *R* v *Clarence* (1888).

QUESTION NINE

B decided to steal a diamond from a local jewellery exhibition. In order to 'case' the exhibition B bought an entry ticket. After inspection B decided it would be too difficult to steal the jewel. On the way out from the exhibition he took a coat from a staff cloakroom. B was challenged by a commissionaire whom B pushed aside before running away.

Advise B of his criminal liability.

Adapted from University of London LLB Examination
(for External Students) Criminal Law June 1985 Q1

General Comment

A straightforward question testing the broad elements of theft and burglary with particular regard to trespassary entry.

Skeleton Solution

Attempted theft – burglary under s9(1)(a) Theft Act 1968 – burglary under s9(1)(b) Theft Act 1968 – theft – robbery – assault and battery.

Suggested Solution

It must be borne in mind that, although the jewel is at an exhibition, any theft of it (ie taking with an intention of permanently depriving the owner) will still be theft and not an offence under s11 of the Theft Act 1968 – removal of articles on display to the public. It is all too easy to assume that the question concerns s11 at first glance.

When B buys the ticket in order to 'case' the exhibition he may commit an offence contrary to s9(1)(a) of the Theft Act 1968. Under s9(1)(a) the offence of burglary is committed where there is entry by an accused into a building as a trespasser with intent to steal. The entry must be 'effective and substantial' and the accused must have intention or at least recklessness as to the facts which make him a trespasser: *R v Collins* (1972). Considering the facts in question there are two main difficulties.

Firstly, B has bought himself a ticket and therefore it could be argued that he has not entered the building as a trespasser. However, B's permission to enter was not given to help plan a theft. B has entered the building for a purpose other than the purpose for which he was given permission and therefore he may have entered 'as a trespasser': *R v Jones and Smith* (1976).

Secondly, it seems doubtful that B entered with intent to steal. B's entry was done with the purposes of assisting him in planning the burglary and therefore the requirement of an intention to steal would not appear to be satisfied unless B had a more general intention to steal anything that took his fancy while in the building: *Attorney-General's References (Nos 1 and 2 of 1979)* (1979).

B could not be liable for an attempt to steal the diamond because he must have done an act which is more than merely preparatory to the full offence with full mens rea, s1(1) Criminal Attempts Act 1981. His acts seem to be just that – ie acts which are preparatory to the theft – and so this would seem unlikely on the facts here, although it is for the jury to decide. If there was an attempt to steal the diamond there may be a further offence under s9(1)(b).

When B removes a coat from the cloakroom he commits the offence of theft contrary to s1 Theft Act 1968. Under s1 a person is guilty of theft if he dishonestly appropriates property belonging to another with the intention of permanently depriving the other of it.

Section 3 provides that an assumption by a person of the rights of an owner will amount to an appropriation. In *R* v *Morris* (1983) the House of Lords held that it was not necessary for the prosecution to prove that an accused assumed all the rights. It is sufficient to prove that he assumed any of the rights.

Furthermore, the concept of appropriation involved an act by way of 'adverse interference with or usurpation of those rights'. The question of dishonesty must be left to the jury who should apply the test as stated in *R* v *Ghosh* (1982).

Additionally, we are told that it is a staff cloakroom and therefore, even if B's ticket were sufficient authority to negative an original trespass, the room is beyond that permission to enter and therefore he would be guilty of entering a part of a building either intending to steal (s9(1)(a)) or having so entered, stealing property (s9(1)(b)).

When B pushes the commissionaire aside he may be liable for assault and battery. Assault is shown where a victim is put in immediate fear of force. A battery is a direct infliction of force. They may be performed either intentionally or recklessly: *R* v *Venna* (1975). There is nothing to indicate that the victim is injured so the more serious assaults under the Offences Against the Person Act 1861 will not be considered. The offence of robbery is committed under s8 of the Theft Act 1968 where a person steals and immediately before or at the time of the theft he uses force on any person in order to steal.

There are two possible problems arising from the definition of robbery. Firstly, it is not entirely clear whether the force was used immediately before or at the time of the theft. While an appropriation of the property may continue for a period of time while the process of stealing is taking place: *R* v *Hale* (1978), on the facts in question it would seem that the theft is over.

Secondly, the force must be 'in order to steal'. It is not sufficient that force is used in order to escape, which seems to be what happened in the facts.

We are not told of any injuries to the commissionaire and, unless he suffers grievous bodily harm, the assault upon him will not suffice to support a charge of burglary (s9(1)(b)) under this head.

QUESTION TEN

C was in D's self service store.

a) She decided to help herself to a tin of salmon which she put in her coat pocket, but whilst in the check-out queue she decided to pay for the salmon and placed it in her basket before doing so.

b) C received excess change from the checkout girl. She put it in her pocket without examining it. She discovered the excess only when she was at home.

c) C decided to take out life assurance on her son and in two proposal forms she described her son as a non-smoker. This C knew to be incorrect. From company X, C obtained additional cover and from company Y a reduced premium because her son was thought to be a non-smoker.

Advise C about her criminal liability.

University of London LLB Examination
(for External Students) Criminal Law June 1986 Q2

General Comment

A new type of question with three distinct and separate parts but all concerned with particular aspects of property offences. Parts (a) and (b) were straightforward. Part (a) in particular could have been anticipated in view of recent case law. Part (c) was not without its difficulties and a careful approach was required in order to deal with the two policies in their different ways.

Skeleton Solution

a) Section 1 Theft Act 1968 – s3 Theft Act 1968 – *R* v *Morris* (1983): appropriation – *R* v *McPherson* (1973).

b) Section 1 Theft Act 1968 : later appropriation – ss5(1) and 5(4) Theft Act 1968.

c) Sections 16(1) and 16(2) Theft Act 1968 – s15(4) Theft Act 1968 – operative deception.

Suggested Solution

a) Section 1 Theft Act 1968 provides that 'a person is guilty of theft if he dishonestly appropriates property belonging to another with the intention of permanently depriving the other of it'.

The question to be decided on the facts as given is whether the offence of theft is satisfied or whether there is merely an attempted theft.

The main issue here is whether, by putting the tin of salmon in her coat pocket, C has appropriated the tin as defined in s3 of the 1968 Act. If she has appropriated the tin she may be guilty of theft if all the other ingredients of the offence are established. If there has been no appropriation she may only be guilty of attempted theft. Section 3 defines an appropriation as 'any assumption by a person of the rights of an owner'. In *Lawrence* v *MPC* (1972) the House of Lords held that an appropriation can occur even if the property has been taken with the owner's consent. However, the House of Lords in *R* v *Morris* (1984) had thrown the issue into some doubt by stating, obiter, that an appropriation can only take place if the property has been taken without the owner's consent. The issue has now been settled by the House of Lords in *R* v *Gomez* (1993) where it was held that *Lawrence* was correct and the absence of consent is not a prerequisite for appropriation. The act of putting the tin of salmon in a coat pocket is of course without the shop's consent and consequently an appropriation would have taken place before or after *Gomez*.

It is submitted that an appropriation took place when C put the tin of salmon in

113

her pocket and all the other ingredients of theft were also present at this time; she was dishonest according to the definition in *R* v *Ghosh* (1982) and intended to permanently deprive the shop of the item. The fact that she subsequently changed her mind is irrelevant as the offence is constituted once all the ingredients are present.

b) When C receives excess change from the checkout girl no offence is shown when she put it in her pocket because at that stage she has no mens rea. Later when she discovers the excess she may be liable for the offence of theft as defined above.

Section 3 of the Theft Act 1968 which defines appropriation as any assumption of the rights of an owner further provides that there can be an appropriation where a person has come by the property (innocently or not) without stealing it, any later assumption of a right to it by keeping and dealing with it as owner can amount to an appropriation. On the facts in question C had appropriated by keeping the money.

The next point to consider is whether the money 'belongs to another' for the purposes of s1 Theft Act 1968.

Section 5(1) provides that property shall be regarded as belonging to any person having possession or control of it or having in it any proprietary right or interest (other than certain equitable interests).

Section 5(4) further provides that where a person gets property by another's mistake, and is under an obligation to make restoration (in whole or in part) then to the extent of that obligation the property shall be regarded as belonging to another, and an intention not to make restoration shall be regarded as an intention to deprive that person of the property.

If ownership of the money remains in someone other than C it is not necessary to rely on s4(4), s5(1) would be appropriate. However if ownership has passed to C then s5(4) will apply but only if the 'obligation to make restoration' is a legal obligation: *R* v *Gilks* (1972).

The last point that requires brief consideration is that of dishonesty. Usually it is for the jury to decide whether a person is or is not dishonest (*R* v *Feely* (1973)) applying where necessary the test as stated in *R* v *Ghosh*. However s2 Theft Act 1968 lists three instances where a jury must acquit. The only one that might be available on the facts in question would be if C believed she had the right in law to keep the property. If this were the case the jury must find that she was not dishonest however unreasonable the belief was.

c) Section 16(1) Theft Act 1968 provides that a person who by any deception dishonestly obtains for himself or another any pecuniary advantage shall commit an offence. Section 16(2) details the type of pecuniary advantages within s16(1) and provides (inter alia) that a pecuniary advantage within the meaning of the section shall be regarded as being obtained for a person where he is allowed to take out any policy of insurances or annuity contract or obtains an improvement of the terms on which he is allowed to do so. This particular aspect of s16(2) would appear to cover exactly the situation where C obtains insurance cover with a reduced premium from company Y but it is less clear whether the additional cover obtained from company X would be within s16(2) as the section appears to apply only where the cover is being taken out and not where it already exists.

In any event it must be remembered that it is still necessary to show that there was a deception which was the effective cause of the obtaining of the pecuniary advantage. Section 15(4) of the Theft Act 1968 defines a 'deception' as any deception (whether deliberate or reckless) by words or conduct as to fact or as to law, including a deception as to the present intentions of the person using the deception or any other person. The false statements in the proposal forms would come within s15(4) and certainly in the case of company Y the deception is the operative reason for the reduced premium being allowed.

There seems little doubt on the facts as given that C is dishonest although, as stated previously it is always for the jury to decide.

QUESTION ELEVEN

P entered O's self-service garage intending to pay for petrol with his credit card. Having filled his tank with petrol P discovered that he did not have his card with him and went to explain to the attendant what had happened. The attendant said that P should leave the car till P returned to pay either with cash or the card. This P refused to do because he needed the car so he drove home and was unable to find his credit card. Later P decided not to pay.

Advise P about his criminal liability. Would it make any difference to your advice if there had been a notice on the pump stating 'Property in the petrol shall not pass till paid for'?

University of London LLB Examination
(for External Students) Criminal Law June 1986 Q6

General Comment

Another 'property' question and a type of question that has appeared before. Providing a student has a firm grasp of basic criminal law principles very good marks could be obtained.

Skeleton Solution

Section 1 Theft Act 1968: actus reus and mens rea not coinciding – s3 Theft Act 1978: *R* v *Allen* (1985) – s2 Theft Act 1978: why not available.

Effect of notice: s5(1) Theft Act 1968: later appropriation within s3 Theft Act 1968.

Suggested Solution

Section 1 Theft Act 1968 defines theft as a dishonest appropriation of property belonging to another with an intention to permanently deprive the other of the property. When P fills his tank with petrol he commits no offence because, although he may satisfy the actus reus of theft, he lacks the mens rea. He would not be regarded as dishonest on the facts as given. When he later decides not to pay at that time a jury would almost certainly regard him as dishonest. However he commits no offence under s1 Theft Act 1968 as mens rea and actus reus do not coincide. The actus reus is complete and the property has passed to P before he becomes dishonest.

When P, having explained the situation to the attendant, refuses to leave the car at the petrol station but drives it home he commits no offence. Undoubtedly there is an existing liability within s2 Theft Act 1978. However it would only be an offence to avoid payment of such existing liability if he did so dishonestly by deception. On the facts as given there is no deception at all.

Section 3 Theft Act 1978 provides that a person who, knowing that payment on the spot for any goods supplied or services done is required or expected from him, dishonestly makes off without payment as required or expected of him and with intent to avoid payment of the amount due commits an offence.

This offence seems the most appropriate to the facts as given. Undoubtedly P has 'made off' for the purposes of s3 because he has passed the spot where payment is required: *R* v *Brooks and Brooks* (1982). Furthermore goods have been supplied to him for which he knows that payment on the spot is required. However two points required further consideration. Firstly is P dishonest and secondly does he intend to avoid payment for the purposes of s3?

P must be dishonest at the time he makes off and it is not sufficient that he becomes dishonest later. It is for the jury to decide whether or not P is dishonest: *R* v *Feely* (1973). The test to be applied is as stated in *R* v *Ghosh* (1982):

1) was P dishonest by the standards of an ordinary person. If no, he is not guilty. If yes;

2) did P realise that he was dishonest by their standards. If yes, he is dishonest. If no, he is not dishonest.

The last requirement under s3 that requires consideration is that of the intent to avoid payment of the amount due. In *R* v *Allen* (1985) the House of Lords considered that these words meant that D must intend to avoid payment altogether and not merely to avoid payment for a short period of time. This would mean that P could not be liable under s3 because at the time he makes off he does intend to pay at a future time and he only later forms the intention never to pay.

If there was a notice on the pump stating that property in the petrol would not pass until it was paid for a different result might occur. However this would only be the case if the notice were effective. In that event ownership of the petrol would remain in someone else until it was paid for and therefore for the purposes of s1 Theft Act 1968 the property would still belong to another. Section 5 of the Theft Act 1968 provides that property shall be regarded as belonging to any person having possession or control of it or having in it any proprietary right or interest. Thus even though P has possession of the petrol someone else has ownership. The initial taking of the property would not amount to theft because, as stated previously, there is no mens rea. However s3 Theft Act 1968 provides that an appropriation of property occurs within s1 where there is any assumption by a person of the rights of an owner and this includes, where he has come by the property (innocently or not) without stealing it, any later assumption of a right to it by keeping or dealing with it as owner. When P drove off without paying at that time there could be a 'later appropriation' within s3 Theft Act 1968. Undoubtedly there is an intention to permanently deprive the owner of the property. The only question is that of dishonesty – he does intend to pay at some time. None of the defences within s2 Theft Act 1968 are available so it is for the jury to decide the question of dishonesty as previously outlined.

At the latest P would most likely come within s1 when he keeps the petrol or uses it after he has decided not to pay for it, providing of course that it has not been fully used by that time.

QUESTION TWELVE

H went into I's self-service store intending to steal salmon. In fact there was no salmon because it had all been sold. H went to the meat counter where her friend J, was serving. H placed an order and J weighed the specified meat before pencilling in a lower price than should have been charged. H, who was not paying attention, did not notice that the price was lower than it should have been. At the checkout the shop girl rang up the lower amount and then it dawned on H that it did seem a little on the low side. However, she said nothing. The cashier gave £5 excess change to H who did not notice this till she arrived at her car. H decided to keep it.

Advise H and J of their criminal liability, if any.

University of London LLB Examination
(for External Students) Criminal Law June 1987 Q3

General Comment

An averagely difficult question. Most of the important aspects of the question are regularly examined and therefore a student who prepared by reference to past papers would have had few difficulties with this question.

Skeleton Solution

H Attempted theft – impossibility – s9(1)(a) and s9(1)(b) – conspiracy – lack of agreement – s15 TA 1968 – s1 TA 1968 – dishonesty – theft of excess change. Section 5(4) contrast s5(1) TA 1968 – coincidence of AR and MR.

J Section 1 TA 1968 – s17 TA 1968 – accomplice to offences by H.

Suggested Solution

When H enters the self-service store intending to steal salmon she may become liable for attempted theft.

Theft is defined in s1 Theft Act 1968 and is established where there is a dishonest appropriation of property belonging to another with intention to permanently deprive the other of the property. The actus reus of attempted theft will be established where there is an act more than merely preparatory towards the full offence, s1 Criminal Attempts Act 1981. It is for the jury to decide whether the act of the accused is more than merely preparatory: *DPP* v *Stonehouse* (1977).

The mens rea for attempted theft is the same as the full offence ie a dishonest intention to permanently deprive. The fact that the salmon has all been sold will not preclude liability. Section 1(2) Criminal Attempts Act 1981 provides that a person may still be liable for attempt notwithstanding that the offence is impossible.

117

Furthermore in deciding whether a person has the necessary mens rea he should be judged on the facts as he believed them to be ie that the salmon was in the store. Section 1(3) CAA 1981.

The more serious offence of burglary requires some consideration. Although in practice this type of factual situation described in the question is not prosecuted as such technically the offence of burglary may be satisfied.

Under s9(1)(a) Theft Act 1968 a person commits burglary if he enters a building or part of a building as a trespasser. H must make a 'substantial and effective' entry and must know or be reckless as to the facts which make him a trespasser: R v *Collins* (1973).

It could be argued that H does not enter as a trespasser as she has the implied consent of I to enter the self-service store. However I only gives permission to enter the store to shop and for such other lawful purposes. H enters to steal and therefore she enters for a purpose in excess of the permission granted to her and could be regarded as entering as a trespasser: R v *Jones and Smith* (1976).

Under s9(1)(a) H must have the necessary intent to steal (or commit rape, grievous bodily harm or criminal damage) at the time of entry. It is immaterial that she never achieves the offence. Furthermore if as here the prosecution would rely on intent to steal all that is required under s9(1)(a) is a general intention to steal – it is immaterial that there turns out to be nothing she wants or that the object that she wants is not there: R v *Walkington* (1978); *Attorney-General's References (Nos 1 and 2 of 1979)* (1979). However if the indictment refers to an intention to steal particular items the prosecution must establish that H had mens rea towards those items.

Section 9(1)(b) provides a further offence of burglary where a person having entered a building or part of a building as a trespasser steals or attempts to steal. Technically this would be satisfied only if the prosecution established that what H did was sufficient to amount to attempted theft.

When J places a lower price on the order J may commit theft. The actus reus is established where there is an 'appropriation of property belonging to another'. Section 3 Theft Act 1968 provides that 'any assumption by a person of the rights of an owner amounts to an appropriation'. In the case of R v *Morris* (1983) the House of Lords held that there could be an appropriation even though all the rights of an owner had not been assumed. It was sufficient to prove that any of the rights had been assumed. Furthermore the concept of appropriation involves an act by way of 'adverse interference with or usurpation of an owner's rights'.

On the facts it would seem that by writing a lower price on the goods the actus reus of theft is satisfied. The mens rea is a dishonest intention to permanently deprive. Considering dishonesty first, J cannot claim any of the limited defences contained in s2 Theft Act 1968. Therefore the question is for the jury to decide. In most cases the jury will not require direction but where there are difficulties the test as stated in R v *Ghosh* (1982) should be applied. The jury must first consider where the person charged was acting dishonestly by the ordinary standards of reasonable and decent people. If it was not dishonest by those standards the prosecution fails. If it was dishonest by those standards the jury must consider whether the person charged realised that what he was doing was dishonest by those standards. If he does he will be dishonest. Furthermore it would be dishonest to act in a way that he knew ordinary people considered to be dishonest even if he believed that he was justified in acting as he did.

A further offence which may be committed by J is that of false accounting. Section 17 Theft Act 1968 provides that where a person with a view to gain for himself and another and with intent to cause loss to another:

'a) Destroys, defaces, conceals, or falsifies any account or any record or document made or required for any accounting purposes shall commit an offence.'

The actus reus of s17 would only be satisfied if the paper on which the lower price was marked could be regarded as an account record or document made or required for any accounting purpose: *Edwards* v *Toombs* (1983).

It should be noted that as H is unaware of what J is doing there is no question of a conspiracy or of H being an accomplice to any offences committed by J at this stage.

When H takes the article at the cash desk she realises that the price marked may be on the low side but says nothing. If J has committed a s17 offence by putting a lower price on the goods H may commit a further s17 offence when she makes use of any account, or record or document which she knows to be misleading, false, or deceptive in a material particular.

Furthermore H could commit a more serious offence under s15 Theft Act 1968 in that she dishonestly by deception obtains property belonging to another with intention to permanently deprive the other of it. The most important question in relation to s15 is whether or not there is a deception by H.

Section 15(4) provides that 'deception' means any deception (whether deliberate or reckless) by words or conduct as to fact as to law, including a deception as to the present intentions of the person or any other person. It could be argued that H recklessly deceived because she knows that there is a risk that the price of the goods is wrong but says nothing.

If there is a deception it must be shown that the deception precedes the obtaining of the property (in this case the point when ownership passes) and that the deception is the operative reason for the obtaining.

It could also be argued that H commits the offence of theft when continuing to purchase the goods realising that the price may be wrong. However, this could only be established if ownership had not passed when she realised that the price could be wrong. Furthermore H must be dishonest both for s15 and for s1. On the facts this is by no means clear and therefore the jury should be directed to approach the question of dishonesty by reference to the test in *R* v *Ghosh*.

Undoubtedly s15 and s1 can overlap on occasions: *Lawrence* v *MPC* (1971). There is a certain amount of confusion as to when this overlap occurs and unfortunately although the House of Lords had opportunity on the *R* v *Morris* (1983) case to consider the relationship between s15 and s1 they failed to consider this point.

If H does commit any offences at the cash desk J may be liable as an accomplice, either as an aider and abettor or as a procurer. An aider and abettor must be present or constructively present at the crime, assisting or encouraging: *R* v *Coney* (1882); *R* v *Clarkson* (1971). Whether this is satisfied on the facts is unclear. Certainly J could only be liable as such if quite a wide interpretation of 'presence' were allowed. Alternatively she could be a procurer. A procurer is a person who assists a principal offender before the crime occurs. A person who is an accomplice is to be treated as a principal offender for the purposes of trial and punishment. Section 8 Accessories and Abettors Act 1861.

When H receives the excess change there is no offence at that time because she has no mens rea. However when later she decides to keep it at that point mens rea and actus reus may coincide and she could be liable for theft. There seems little doubt that H would be regarded as dishonest: *R* v *Ghosh*. Furthermore, there is an intention to permanently deprive. The actus reus of theft requires further consideration. Section 3(1) provides that an appropriation may take place at a later stage where a person comes by property (innocently or not) without stealing it but later assumes a right to it by keeping or dealing with as owner. Applying this H would appropriate at the time she decides to keep it.

The next question to be considered is whether the money belongs to another. Obviously this depends on whether ownership of the money has passed to H as a result of the mistake. If it has not then the property will still belong to another within s5(1) because H will not own the money even though she has possession and control of it. If ownership of the money has passed to H it is necessary to consider s5(4) which provides that where property is got by another's mistake, and is under an obligation to make restoration of the property to the extent of that obligation the property shall be regarded (as against him) as belonging to the person entitled to restoration and an intention not to make restoration shall be regarded accordingly as an intention to deprive that person of the property. It must be noted that under s5(4) it is not sufficient that property passes by mistake. The obligation within s5(4) must be a legally enforceable obligations: *R* v *Gilks* (1972).

If the actus reus were satisfied then at the time H decided to keep the money the offence of theft would be complete.

QUESTION THIRTEEN

L entered M's supermarket intending to take some bottles of Brecon beer. When L arrived at the beer counter she found that Brecon beer was out of stock. L did the rest of the shopping and noticed that there was a tin of salmon which had obviously been underpriced. L put it in her basket. L removed a 24p label from a tin of beans and put it on a £3 tin of asparagus before placing it in her basket. Before going to the checkout L decided to return the tin of asparagus to its shelf. At the checkout the shop girl rang up the incorrect price for the salmon. Also she gave L too much change though L did not notice this until later.

Advise L of her criminal liability.

> Adapted from University of London LLB Examination
> (for External Students) Criminal Law June 1988 Q5

General Comment

You will need to consider both theft and burglary in this question, but note especially that the facts do not indicate beyond reasonable doubt that L had the required mens rea, ie dishonesty and an intention to permanently deprive, and the mens rea of a trespasser.

When she switches labels on the tin, the issue is whether that constitutes an appropriation and whether it was done with the required mens rea, and when the offence is complete.

The underpriced tin of salmon raises the issue of deception, and the excess change the issue of appropriating property belonging to another.

Skeleton Solution

Entering supermarket – burglary contrary to s9(1)(a) Theft Act 1968, mens rea of theft and trespasser, offence committed at time of entry – irrelevant that supermarket was out of stock.

Underpriced tin of salmon – when was there an appropriation – was there a deception – was there dishonesty.

Switching labels – act of appropriation – did she have mens rea.

Given excess change – when did L appropriate it – did it at that point still belong to another – did she have mens rea.

Suggested Solution

When L entered M's supermarket intending to take some bottles of Brecon beer, L may be guilty of burglary, contrary to s9(1)(a) Theft Act 1968, which states that a person is guilty of burglary if he enters a building or any part of a building as a trespasser and with intent to commit theft.

The actus reus of burglary consists of an entry, as a trespasser, of any building or part thereof.

Whether a person can be properly described as being outside a building or in the process of entry or as being inside the building must be determined in a commonsense way by the jury, who must determine whether the defendant had made an 'effective entry': *R* v *Brown* (1985); *R* v *Collins* (1973).

A defendant must enter as a trespasser. Trespass is a legal concept and the law of tort must be considered. As a matter of civil law any intentional, or reckless or negligent entry into a building would constitute a trespass if the building was in the possession of a person who did not consent to the entry. If there is no civil trespass there can be no burglary but liability in tort is not sufficient for the criminal law. To commit burglary requires mens rea, ie the defendant must know or be reckless as to the facts which make him a trespasser: *R* v *Collins*. Once a defendant has entered as a lawful visitor, he cannot commit burglary thereafter for the criminal law does not accept the civil law doctrine of trespass ab initio: *R* v *Collins*. Burglary requires entry as a trespasser of a building or part thereof. If a person is authorised to enter premises for one purpose but enters with another, he enters as a trespasser so that a shoplifter could be guilty of burglary as soon as he has entered a shop as he enters for a purpose alien to the shopkeeper's invitation: *Barker* v *R* (1983).

To constitute a 'building' for the purposes of burglary, the structure must have some degree of permanence: *R* v *Manning and Rodgers* (1871).

On the facts, the relevant ulterior offence which L appears to have intended to commit is theft, contrary to s1 Theft Act 1968. An offence under s9(1)(a) Theft Act 1968 is committed at the time of entry so that it would be irrelevant that there was no Brecon beer to steal – this would not be a case of attempting the impossible as the full crime would have been committed. However it is not clear that L had the mens rea of theft, ie dishonesty and an intention of permanently depriving the owner of his property.

Section 2 of the Theft Act provides a partial definition of dishonesty by stating that a belief in legal right or a belief in the owner's consent or a belief that the property had been lost is not to be regarded as dishonest. Apart from this guidance, the matter is one entirely for the jury who must find a defendant dishonest if his conduct would be regarded as dishonest by the ordinary standards of reasonable and honest people and if the defendant realised that his conduct would be so regarded: R v Ghosh (1982).

There must be an intention to permanently deprive and the best evidence of this will usually be what the defendant did with the goods.

Therefore, L will be guilty of burglary contrary to s9(1)(a) Theft Act 1968 if, when she entered, she entered with the mens rea of a trespasser and the mens rea of theft.

When L removed a 24p label and placed it on a £3 tin, she appears to have committed theft contrary to s1 Theft Act 1968. The fact that she put the tin back onto the shelf cannot affect her then existing liability.

The actus reus of theft consists of an appropriation of property belonging to another. Clearly, the tin is property: s4 Theft Act 1968. It clearly belongs to another: 5(1) Theft Act 1968. By s3(1) Theft Act 1968, an appropriation is 'any assumption by a person of the rights of an owner'. By swapping the labels L has clearly assumed the owner's right to decide at what price to sell the goods. Therefore, the theft was complete when the appropriation was complete, ie when the label was switched.

However, L will also require the mens rea of theft, ie dishonesty and an intention to permanently deprive the owner of his property.

When L purchases a tin of salmon which she knows was underpriced, she does not appear to be guilty of theft because she has not committed an essential element of the actus reus of theft, namely an appropriation. If the essence of appropriation lies in the conduct of the defendant which is observable as conduct which is inconsistent with or is an usurpation of the owner's rights, then L has done nothing which was she was not authorised by the owner of the tin to do: Dip Kaur v Chief Constable for Hampshire (1981). As L had not put the label on the tin, there can be no deception offence for there is generally no liability for deception by omission to undeceive where the defendant has not caused the misapprehension.

L was given too much change by the shop girl but found this out after the event. The actus reus of theft does not appear to have been committed as when and if L decided to keep the excess change (and thereby appropriate it), it was no longer property belonging to another. The shop girl's mistake did not prevent ownership in the money passing immediately upon delivery: Moynes v Cooper (1956). By s5(4) Theft Act 1968, where property is got by mistake, a defendant can steal if if he dishonestly appropriates it if he is under a legal obligation to make restoration, despite being the owner of it. Whether a defendant is under a legal obligation to make restoration depends on the civil law.

Therefore, L can only steal the excess change if it still remained property belonging to another when she discovered that she had it and if she decided to keep it dishonestly and with an intention to permanently deprive the owner of it.

By having the basket with her for use in the course of or connection with the burglary or theft L may also commit the offence of 'going equipped' under s25 of the Theft Act 1968 (see Chapter 7).

QUESTION FOURTEEN

C entered the local antique shop to make enquiries about a clock he had seen in the shop window. Inside the shop he decided to look round to see if there was anything worth stealing. He saw a Swansea teapot and decided to try to steal it. While the shopkeeper was serving another customer, C put the teapot in his bag. He felt guilty and replaced it before the shopkeeper returned. C left the shop having purchased the clock. C had paid the price requested by the shopkeeper which was less than on the price label because, as C knew, the shopkeeper by mistake had misread the price label.

Advise the parties. What difference, if any, would it make to your advice if the teapot had been kept behind the shop counter?

University of London LLB Examination
(for External Students) Criminal Law June 1990 Q2

General Comment

The question clearly requires a sound grasp of the law of theft, not least the current debate as to the nature of appropriation, and the complexities of s5(4) of the 1968 Act.

It is necessary to consider burglary, if only to explain why such a charge could not be sustained. Given the difficulties in establishing liability for theft of the clock, it is suggested that alternatives such as deception ought to be considered.

Skeleton Solution

Attempted theft of items unknown – theft of the teapot: consider intent to deprive – burglary, no liability – theft of the clock on alternative assumptions – consider s5(4) – consider appropriation debate – consider problems with dishonesty – consider alternative charges.

Suggested Solution

When C enters the shop he decided to look around to see if there is anything worth stealing. In theory the prosecution could charge him with attempted theft of property unknown. The indictment does not have to specify the property C was attempting to steal; see *Scudder* v *Barret* (1979). Neither will it avail C to argue that there was nothing in the shop worth stealing. Impossibility is not a defence to a charge of attempted theft; see the Criminal Attempts Act 1981, as interpreted by the House of Lords in *R* v *Shivpuri* (1987). The major problem in actually securing such a conviction would be proof that he had taken steps more than merely preparatory to stealing, simply by looking around the shop; see *R* v *Gullefer* (1990).

C is more likely to be convicted of theft following his act of placing the teapot in his own bag. The teapot is property belonging to another as against C; see ss4(1), and 5(1) of the Theft Act 1968. In placing the teapot in his bag, C is assuming one of the rights of the owner; see the definition of appropriation provided by s3(1) of the 1968 Act. In *R* v *Morris* (1984) the House of Lords held that an appropriation occurred when any of the owner's rights were usurped; it was not necessary that all of the rights were usurped or infringed. By putting the teapot in his bag he has assumed the owner's right of possession even though he is still inside the shop. If any difficulty arises in relation to this theft charge it must be as regards the defendant's mens rea. Firstly he must be dishonest. C does not appear to come within any of the negative concepts of dishonesty as determined by s2 of the 1968 Act. It is submitted that, applying the common law definition of dishonesty provided by the Court of Appeal in *R* v *Ghosh* (1982), ordinary decent people would regard such behaviour as dishonest, and that C must surely have realised this. The remaining issue is that of C's intention to permanently deprive. C will undoubtedly contend that the fact that he replaced the teapot is evidence that he did not intend to keep it. Whilst his actions might be evidence of his remorse, and thus might be of relevance in considering the appropriate sentence, they are of little relevance to the substantive offence. The crucial issue is whether or not C intended to permanently deprive the owner of the teapot at the moment when he appropriated it by placing it in his bag. If he did, the theft is complete at that moment. Once the theft is complete it cannot be undone. It is submitted, however, that his action of replacing the teapot will create some evidential difficulties for the prosecution.

The question of whether or not C can be charged with burglary needs to be considered. That he has committed a theft seems likely for the reasons given above, but there may be difficulties with other elements of the offence.

Burglary requires proof that the defendant has entered a building as a trespasser. A shop is presumed to be open to the general public, and members of the public have a licence to enter. If a defendant enters a shop in order to steal an item within, it might be contended that he is entering for a purpose in excess of his implied permission, and thus enters as a trespasser; for further evidence in support of this approach see *R* v *Jones and Smith* (1976).

The difficulty for the prosecution in C's case is that he does not appear to have formed the intention to steal until he had already entered the shop. Once he had decided to steal he would have become a trespasser, but the wording of the two offences created by s9 of the 1968 Act requires proof that he either 'entered as a trespasser', or that he stole 'having entered as a trespasser'. There is no evidence to suggest that he enters any other part of the building occupied by the shop with an intent to steal, hence it is submitted that a charge of burglary would fail.

If one assumes that C picked the clock up and presented it at the counter, it is submitted that he cannot have committed any act of appropriation by selecting it. The item is correctly priced, hence the issues raised in the Divisional Court decision in *Dip Kaur* v *Chief Constable for Hampshire* (1981), do not arise.

Having purchased the clock, albeit at the wrong price, C will contend that the clock became his, and that a charge of theft could not be sustained because the clock was no longer property belonging to another. This argument will succeed unless the prosecution can establish that property in the clock did not pass to C. Section 5(4) of the 1968 Act states that where a defendant gets property by another's mistake and is under an obligation to make restoration of that property or its proceeds, then to the extent of that obligation the property or its proceeds shall be regarded (as against him) as belonging to the person entitled to restoration. Prima facie this section would seem to apply to C, thus effectively preventing property in the clock from passing to him, for the purposes of theft, because of the shopkeeper's mistake. The difficulty for the prosecution, however, is that s5(4) does not of itself create an obligation to restore goods obtained by another's mistake. Such an obligation must already exist in law. It is beyond doubt that such an obligation does exist where one obtains money as a result of another's mistake, but it is far less clear that any such obligation arises where the property so obtained takes some other form. It is instructive to note that s5(4) was specifically drafted to deal with the problem that arose from the decision in *Moynes* v *Cooper* (1956), ie a defendant receiving too much cash in his wage packet. It has been applied to similar situations since its enactment, eg *Attorney-General's Reference (No 1 of 1983)* (1984), but has not been applied to a situation where a defendant has received goods by mistake. On this basis it is suggested that a charge of theft would founder on the prosecution's inability to prove that the clock was property belonging to another when C left the shop.

It should be noted that it will no longer be open for C to argue that he could not be guilty of theft as he had taken the vase with the owner's consent; *R* v *Gomez* (1993) disapproved of the obiter in *R* v *Morris* (1983) and established that an appropriation can take place if the accused dishonestly assumes any of the owner's rights with or without the owner's express or implied permission. The difficult question remains of whether or not the defendant was dishonest. It is submitted that C might raise two arguments by way of defence on this point. First, that he honestly believed he had a right in law to take the item; see s2(1)(a) of the Theft Act 1968. In contract law terms he would surely have acquired voidable title. Secondly, C could argue that, following *R* v *Ghosh* (above), ordinary decent people would not regard his actions as dishonest, or at least that he did not realise that they would regard them as dishonest. Whether or not this latter argument succeeds would depend largely upon the amount by which the price of the clock was mis-stated by the shopkeeper. C's intention to permanently deprive the owner of the clock is evident.

If one assumes that the shopkeeper took the item from a shelf behind the counter and handed it to C, there is no question of C having appropriated it until he takes it from the store. It is submitted that the difficulties outlined above in relation appropriation would also arise in this case. C will not have assumed the rights of the owner until he takes possession of the clock, by which time he will have paid for it. C will contend that he had at least voidable title to the clock, and that until this is avoided by the shopkeeper he cannot commit an act of appropriation in relation to it. The law on this issue is currently rather confused. In *R* v *Morris* Lord Roskill rejected the introduction into the law of theft of such concepts as void and voidable contracts, but did not indicate how else such problems might be resolved. Arguably one could apply *Lawrence* and contend that C is appropriating the clock when it is handed to him, even though the owner consents to his actions, and even though he is becoming the owner of it. Such an analysis derives support from cases such as *Dobson*. Were this view to be accepted, there would still be the difficulty of establishing dishonesty on the part of the defendant for the reasons outlined above. Moreover, had C gone behind the counter he would have entered a 'part of the building' as a trespasser (there being no implied invitation to shoppers to go behind the counter) and therefore the above offences of burglary may have been committed.

There is the possibility that C could be guilty of obtaining the clock by deception, contrary to s15 of the 1968 Act, but the difficulty would lie in establishing a deception on his part. The prosecution may cite *DPP* v *Ray* (1974), and contend that by remaining silent C was representing that he honestly believed the price requested by the shopkeeper to be correct when this was not the case. The chief difficulty here is of course the fact that the price of the clock was determined by the shopkeeper, not C! Proving dishonesty would also be problematic, for reasons already given.

QUESTION FIFTEEN

D borrowed his father's car and took his girlfriend to a circus. D believed that his father would have given permission if asked although his girlfriend knew that no such permission would have been granted. D climbed over a barrier and entered the circus but D's girlfriend refused to join him and entered by paying for her admission. Inside, D bought ice creams for himself and his girlfriend and he received an excess of change which he did not notice till he returned home.

Advise the parties of their criminal liability.

University of London LLB Examination
(for External Students) Criminal Law June 1990 Q3

General Comment

A fairly straight forward question. The most difficult point being D's liability for not paying his entrance fee. This must be considered even if the conclusion is that he incurs no liability. Similarly with burglary. Note that the s5(4) point arises for the second time in this paper. In the interests of clarity the liabilities of the parties should be considered separately.

Skeleton Solution

D's liability for s12 – theft of the petrol – deception offences – making off without payment – theft of excess change – liability of D's girlfriend under s12 and for theft of the petrol.

Suggested Solution

D may be charged with taking a conveyance without the consent of the owner contrary to s12(1) of the Theft Act 1968. To establish a taking of the car, the prosecution must prove that there has been some movement of it, which is evident here; see *R* v *Bogacki* (1973). Secondly, it must be shown that the taking of the vehicle was for the defendant's or another's own use. This essentially requires proof that the defendant used the car as a conveyance; see *R* v *Bow* (1976). Again it is evident that D has been carried in the car. It would appear from the facts given that the owner, D's father, has not granted permission for the car to be driven by D, hence the actus reus of the offence is made out. D has taken the conveyance without having the consent of the owner. D will rely, however, on s12(6) of the 1968 Act which provides that a person does not commit an offence under s12, if he takes a conveyance in the belief that he would have the owner's consent if the owner knew of his doing so and the circumstances of it. The test for this belief appears to be subjective; see *R* v *Clotworthy* (1981).

In driving the car D will be appropriating the petrol in the car's petrol tank, which is property belonging to his father. By driving the car he evidently intends to deprive his father of the petrol. D is unlikely to be convicted of theft of the petrol, however, as the prosecution will have great difficulty in establishing dishonesty. D would presumably rely on s2(1)(b) of the 1968 Act, in claiming that he honestly believed he had the owner's consent to taking the property.

By climbing over the barrier and entering the circus without paying, D enters the circus as a trespasser. On the assumption that the circus is housed in a tent of some description, the question arises as to whether or not this constitutes a building for the purposes of s9(1)(a) and (b) under the 1968 Act. It would appear that in order to qualify as a building for the purposes of burglary, the property entered must have some degree of permanence. The weight of academic opinion seems to suggest that a tent would not satisfy the definition of a building, even if it was being used as a home. Even if the court was willing to concede this point in the prosecution's favour, there would still be the difficulty of proving that D had any of the ulterior intents required under s9(1)(a), such as an intent to steal, rape, commit grievous bodily harm, or criminal damage, none of which is evident here.

When D climbs over the barrier to evade the entrance fee, he may have committed the offence of making off without payment, contrary to s3 of the Theft Act 1978. Payment for the service supplied by the circus is due at the point of entry, and by climbing in D could be described as making off from the spot where payment is due. A technical difficulty, however, is that s3 refers to a 'service done' and a 'service which has been provided'. There is, therefore some doubt as to whether the section extends to cover avoiding payment for service to be provided at some point in the future.

Prima facie it may appear that D, by avoiding payment of the entrance fee, has either obtained a service by deception, contrary to s1 of the 1978 Act, or has dishonestly, by deception, obtained exemption from liability to make a payment, contrary to s2(1)(c) of the 1978 Act. The difficulty in both cases would be in proving some deception on D's part either before obtaining the services, or before obtaining exemption from a liability. There is no evidence that he is trying to deceive anyone by his conduct. Arguably he is seen by members of staff once inside the circus, and is allowed to stay there because he is making the implied representation that he has paid the proper entry fee. On this basis there is the possibility of a s1 offence under the 1978 Act once he is allowed to remain by someone who believes he has paid; see *DPP* v *Ray* (1974). There is insufficient information in the question to be able to pursue this point in more depth.

Section 5(4) of the 1968 Act states that where a defendant gets property by another's mistake and is under an obligation to make restoration of that property or its proceeds, then to the extent of that obligation the property or its proceeds shall be regarded (as against him) as belonging to the person entitled to restoration. Prima facie this section would seem to apply to D, thus effectively preventing property in the change from passing to him. Section 5(4) does not, of itself, create an obligation to restore property obtained by another's mistake. Such an obligation must already exist in law. It is beyond doubt that such an obligation does exist, in quasi contract, where one obtains money as a result of another's mistake. Section 5(4) was specifically drafted to deal with the problem that arose from the decision in *Moynes* v *Cooper* (1956), ie a defendant receiving too much cash in his wage packet. It has been applied to similar situations since its enactment, eg *Attorney-General's Reference (No 1 of 1983)* (1985) (policewoman receiving too much in wages via a bank giro credit). Thus D appropriates property belonging to another when he leaves with the excess change, but at the time he is unaware of the overpayment, and thus would be able to claim that he was not dishonest. He may be guilty of theft if he later realises that he has been given too much change but fails to return it. Retaining the money could be a dishonest appropriation, subject to two caveats. Firstly, D may wrongly, although honestly believe that he has the right in law to keep the money; see s2(1)(a) Theft Act 1968. Secondly, if the sum involved is small, he may not be regarded as dishonest under the test laid down in *R* v *Ghosh* (1982).

D's girlfriend may have committed an offence contrary to s12 of the 1968 Act in allowing herself to be carried on a conveyance she knows to have been taken without the consent of the owner.

In theory D's girlfriend could be regarded as having stolen the petrol, as unlike D, she does not honestly believe that the owner would consent to its being taken, and she may be regarded as dishonest under the test in *R* v *Ghosh*.

7 OTHER THEFT ACT AND RELATED OFFENCES

7.1 Introduction

7.2 Key points

7.3 Recent cases and statutes

7.4 Analysis of questions

7.5 Questions

7.1 Introduction

In addition to the offences of theft and deception there are several related offences that must be known in order to have a complete understanding of the offences against property. These offences will invariably be examined within questions that relate mainly to the areas covered in the proceeding chapter, and they provide an opportunity to gain extra marks for the well-prepared student.

7.2 Key points

a) *Robbery – s8 Theft Act 1968*

The accused must commit theft fulfilling all the requirements under s1 of the Theft Act 1968. For example, if the accused believed he had the right to take the property he cannot be convicted of robbery (although he may of course be convicted of offences against the person): *R v Robinson* [1977] Crim LR 173. Note that the force must be used before or at the time of the theft and in order to steal: *Corcoran v Anderton* [1980] Crim LR 385. Thus force used after the theft has taken place (eg in order to escape) would not sustain a charge of robbery. However, the doctrine of 'continuing appropriation' should be noted in this respect: see *R v Hale* (1978) 68 Cr App R 415. What amounts to force is a question of fact for the jury: *R v Dawson and James* (1976) 64 Cr App R 170.

b) *Blackmail – s21 Theft Act 1968*

Note the different ways in which 'demands' may be made (*Treacey v DPP* [1971] AC 537) and what will constitute a 'menace': *R v Harry* [1974] Crim LR 32; *R v Garwood* [1987] Crim LR 476.

Note also the occasions where an accused's belief that he was entitled to get his property back from another by these methods may provide a defence – *R v Harvey* (1980) 72 Cr App R 139.

c) *Taking a conveyance – s12 Theft Act 1968*

Again the definition must be known and the component parts understood.

'Taking' – *R v Bogacki* [1973] QB 832; *R v Bow* (1977) 64 Cr App R 54; *R v*

Marchant (1985) 80 Cr App R 361; 'owner's consent' or 'lawful authority' – *R* v *McGill* [1970] RTR 4; *Whittaker* v *Campbell* [1984] QB 318; *R* v *Peart* [1970] 2 QB 672.

'Conveyance' – *Neal* v *Gribble* (1977) 64 Cr App R 54. Note also that it is an offence to allow oneself to be carried in or on a conveyance knowing it has been so taken, and the offence of unauthorised taking of a pedal cycle.

d) *Removal of articles*

Students should be aware of the specific offence under s11 of the 1968 Act dealing with removal of articles displayed to the public and how it differs from theft and burglary. Most importantly, the lack of a requirement for intention permanently to deprive must be appreciated (as with taking a conveyance).

e) *Going equipped*

The offence of 'going equipped', ie having with one any article for use in connection with any burglary, theft or cheat – s25 Theft Act 1968 is one which is often overlooked in answering questions: *R* v *Rashid* [1977] 2 All ER 237; *R* v *Bundy* [1977] 2 All ER 382; *R* v *Minor* (1987) 52 JP 30.

f) *Handling*

i) This is an important and relatively complex offence and its elements ought to be known in some depth.

The concept of 'handling stolen goods' must be appreciated – the feeling among legislators is that, without 'fences' – ie receivers and handlers – there would be little theft. Therefore handling is viewed more seriously, and punished more harshly than theft. It follows that the thief cannot be the handler.

ii) The offence can be committed in many different ways (18 to be precise).

The handler must be dishonest. He must also 'know or believe' the goods to be stolen and these words are to be given their ordinary meaning: *R* v *Harris* (1987) 84 Cr App R 75. In *R* v *Hall* (1985) 81 Cr App R 260 the Court of Appeal laid down guidelines for directing juries on this matter and it was held that where the accused 'cannot say for certain that goods are stolen but there can be no other reasonable conclusion in the light of all the circumstances', such knowledge would suffice. Mere suspicion is not enough.

iii) The various ways in which the offence may be committed must be known:

• receiving (or arranging to do so). The meaning of 'receive' should be clearly understood: see *R* v *Cavendish* [1961] 1 WLR 1083; *R* v *Kanwar* [1982] 1 WLR 845; *R* v *Smith* (1850) 1 Den 510;

• undertaking the retention, removal, realisation or disposal by or for the benefit of another (or arranging to do so). On the meaning of 'assisting' (which like 'receiving' often occurs in examinations) see *R* v *Brown* [1969] 3 WLR 370; *R* v *Pitchley* [1972] Crim LR 705; *R* v *Kanwar* [1982] 1 WLR 845;

- assisting in the retention, removal, realisation or disposal by or for the benefit of another (or arranging to do so).

iv) 'Stolen goods' must be understood – ie goods obtained by theft, blackmail, deception, or similar offences abroad which would have constituted theft, blackmail or deception had they been committed in England.

Note should be taken of when goods cease to be 'stolen' and the arguments arising in *Haughton* v *Smith* [1975] AC 476 and *R* v *King* [1938] 2 All ER 662.

v) Note that an accused may only be convicted of handling by any method other than receiving if the handling is done for the benefit of someone other than the accused himself: see *R* v *Bloxham* [1983] 1 AC 109.

vi) Note that 'stolen goods' are not confined to the goods which were originally stolen but also include anything exchanged for those goods and which then 'represent stolen goods': see s24(2) Theft Act 1968.

vii) Note the circumstances in which money drawn from a bank account may be stolen goods: see *Attorney-General's Reference (No 1 of 1974)* [1974] 2 WLR 891.

g) *Forgery and counterfeiting*

Very briefly, it is useful to remember that there exist separate offences of forgery and counterfeiting. Forgery is basically making or using a document, stamp, tape etc which 'tells a lie about itself'. Counterfeiting involves making or using counterfeit currency or coins.

7.3 Recent cases and statutes

There have been no major recent developments in this area.

7.4 Analysis of questions

There will usually be several of these theft-related offences hidden within the facts of questions and it is easy to remain pre-occupied with the obvious crimes revealed at first glance.

Occasionally a question will be largely concerned with one of these related offences usually taking a conveyance or blackmail.

7.5 Questions

QUESTION ONE

Xeres and Yella decided that they would try to borrow a car to go for a drink. Xeres asked his brother for a loan of a car to go to town. In fact he wanted to borrow it and take Yella for a drink in a nearby village and he knew that if he told his brother the truth he would not lend it.

What crimes have Xeres and Yella committed?

Adapted from University of London LLB Examination
(for External Students) Criminal Law June 1983 Q6

General Comment

A straightforward question on s12 of the Theft Act 1968 with consideration of a possible deception.

Skeleton Solution

Taking a conveyance or being carried thereon: s12 TA 1968 – obtaining property/service: s15 TA 1968 and s1 TA 1978.

Suggested Solution

When Xeres and Yella borrowed Xeres' brother's car to go for a drink at a nearby village they may both have committed offences contrary to s12 of the Theft Act 1968. Section 12 provides that a person shall be guilty of an offence if without having the consent of the owner or other lawful authority he takes any conveyance for his own or another's use, or knowing that any conveyance is to be taken without such authority, drives it or allows himself to be carried in it or on it.

There is not a 'taking' of a conveyance until there is movement, *R* v *Bogacki* (1973) and furthermore the taking of the conveyance must be for use as a conveyance: *R* v *Bow* (1976). These elements of the offence would be satisfied on the facts in question. However, what may not be satisfied is whether the taking is 'without the consent of the owner'.

On the facts in question the consent is obtained by fraud. In this respect two particular cases must be considered. In *R* v *Peart* (1970) D persuaded P to lend him a van in order to go to A. In fact he wanted the van to go to B where he was found by police some time after the expiry of the period within which he should have returned the van. The conviction under s12 was quashed by the Court of Appeal because the consent which P had obtained was not vitiated by the deception. In that case the deception did not relate to a fundamental matter and therefore still operated. However, the court left open the question of whether a deception relating to a fundamental aspect would nullify consent.

In *R* v *McGill* (1970) it was held that D may be convicted of an offence if he has obtained consent to use a conveyance for a particular purpose and for a given time but uses it beyond that time for a different purpose. At the moment when he has completed the purpose for which the consent was originally given and he goes on to use the vehicle for a different purpose there will be a fresh 'taking' of the conveyance under s12.

It is difficult to reconcile these two cases and it is submitted that the facts in question are more akin to those of *R* v *Peart* (1970) than *R* v *McGill* (1970). On that basis the deception is not fundamental and therefore the consent would still operate. However if this were not the case and the court found that there was a taking of the conveyance without consent, Xeres could be charged with taking and driving the conveyance contrary to s12 and Yella could be charged with allowing himself to be driven contrary to s12, but only if he knew that the taking was without consent. There would be no possibility of charging either party under s1 of the Theft Act 1968 (theft) or s15 of the Theft Act 1968 (obtaining property by deception) because although they have satisfied the actus reus and it is possible that they would be viewed as dishonest, they did not possess the necessary 'intention to permanently deprive'.

Similarly, a charge of obtaining a service from the brother under s1 of the 1978 Theft Act would be inappropriate as, although there is a 'benefit' conferred upon X and Y, it was not made on the understanding that it has been or will be paid for.

QUESTION TWO

N and O, aged 17 years and 13 years, decided to borrow their father's car without asking. They suspected, though they did not know, that he would have refused. N drove them to a nearby cafe.

Advise N and O.

Adapted from University of London LLB Examination
(for External Students) Criminal Law June 1984 Q5

General Comment

Again, a fairly simple examination of s12 with particular regard to 'consent' and the aggravating factor of the age of the accused.

Skeleton Solution

Conspiracy: CLA 1977 – mischievous discretion – taking a conveyance and being carried thereon: s12 TA 1968.

Suggested Solution

When N and O decide to borrow their father's car without his approval, they may commit a conspiracy contrary to s1 of the Criminal Law Act 1977 in that they have agreed on a course of conduct which if carried out in accordance with their intention will necessarily amount to the offence contained in s12 of the Theft Act 1968. N is 17 years old and therefore for the purpose of criminal law is treated as an adult. However, O is 13 years old and because of this will only be a party to the conspiracy if it can be shown that he has 'mischievous discretion': *R* v *Gorrie* (1918); *McC* v *Runneckles* (1984) and *C (a minor)* v *DPP* (1995). The fact that they suspected, although they did not know, their father would have refused would not give them a defence to any change contrary to s12. Under s12(6) a person would not commit the offence of taking a conveyance if:

a) he believed he had lawful authority to take the conveyance; or

b) he believed that he would have the owner's consent if the owner knew of the circumstances.

Neither of those requirements are satisfied on the facts in question.

When N drives the car and O is carried in the car they commit offences under s12 of the Theft Act 1968. N would be liable for taking and driving a conveyance without the consent of the owner and O would be liable, presuming that he has mischievous discretion, for allowing himself to be driven in a conveyance, knowing that it has been taken without the consent of the owner. The 'taking' of the conveyance occurs at

133

the moment of some movement: *R* v *Bogacki* (1973). Furthermore, the taking and driving was in this case for use as a conveyance in that both N and O were transported in the vehicle: *R* v *Bow* (1976) and *R* v *Stokes* (1982).

QUESTION THREE

G and I were students at the same college. G wrote to H, I's millionaire father, demanding payment to rag funds in return for I's release. I agreed to write to H saying that he had been held against his will. This was not true. On receipt of these letters H was very alarmed and told his wife what had transpired. She had a nervous condition and suffered a heart attack.

H paid the money to the rag fund. Earlier, G and friends had blocked the roads near the college demanding payment before permitting vehicles to pass.

Advise G, I and H on their criminal liability.

Adapted from University of London LLB Examination
(for External Students) Criminal Law June 1985 Q3

General Comment

A fairly straightforward examination of making 'demands with menaces' and the possible overlap with deception.

Skeleton Solution

Blackmail: s21 TA 1968 – attempted deception: s15 TA 1968 – deception: s15 TA 1968 – robbery: s8 TA 1968.

Suggested Solution

When G writes to I's father demanding payment to rag funds in return for I's release he may commit the offence of blackmail contrary to s21 Theft Act 1968. A person is guilty of blackmail if he makes an unwarranted demand with menaces with a view to gain for himself or another or to cause loss to another in money or other property.

A 'demand' can be made in any number of ways and on the facts in question it would be complete when the letter is posted. It is immaterial whether or not it is received by the victim: *Treacy* v *DPP* (1971). The term 'menaces' is not defined in the Act. In *R* v *Clear* (1968) it was held that the demand was only menacing if it was accompanied by threats of such nature and extent that an ordinary person of normal stability would be influenced so as to accede to the demand. In *R* v *Harry* (1974) the organisers of a student rag wrote letters to local shopkeepers offering them immunity from rag activities if they contributed to rag funds. While some shopkeepers complained this was held not to be menacing because an average person would not have been affected. Possibly if G and I had appreciated the wife's nervous condition that would have been taken into account.

A demand with menaces is unwarranted unless:

a) the accused believes that he has reasonable grounds for making the demand; and

b) the accused believes that the use of menaces is a proper means of reinforcing the demand.

When I writes to his father saying falsely that he is being held against his will he may be liable for an attempt to obtain money by deception contrary to s15 Theft Act 1968. Section 15 of the Theft Act 1968 provides that a person who by any deception dishonestly obtains property belonging to another with intention to permanently deprive shall commit an offence. The deception must satisfy s15(4) and therefore must be either intentional or reckless and can be by words or conduct, as to fact or as to law, including a deception as to the present intentions of the person using the deception, or any other person.

The deception must be shown to be the operative reason for the obtaining of the property (in this case the money).

Undoubtedly, there is an intention to permanently deprive although it may not be so easy to satisfy the requirement for dishonesty. The question of dishonesty must be left to the jury to decide. In R v Ghosh (1982) the Court of Appeal adopted an essentially subjective approach. When deciding whether or not a person was acting dishonestly the jury had to decide whether according to the ordinary standard of reasonable and honest people the accused's conduct was dishonest. If it was not then the accused should be acquitted. If it was the jury should then consider when the accused viewed his conduct as dishonest by ordinary standards. If he realised that his conduct was dishonest by these standards he would still be dishonest even if he believed that he was morally justified in acting in the way he did act.

When H pays the money to the rag fund a full offence contrary to s15 of the Theft Act 1968 may have been committed. While the House of Lords was of the opinion in Lawrence v MPC (1971) that there was a certain overlap between s15 of the Theft Act 1968 and s1 of the Act it did not make clear when that overlap would occur. No further clarification was given to this point in R v Morris (1983). If ownership of the money has passed from H it seems most likely that s15 alone is satisfied as the overlap between s15 and s1 would more obviously occur if ownership of the money remained in H while possession and control passed to the rag fund.

When G and friends blocked the road demanding payment before allowing vehicles to pass, a further offence under s21 may be shown although it seems much less likely that their demands would be found to be menacing. As we are not told of any force or threatened force used towards the drivers it is unlikely that a charge of robbery under s8 of the Theft Act 1968 would be made out.

QUESTION FOUR

E went into F's camera shop to steal a 'Flashman' camera. He could not find one there and left having been told by a sales assistant that they did not have one in stock. Next E went into Gutrum Cameras to see if there was a 'Flashman' on the premises to steal on a subsequent visit. He found the camera and while the sales assistant's attention was elsewhere E changed the price labels on the camera putting a lower price label on the 'Flashman' camera. He then realised that the shop was protected by closed circuit television. E left the camera and rushed out of the store, forgetting to pay for a roll of film which he had picked up. As he was leaving, E pushed aside a customer who was entering the shop. Advise E.

University of London LLB Examination
(for External Students) Criminal Law June 1991 Q2

General Comment

There are a number of points to watch in attempting this question. E does not intend to steal the camera when he visits the second shop but is planning to return on another occasion. How does this affect his liability? What is his state of mind when he leaves the shop with the film? We are not given clear guidance on this. It is suggested that the examiner clearly wanted candidates to consider robbery, although on the facts it seems unlikely that such a charge could succeed.

Skeleton Solution

Section 9(1)(a) burglary in both shops – label switching as theft – attempted s15 – effect on burglary – not paying for the film – theft. problem with dishonesty – making off – battery – robbery.

Suggested Solution

a) *Section 9(1)(a) burglary*

E may have committed burglary contrary to s9(1)(a) of the Theft Act 1968, when he entered F's camera shop intending to steal the 'Flashman' camera. The shop is clearly a building. Byles J, in *Stevens* v *Gourley* (1859), stated that a building was 'a structure of considerable size and intended to be permanent or at least to endure for a considerable length of time'. E has clearly entered the shop; *R* v *Brown* (1985). Section 9(1)(a) requires proof that E entered the shop as a trespasser. Clearly an honest shopper has permission to enter a shop and thus does not commit trespass as that concept is understood at civil law. In *R* v *Smith and Jones* (1976), the defendants visited the house of Smith's father and stole his television set. They were convicted under s9(1)(b) and appealed on the basis that they had permission to go into the house and thus could not have been trespassing. The court held that the defendants were rightly convicted under the subsection, on the basis that a person enters a building as a trespasser where he realises he has exceeded his permission, or is reckless as to whether he has done so. The defendants might have had permission to enter the house for normal domestic purposes, but not to enter in the middle of the night to steal.

Similarly E will not have had intention to enter the shop in order to steal and will have been aware of this. The fact that the camera he sought was not available will not affect E's liability. The Court of Appeal's decision in *Attorney-General's References (Nos 1 and 2 of 1979)* (1979) establishes that the essence of the offence is the defendant's state of mind at the time of entry, the intent to steal can exist quite independently of any property that he can or wants to steal.

E may also incur liability under s9(1)(a) in respect of his visit to 'Gutrum' cameras, although he may contend that as he does not intend to steal the camera there and then he does not have the present intention to steal which is one of the ulterior intents required for liability under s9(1)(a).

b) *Label switching: theft and burglary*

In switching labels on the cameras E may have committed theft. The cameras are obviously property belonging to another. Section 3(1) of the Theft Act 1968 defines appropriation as '... any assumption by a person of the rights of an owner ...'. In *R* v *Morris* (1983) this was held to extend to label switching on the basis that the defendant was assuming the owner's right to determine the price to be paid for the goods. In acting in this way E is clearly dishonest; see s2(1) of the 1968 Act and *R* v *Ghosh* (1982). There remains the question of whether or not he has intention to permanently deprive the store of its property. If he intended to take the camera to the counter there and then the answer would be 'yes', but the difficulty here is the evidence that he intends to return on another occasion to steal it. In this situation it may be wiser to charge E with the alternative offence of attempting to obtain property by deception. If he had presented the camera to the assistant with the lower price label and been permitted to purchase it at this lower price he would have obtained the camera by deception, hence his actions in swapping labels are acts more than merely preparatory to the deception offence; see s1(1) Criminal Attempts Act 1981, and comments by Lord Roskill in *R* v *Morris* (above). The fact that E changes his mind once he realises he has been observed is irrelevant. he has already committed the attempt, and possibly the theft, if he swapped labels with the requisite mens rea.

c) *Not paying for the film*

When E picked up the film he may have committed theft if he intended not to pay for it. In *R* v *Gomez* (1993) the House of Lords held that an authorised act could amount to appropriation if it was done dishonestly. *Lawrence* v *MPC* (1971) was approved and *R* v *Morris* (1983) was disapproved. However, we are told that E 'forgot' to pay for the film. If E had a genuine intention to pay for the film but forgot it is submitted that he would not be dishonest under *R* v *Ghosh* (1982). If a charge of theft cannot be sustained, then no question of liability under s9(1)(b) arises (entering as a trespasser and stealing).

As an alternative the prosecution may contemplate a charge under s3(1) of the Theft Act 1978, which creates the offence of making off without payment. Under s3 a person who, knowing that payment on the spot for any goods supplied or service done is required or expected from him, dishonestly makes off without having paid as required or expected and with intent to avoid payment of the amount due is guilty of an offence. A number of difficulties are evident with such a charge. First does E make off dishonestly? The test here is that laid down in *R* v *Ghosh* (above). If he thinks he has paid would he realise that ordinary and decent people would regard his actions as wrong? Secondly, does he make off with intent to avoid payment? Again, if he thinks he has paid, or even if he has simply forgotten, the answer must be 'no'.

d) *Robbery?*

The fact that E pushes aside a customer as he is leaving the shop is unlikely to give rise to a criminal charge. Technically E could be charged with battery as he has inflicted unlawful force on another; see *Cole* v *Turner* (1705), but the police are unlikely to entertain such a complaint. A private prosecution would have to be brought to pursue the matter. If prosecution form the view that E is committing theft of the film in leaving the store without paying for it, the matter becomes more serious. E could then be charged with robbery. Under s8 of the 1968 Act, a person is guilty of robbery 'if he steals, and immediately before or at the time of doing so, and in order to do so, he uses force on any person or puts or seeks to put any person in fear of being then and there subjected to force.'

There is no doubt here that force has been used (on the customer) but the question would arise as to whether or not it coincided with the theft. E may contend that the theft had already occurred, but the prosecution will rely upon the Court of Appeal's decision in *R* v *Hale* (1978), to the effect that appropriation could be a continuing act, the point at which it ceased was being determined by the jury on the facts of each case. Where, therefore, D steals property belonging to P, is discovered by P, and threatens P that unless he is allowed to escape without the police being called he will assault P, D will be guilty of robbery. The threats to P are made whilst the theft (appropriation) is continuing, and are made in order to accomplish the theft. It is submitted that even if the prosecution does persist in a charge of theft, E will rely upon the decision in *R* v *Robinson* (1977), in which the Court of Appeal held that a defendant should be found not guilty of robbery where he honestly believed he had a right in law to take the property, ie where the defendant falls under s2(1)(a) of the 1968 Act.

QUESTION FIVE

Whilst waiting in a bank, T saw V make a large withdrawal which he decided to steal. T threatened to hit V and snatched the money. He then ran out of the bank pushing two customers out of the way. T stopped a passing motorist, X, telling him a lie that he urgently needed to visit his wife who had been taken into a local hospital after an accident. X drove T to the hospital where he was apprehended.

Advise T.

Adapted from University of London LLB Examination
(for External Students) Criminal Law June 1985 Q8

General Comment

A fairly detailed question made simpler by the fact that there is only one accused. A well-prepared student would be able to get very good marks here.

Skeleton Solution

Robbery: s8 TA 1968 – assault and battery – obtaining service by deception: s1 TA 1978 – taking a conveyance: s12 TA 1968.

Suggested Solution

When T removes the money from V's bag he commits the offence of theft contrary to s1 Theft Act 1968. Under s1 there is theft when there is an appropriation of property belonging to another with a dishonest intention to permanently deprive the other of the property. Section 3 provides that an assumption by a person of the right of an owner will amount to an appropriation. In *R* v *Morris* (1983) the House of Lords held that it was not necessary for the prosecution to prove that an accused assumed all the rights. It was sufficient to prove that he assumed any of the rights. Furthermore, the concept of an appropriation involved an act by way of 'adverse interference with or usurpation of those rights'. The question of dishonesty must be left to the jury who should apply the test as stated in *R v Ghosh* (1982).

However, the theft here is aggravated by T's use of threats toward V.

Section 8 of the Theft Act 1968 makes it an offence of robbery where a person steals and immediately before or at the time of doing so, and in order to do so, he uses force on any person, or puts or seeks to put any person in fear of being then or there subjected to force.

In threatening V, T commits a common law assault and also, as he puts V in fear of being subjected to force in order to facilitate his theft, T commits robbery.

His use of force on the customers appears to come after the theft is complete in which case he would only commit an assault and battery at common law against them.

However, in *R v Hale* (1978) the Court of Appeal held that an appropriation could be regarded as a continuing act and when considering the time at which force was used, and the purpose therefor, it may be open to a jury so to conclude.

It is submitted that in this case the appropriation by T is complete before he pushes the customers.

When T stops a passing motorist and tells him a lie to persuade him to give him a lift, he may commit an offence contrary to s1 Theft Act 1978. Under s1(1) a person who by any deception dishonestly obtains services from another shall be guilty of an offence. The phrase 'deception' is defined in 15(4) Theft Act 1968 as any deception (whether deliberate or reckless) by words or conduct as to fact or as to law, including a deception as to the present intentions of the person using the deception or any other person.

The deception must be the operative reason for the obtaining of the services: *R v Clucas* (1949).

The term 'service' is defined in s1(2) of the Theft Act 1978 which provides that it is an obtaining of services where the other is induced to confer a benefit by doing some act, or causing or permitting some act to be done on the understanding that the benefit has been or will be paid for.

It is this last element of payment that does not on the facts appear to be satisfied.

T may also commit the offence of taking a conveyance without the owner's consent or other lawful authority contrary to s12 of the Theft Act 1968.

The question to be determined here would be whether T had 'taken' the conveyance. He has certainly used it as such, satisfying the requirements in *R v Bow* (1977).

Another requirement for the offence is that the taking is without the owner's consent. X here consents to the use of the vehicle but that consent is obtained by T's false representations. Does that vitiate the consent.

In *Whittaker v Campbell* (1984) it was held that in such circumstances it could not be said that the owner had not consented.

In *R* v *Peart* (1970) D made a false representation of an urgent need to make one journey, knowing that the owner would not have consented to the taking had he known of D's real intended journey. It was held that such a deception did not vitiate the owner's consent.

Therefore it appears that, even if a 'taking' could be established, T does not do so without the owner's consent.

QUESTION SIX

a) T took £450 from her boss's till despite having been expressly instructed not to do so. T intended to replace the money. T used the money to buy groceries from T's friend U having explained to U how she had come by the cash.

b) T believed that V had agreed to lend T his car to visit T's mother. In fact V had agreed to lend the car but only if T's husband drove it. T did in fact drive the car. Later, T went to a multi-storey car park to look for a car to take for a joyride. T took a set of duplicate ignition keys with him in the hope that one of them might fit one of the parked cars.

Advise T and U of their criminal liability if any.

Adapted from University of London LLB Examination
(for External Students) Criminal Law June 1986 Q8

General Comment

A fairly straightforward question. Part (a) in particular covers an area of the syllabus that has frequently been examined. Part (b) deals with an area not quite so commonly examined. However an averagely well prepared student should be able to pick up good marks on this question.

Skeleton Solution

a) Section 1 Theft Act 1968 – s2 Theft Act 1968: cases on dishonesty – s22 Theft Act: definition of stolen goods.

b) Section 12(1) Theft Act 1968 – s12(6) Theft Act 1968 – going equipped – s25 TA 1968.

Suggested Solution

a) When T took £450 from her employer's till having been expressly instructed not to do so she may commit the offence of theft contrary to s1 Theft Act 1968. Under s1 a person is guilty of theft if he dishonestly appropriates property belonging to another with the intention of permanently depriving the other of it.

Undoubtedly on the facts there is the actus reus of theft. Furthermore she has an intention to permanently deprive because although she intends to return an equivalent sum of money she has the intention to use the money she removed for her own purposes. This would be an example of an intention to permanently deprive. The borrowing of the money is equivalent to an outright taking within s6(1) because T treats it as her own to dispose of regardless of the other's rights. (*R* v *Velumyl* (1989)).

The only question remaining is whether T is dishonest.

Section 2 Theft Act 1968 lists three instances when a person is not to be regarded as dishonest. These are:

a) if he believed he had the right in law to take the property;

b) where the accused believes the owner would consent if he knew of the circumstances; or

c) if he believed the owner cannot be found by taking reasonable steps.

None of these is available on the facts as given. It is therefore for the jury to decide whether T is dishonest: *R* v *Feely* (1973). The test to be applied is as stated in *R* v *Ghosh* (1982) and, if T claims that her behaviour was honest even though the majority of people would think it dishonest, a *Ghosh* direction is appropriate: *R* v *Price* (1990):

i) was T dishonest according to the standards of reasonable honest people? If no, T will not be guilty. If yes;

ii) did T realise that reasonable and honest people would regard what she did as dishonest? If yes, she is guilty. If no, she is not guilty.

U may commit an offence within s22 Theft Act 1968 when she accepts the money in payment for groceries knowing how T came by the cash. However before this offence is shown a number of points would have to be satisfied. Under s22 Theft Act 1968 U would be liable for handling stolen goods if (otherwise than in the course of the stealing) knowing and believing them to be stolen goods she dishonestly receives the goods, or dishonestly undertakes in their retention, removal, disposal or realisation by or for the benefit of another, or arranges to do so.

The first question to consider is whether the money can be regarded as 'stolen goods'. For the purposes of s22, 'stolen goods' includes goods taken contrary to s1 Theft Act 1968. Therefore only if T was dishonest in her appropriation – so that T is liable for theft, can the money be regarded as stolen and U be regarded as receiving stolen goods. However it must still be shown that U acted dishonestly (*R* v *Feely* and *R* v *Ghosh*) and that she had knowledge or a belief that the money was stolen. It should be noted that if the money is stolen the groceries purchased with the money may themselves be 'tainted'. Within s24(2) Theft Act 1968 'stolen goods' shall include any other goods which are directly or indirectly stolen goods in the hands of the thief.

Technically U may also commit the offence of theft as defined above at the same time as any s22 offence: *R* v *Sainthouse* (1980). However, U cannot on the same circumstances and facts, be convicted of both offences: *R* v *Shelton* (1986).

If U committed an offence under s22 T would be liable as an aider and abettor to the offence in that she was present assisting and encouraging at the scene of the crime *R* v *Coney* (1882) with full knowledge of the facts that constitute the offence: *Johnson* v *Youden* (1950).

b) It is necessary to consider the offence of taking a conveyance under s12 Theft Act 1968. Section 12 Theft Act 1968 provides that a person shall be guilty of an offence if, without having the consent of the owner or other lawful authority, he takes or drives any conveyance for his own or another's use. T had undoubtedly committed the actus reus of the offence. The car is a 'conveyance' within s12(3) and T takes it for use as a conveyance: R v Bow (1977). However, s12(6) provides that a person does not commit the offence of taking a conveyance if he believes that he had lawful authority to take the conveyance. Such belief need not be reasonable provided it is honestly held.

When T goes to the car park armed with the keys he may commit the offence under s25 of the Theft Act 1968, of going equipped as he, when not at his place of abode, has with him articles for use in the course of or in connection with a theft. Although taking a car for a joyride would not amount to 'theft' per s1 of the Act, it is sufficient for the purposes of s25 that his intention is to take a conveyance without consent.

QUESTION SEVEN

Wally decides to get himself some money to pay off gambling debts. He goes to a nearby shopping precinct, taking a child's halloween mask with him from his house.

Seeing Lindsey pushing a pram containing her three month old baby, Wally puts on the mask. He stops Lindsey and shouts 'Give me your purse or the baby gets it!'

Lindsey is terrified for her baby's safety and hands over the purse.

What offences, if any, has Wally committed?

Written by Editor

General Comment

This question is a straightforward test of a student's knowledge of robbery and blackmail and the distinction between the two.

Skeleton Solution

Robbery: s8 TA 1968 – blackmail: s21 TA 1968 – theft: ss1–7 TA 1968 – going equipped: s25 TA 1968.

Suggested Solution

When Wally leaves his house with the mask in his possession, he commits an offence under s25 of the Theft Act 1968 which states that:

'a person shall be guilty of an offence if, when not at his place of abode, he has with him any article for use in the course of or in connection with any burglary, theft or cheat.'

The term 'article' is very wide: R v Rashid (1977) and would cover the halloween mask under these circumstances.

Wally intends to use the mask in a future theft and therefore he has sufficient mens rea for this offence: R v Ellames (1974).

When Wally puts on the mask and threatens the baby, getting Lindsey to hand over her purse, he may be guilty of robbery under s8 of the Theft Act 1968.

142

A person is guilty of robbery if he steals, and immediately before or at the time of doing so, and in order to do so, he uses force on any person or puts, or seeks to put any person in fear of being then and there subjected to force.

In appropriating the purse, Wally 'steals' ie he dishonestly appropriates property belonging to another with the intention of permanently depriving the other of it (s1 Theft Act 1968). The question here is whether he has used force or sought to put a person in fear of being subjected to force.

It can be argued that he uses no force on Lindsey, neither does he seek to put her in fear of its use on her. Moreover, Wally cannot realistically be said to put the baby in fear of being subjected to force as, it is submitted, the baby is too young to appreciate the situation.

Therefore it is arguable that the fear instilled in Lindsey by Wally is insufficient to support a charge of robbery. Had he used force on the baby, that may have sufficed.

More appropriate would be a charge of blackmail contrary to s21 of the Theft Act 1968 which makes it an offence for a person, with a view to gain for himself or another, or with intent to cause loss to another, to make any unwarranted demand with menaces.

Here the demand is quite clear and it is made with a view to gain.

'Menaces' is to be given its ordinary meaning: *R* v *Lawrence and Pomroy* (1971) and in *Thorne* v *Motor Trade Association* (1937). Lord Wright held a menace to be a threat of 'any action detrimental to or unpleasant to the person addressed'.

This is clearly the case here and Wally's threat would be 'of such a nature and extent that the mind of an ordinary person of normal stability and courage would accede to the demand: *R* v *Clear* (1968).

Wally would not be able to avail himself of the provisions of s21 by claiming a belief that he has reasonable grounds for making the demand and that the use of the menaces is a proper means of reinforcing it.

If Wally knows that what he is threatening is a crime he cannot maintain that such a threat is proper: *R* v *Harvey, Ulyett and Plummer* (1980).

QUESTION EIGHT

'There is no overlap between theft and handling.'

Discuss.

University of London LLB Examination
(for External Students) Criminal Law June 1990 Q7

General Comment

A straightforward question requiring a comparison of the elements of theft and handling. Some explanation of *Pitham and Hehl* is clearly needed, as well as a more general explanation of why the two offences need to co-exist.

Skeleton Solution

Explain elements of both offences – provide examples of cases where there may be an overlap – look at the judicial response – consider wider issues.

Suggested Solution

Theft, as defined by s1(1) of the Theft Act 1968 involves the dishonest appropriation of property belonging to another with intention to permanently deprive that other of it. A central concept within this definition is that of appropriation. Section 3(1) of the 1968 further defines appropriation as an assumption of the owner's rights. Lord Roskill, in *R* v *Morris* (1983), explained that this could be any assumption of any of the owner's rights. Appropriation can take place, therefore, where a defendant sells another's property, pledges it, gives it away, uses it up, or merely takes it into his own possession.

Section 22(1) of the 1968 Act defines handling as occurring where a defendant who knows or believes goods to have been stolen, dishonestly receives them, or dishonestly undertakes or assists in their retention, removal, realisation, or disposal, for another's benefit, or by another person. Crucially, the section adds, in parenthesis, that all of this must occur otherwise than in the course of stealing.

It was clearly the intention of the legislators, therefore, that there should be a distinction between handling and theft. Prima facie they were to be mutually exclusive. If a defendant was stealing goods he could not at the same time be handling them. In reality the law has cause confusion. A number of scenarios need to be considered.

Where a defendant steals another man's wallet, he commits an offence contrary to s1(1) of the 1968 Act, but not s22(1). Although he has received stolen property he has done so in the course of stealing it, and thus is excluded from the ambit of s22(1). In a simple case such as this there is no problem. In any event the prosecution would be content to charge the defendant with theft.

Complications emerge where the defendant is accompanied by a friend. Let us supposed that D1 takes P's wallet whilst D2 keeps watch. Once he has taken the wallet, D1 passes it immediately to D2. Is D2 guilty of theft, handling, or both ? The correct answer would perhaps be either. D2 could be charged with theft as an accomplice to D1. He is clearly aiding in the commission of the offence, and has the necessary mens rea. Alternatively he could be charged with receiving stolen goods contrary to s22(1). In *R* v *Pitham and Hehl* (1976), D1 invited D2 and D3 to the house of X who was in prison at the time. D1 invited D2 and D3 to purchase some of the contents of the house, which they agreed to do. It was held that D1 was guilty of theft because he had offered to sell property belonging to another. D2 and D3 were held to be guilty of stealing the property. The theft, in the view of the court, was complete once the act of appropriation had been committed, ie once the offer to sell had been made. D2 and D3 could thus be charged with arranging to receive stolen property otherwise than in the course of stealing since the theft had ceased. It has been argued that the effect of this ruling has been to render the words 'otherwise than in the course of stealing' redundant. What it certainly illustrates is that the statement suggesting that theft and handling cannot overlap is somewhat dubious.

A further difficulty arises where stolen property passes from one defendant to another. Suppose that D1 steals a camera, and sells it to D2 at a considerable undervalue. D2 knows that the camera is stolen. That D1 is guilty of theft but not handling is evident from what has already been explained above. What of the liability of D2? By taking the stolen property into his possession, knowing it to have been stolen, D2 is clearly receiving stolen property contrary to s22(1). But is he not also committing theft? He cannot claim to have acquired good title to the camera, since he was not a bona fide purchaser for value without notice, hence the camera remains property belonging to another as against D2. By taking it into his possession he assumes the rights of the owner, and one can assume from the facts that he has the necessary mens rea. Prima facie it would appear that he cannot be convicted of handling the stolen camera, since he is at the same time stealing it, and the statute, as explained above, endeavour to keep the two offences apart. The same problem arises in relation to other forms of handling under s22(1). Disposal, retention, realisation, and removal of another's property could all be acts amounting to appropriation for the purposes of theft. Taken to its logical conclusion this argument would limit the scope of handling stolen goods to such an extent that the offence could become redundant. The courts have supplied at least a partial solution by way of decisions such as *R* v *Sainthouse* (1980), where it was held that the term 'otherwise than in the course of stealing' was meant to prevent the original thief from being charged with handling stolen goods whilst 'on the job'. The expression was not to be taken as preventing charges under s22(1) from being brought against a subsequent handler of those goods, even though technically he might be appropriating them.

On a more general level there are two good arguments for maintaining a separate offence of handling stolen goods, even though the offence may overlap with theft. Firstly, there may be some cases where it is debatable whether or not a handler is necessarily appropriating stolen goods, eg cases where D arranges to receive stolen property. Secondly, there may be cases where the original thief has obtained voidable title to the goods, for example where he has obtained them by deception, and as a result, the goods might not represent property belonging to another, as against the handler.

8 CRIMINAL DAMAGE

8.1   Introduction

8.2   Key points

8.3   Recent cases

8.4   Analysis of questions

8.5   Questions

8.1 Introduction

Criminal damage is an area of criminal law that is relatively straightforward and which usually forms the basis of at least one examination question. As with the Theft Acts offences, definitions should be learnt together with statutory defences.

8.2 Key points

a) The elements of the basic offence of criminal damage under the Criminal Damage Act 1971 are:

i) Property – note the definition in s10(1).

ii) The property must belong to another – see s10(2) and note especially that a person may be guilty of damaging his own property if it is co-owned, if another has lawful custody and control of it or has a charge on it: *R* v *Denton* [1982] 1 All ER 65.

iii) The property must be destroyed or damaged (defined in *Morphitis* v *Salmon* [1990] Crim LR 48 as including 'not only permanent or temporary harm but also permanent or temporary impairment of value or usefulness').

iv) 'Without lawful excuse' – under s5(2)(a) the accused will have a lawful excuse if he believed that the person entitled to give consent would have consented had he known of the circumstances. Note that the accused need only have a genuine belief, the belief need not be reasonable: s5(3) and *Jaggard* v *Dickinson* [1980] Crim LR 717.

Under s5(2)(b) the accused will have a lawful excuse if he believed the property was in need of immediate protection and if he believed that the measures he took were reasonable. Note again that the accused need only have the requisite belief, whether it is reasonable or not is irrelevant. The accused must believe that the property is in immediate need of protection: *R* v *Hunt* [1977] Crim LR 740; *Johnson* v *DPP* [1994] Crim LR 672. See also: *R* v *Ashford and Smith* [1988] Crim LR 682; *Lloyd* v *DPP* [1991] Crim LR 904.

v) Note that there are *two* alternative mens rea to the offence and a candidate should endeavour to specify which he thinks is appropriate when answering a question, ie the accused intended to damage property or was reckless as to whether property was damaged in the *Caldwell* sense (*R* v *Caldwell* [1981] 2 WLR 509). The ingredients of *Caldwell* recklessness (see Chapter 2) must be analysed if the candidate believes the accused has recklessly as opposed to intentionally damaged property.

b)   Note that criminal damage by fire is charged as arson (s1(3)).

c)   Under s1(2) a person may be guilty of the more serious offence of 'aggravated criminal damage' if he commits criminal damage and intended or was reckless (in the *Caldwell* sense) as to whether life would be endangered. Note that it is not necessary that life is actually endangered, it being sufficient that the accused had the requisite mens rea with respect to the endangerment: *R* v *Parker* [1993] Crim LR 856.

d)   Note the offences of making threats to damage property (s27) and possession of articles intended for use to damage property (s3).

8.3   Recent cases

Johnson v *DPP* [1994] Crim LR 672

R v *Parker* [1993] Crim LR 856

8.4   Analysis of questions

Criminal damage questions rarely appear alone and the offences are usually included among other crimes eg burglary and theft. In many cases the destruction of property may also amount to a theft and the overlap between the offences must be appreciated.

8.5   Questions

QUESTION ONE

C and E were out poaching on D's land. C fell and injured himself and lay in the undergrowth for several hours. Eventually another poacher found C and alerted E who came onto the land deliberately damaging a fence, to take C to hospital.

Advise E of his criminal liability.

> Adapted from University of London LLB Examination
> (for External Students) Criminal Law June 1988 Q2

General Comment

The issue of criminal damage needs to be considered carefully, step by step, especially whether E has any lawful excuse for what he did. Note that there is no defence of necessity in English law.

Skeleton Solution

Fence damaged – Criminal Damage Act 1971 – 'damage' – 'property' – 'belonging to another' – mens rea – intention – recklessness – defences.

When E deliberately damaged a fence in entering D's land in order to take C to hospital, he may have committed criminal damage contrary to s1(1) Criminal Damage Act 1971.

The actus reus of the offence consists of 'destroying' or 'damaging' 'property' 'belonging to another'.

The terms 'destroy' and 'damage' contemplate actual destruction or damage, ie some physical harm, impairment or deterioration which can be perceived by the senses. The actual damage need only be slight but there must be actual damage: *Eley* v *Lytle* (1885); *Gayford* v *Chouler* (1898); *Laws* v *Eltringham* (1881). How the defendant regards his conduct will be irrelevant if, in fact, damage was caused: *R* v *Fancy* (1980).

On the facts of the question, 'damage' appears to have been committed.

By s10(1) Criminal Damage Act 1971, property is widely defined so as to include all 'property of a tangible nature, whether real or personal'.

Clearly, a fence constitutes 'property' for the purposes of the Criminal Damage Act 1971.

An offence under the Criminal Damage Act can only be committed against property 'belonging to another'. By s10(2) Criminal Damage Act 1971, property will belong to another if that other has some proprietary interest in the property. There is no need for that other to own it.

From the facts, the fence appears to 'belong to another' within the meaning of the Criminal Damage Act 1971.

The mens rea of the offence of criminal damage consists of intention or recklessness, and an absence of lawful excuse. A person intends to cause a result if he acts with the purpose of doing so: *R* v *Moloney* (1985); *R* v *Hancock and Shankland* (1986); *R* v *Nedrick* (1986). The defendant must not only intend to do the act which caused the damage but also must have intended to cause the damage.

From the facts, it appears that E had the required mens rea.

By s5(2) Criminal Damage Act 1971, two grounds of justification are given for damage deliberately done, namely a belief in the consent of the person entitled to consent to the destruction or damage of the property and action taken in defence of property.

On the facts, E knew that D, the person who was entitled to consent had refused his consent.

As E damaged the fence in order to help C, he clearly cannot argue that he was acting in defence of property.

Therefore, these two limbs of the defence of lawful excuse are not available to E.

However, by s5(2) Criminal Damage Act 1971, the law recognises that there may be other circumstances, apart from a belief in consent or acting in defence of property, which could constitute a lawful excuse for it provides that 'this section shall not be construed as casting any doubt on any defence recognised by law as a defence to criminal charges'.

On the facts, it does not appear that E could avail himself of any defence recognised by law, eg infancy, insanity, duress. Therefore, E appears to have committed criminal damage.

QUESTION TWO

N, aged 13 years, was pedalling his bicycle along a busy pavement, crashed the cycle through a shop window. N caused an electrical cable to short and a fire started in the shop window, spreading quickly to the interior.

Assess N's criminal liability.

Adapted from University of London LLB Examination
(for External Students) Criminal Law June 1985 Q5

General Comment

This question, although complicated slightly by causation and mischievous discretion, is really a test of knowledge of the elements of criminal damage.

Skeleton Solution

Criminal damage to shop – and causing fire – s1(1), 1(2) and 1(3) of the Criminal Damage Act 1971.

Suggested Solution

When N crashes his bicycle into a shop window thus causing a cable to short and a fire to start he may commit a number of offences under the Criminal Damage Act 1971.

Section 1(1) of the Act provides that a person who without lawful excuse destroys or damages property belonging to another intending to destroy or damage any such property or being reckless as to whether any such property would be destroyed or damaged commits an offence.

Section 1(2) of the Act provides that a person who without lawful excuse destroys or damages property, whether belonging to himself or another with intent to endanger life or being reckless as to whether life is endangered shall commit an offence.

Section 1(3) of the Act provides that an offence under s1(1) or (2) committed by the use of fire is to be charged as 'arson'.

The test for recklessness was given by the House of Lords in *MPC* v *Caldwell* (1981). A person charged with an offence under the Criminal Damage Act 1971 is reckless if:

1) he does an act which in fact creates an obvious risk (of property being destroyed or damaged); and

2) when he did the act he either has not given any thought to the possibility of there being any such risk or he had recognised that there was some risk involved and has nonetheless gone on to take it.

149

In *Elliott* v *C (a minor)* (1983) it was held that the phrase 'creates an obvious risk' requires only that the risk would be obvious to a reasonably prudent man, not necessarily that the accused would have seen the risk had he given thought to it. Thus the fact that an accused was, for example, of subnormal intelligence or a child would not be taken into account.

Here, N's cycling down a busy pavement may amount to such an obvious risk.

It is submitted that, even if N were reckless under these circumstances, he would not be guilty of arson. Arson is a distinct and separate offence which, according to Smith and Hogan (6th Ed p687) requires intention or recklessness not merely that property would be damaged but that it would be damaged *'by fire'* and this is clearly not the case here.

It could not be said that N's conduct created an obvious risk of the shop being destroyed or damaged by fire although N, having started the fire, may have a duty to take some action to extinguish it: *R* v *Miller* (1983).

A defence may be available to N because he is only 13 years old. The defence of infancy is available to a child aged between 10–14 if it can be shown that he lacked 'mischievous discretion' ie a comprehension of the difference between right and wrong: *R* v *Gorrie* (1918); *McC* v *Runneckles* (1984); *C (a minor)* v *DPP* (1995), although the objective test in *Elliott* v *C* would apply to N's 'recklessness'.

QUESTION THREE

P, an anti-bloodsports demonstrator, spread chemicals·on fields to make the hounds sneeze and to impair their sense of smell.

Advise P of his criminal liability if any.

> Adapted from University of London LLB Examination
> (for External Students) Criminal Law June 1985 Q6

General Comment

A straightforward examination of simple damage and its component parts.

Skeleton Solution

Criminal damage under s1(1) Criminal Damage Act 1971 to land – attempted criminal damage to hounds – s1(2) of the Criminal Damage Act 1971 – possessing articles – s3 CDA 1971.

Suggested Solution

When P spreads chemicals on the land in order to divert the hounds from their trail he may commit an offence contrary to s1(1) of the Criminal Damage Act 1971

Section 1(1)provides that a person who without lawful excuse destroys or damages any property belonging to another intending to destroy or damage any such property or being reckless as to whether any such property would be destroyed or damaged shall commit an offence.

The expression 'destroy or damage' speaks for itself to a great extent although it should be noted that an article or object may be damaged even though it is not actually broken in any way and can serve to carry out its normal purpose: *Hardman* v *Chief Constable of Avon and Somerset* (1986).

Section 10(1) of the Criminal Damage Act contains the definition of property for the purposes of criminal damage. 'Property' means property of a tangible nature whether real property or personal property.

Applying these principles to the facts in question when P spread chemicals onto the land he was damaging property belonging to another in that the chemicals were to a degree spoiling the property. Undoubtedly P would wish to claim that he was acting with lawful excuse and therefore not liable for any offence.

A partial definition of 'lawful excuse' may be found in s5 of the Act. P's conduct would not fall within any of the specific situations mentioned in s5 ie belief that the owner would consent or defence of property. It would therefore be up to the jury to decide whether they thought he had a lawful excuse for his conduct. The mens rea of s1(1) is satisfied where in addition to acting without lawful excuse the destruction or damage of the property is shown to be either intentional or reckless in the *MPC* v *Caldwell* (1982) sense.

While D may not intentionally damage the land he would be 'reckless' within the *MPC* v *Caldwell* definition in that he created an obvious risk that the property would be damaged and either he had given no thought to the possibility of the risk or he had seen the risk but had nevertheless gone on to take it.

P may commit a further offence under the Criminal Damage Act by attempting to damage property belonging to another. When he spreads the chemicals he does so in order to make the hounds sneeze and impair their sense of smell. The hounds would be 'property belonging to another' and what he intended would be sufficient to amount to 'damage'. In order to establish an attempt it must be shown that his act is more than merely preparatory: s1 Criminal Attempts Act 1981. This is for the jury to decide. Furthermore the mens rea for any attempt is generally the same as for the full offence except that as this is a result crime it must be shown that P intended the damage. Recklessness is not sufficient.

Additionally, by having the chemicals in his custody or under his control intending, without lawful excuse to use it to destroy or damage property belonging to some other person, P commits an offence under s3 of the Act.

QUESTION FOUR

X and Y were members of a peaceful sect who were strongly opposed to war and violence of any description. Intending to cut holes in a perimeter fence of a military establishment, X and Y set off across nearby moorland armed with pliers.

They were apprehended before reaching the fence.

Advise X and Y of their criminal liability, if any, under the Criminal Damage Act 1971.

X and Y tell you that they intend to use the defence that they were acting in defence of their nearby property which would be endangered by the presence of the establishment in the event of war.

How far are they likely to succeed in this defence and would it make any difference if X and Y had carried out their damage?

Written by Editor

General Comment

A fairly detailed question covering recent cases on criminal damage and in particular the statutory defence.

Skeleton Solution

Possessing articles – s3 CDA 1971; lawful excuse – s5(2) and (3) CDA 1971.

Suggested Solution

Where X and Y take up the pliers intending to cut the fence they commit the offence under s3 of the Criminal Damage Act 1971.

Under s3 a person who has anything in his custody or under his control intending without lawful excuse to use it or to cause or permit another to use it, to destroy or damage property belonging to some other person shall be guilty of an offence.

It is not necessary that they leave their house with the pliers or even that they have them with them, and the offence is complete as soon as they have custody or control of the implements with the relevant intention.

X and Y may argue that, although they did intend to cause damage to the fence, it was with a view to causing the military base to close, thereby removing the likelihood of a hostile attack on the area in the event of war. That being the case, X and Y may argue that they fall under the protection of s5(2)(b) which states that a person shall have a lawful excuse if he intended to cause damage in order to protect property belonging to himself or another and at the time he believed that the property was in immediate need of protection. Moreover, s5(3) states that such a belief, if honestly held, need not be justified.

However, it was held by the Court of Appeal in *R v Ashford and Smith* (1988) that such circumstances did not give rise to 'lawful excuse' and that the question of whether an act was done to protect property must be an objective one.

In *R v Hill; R v Hall* (1989) the Court of Appeal decided that the tests were twofold:

i) what was in the accused's mind – a subjective test; and

ii) whether it could be said, as a matter of law, that on the facts as believed by the accused, the action would amount to something done to protect his/her home or that of others.

In similar circumstance to those encountered here it was held that the proposed act was too remote from the eventual aim and also that there was no evidence that there was a belief that the property was in need of immediate protection.

Therefore the defence would fail.

Section 5(2) and (3) also applies to actually damaging or destroying property and therefore the same test would be applied in determining whether or not X and Y had acted without lawful excuse.

QUESTION FIVE

E, a school bully, threatened F who was very shy. E said he would beat up F unless F brought money to school to give to E. F, who was very frightened, took some money from the till of the shop in which he worked at weekends, intending to replace it later. The following Monday F took the money to school and gave it to E. To get his own back, F let air out of the front tyre of E's bicycle and E was severely injured on his way home from school.

Advise the parties. What difference, if any, would it make to your advice if E had died from the accident?

University of London LLB Examination
(for External Students) Criminal Law June 1992 Q2

General Comment

The question raises a wide range of issues. There is firstly the question of blackmail on the part of E. The next issue is whether F can provide a defence to theft from his employer. Possible defences include the absence of dishonesty and duress, although the lapse of time between the threat and the commission of the offence will be material. F's tampering with E's bicycle leads to the tricky issue of what exactly constitutes 'damage'. F's mental state at the time of letting down the tyres provides the key to defining his liability for the injury of E. If E's death had resulted from the accident, the further question of constructive manslaughter will arise.

Skeleton Solution

Blackmail – F's shyness, whether person of normal stability and courage – whether E knew of the effect on F.

Burglary/theft – intent permanently to deprive – dishonesty – s2 Theft Act 1968 and R v Ghosh – duress chance to escape.

Criminal damage – impairing usefulness: Cox v Riley – risk of endangering life.

Grievous bodily harm/assault on E – intent – causation – s20 grievous bodily harm – foreseeing the risk of some harm: R v Savage; R v Parmenter.

Manslaughter of E – unlawful and dangerous act – R v Church – criminal damage sufficient unlawful act?

Suggested Solution

a) *Blackmail*

E potentially committed the offence of blackmail when he threatened to beat up F unless F brought money to school to give to him. The offence of blackmail (s21 of the Theft Act 1968) requires an unwarranted demand with menaces with a view to gain. E clearly sought to receive money from F and made an unwarranted demand coupled with a threat of violence, either express or implied, against F if the demand was not met. The first question here is, does E have a reasonable excuse for this demand? – the answer is clearly no. The second question concerns the nature of the threat. In R v Clear (1968) Sellers LJ stated

153

that the threat must be 'of such a nature and extent that the mind of an ordinary person of normal stability and courage might be influenced or made apprehensive so as to accede unwillingly to the demand'. F is described as very shy and as such may not reach the standard of the person of normal stability. However, if E was aware of the likely effect of his actions on F then the threat will amount to menaces: see *R* v *Garwood* (1987). It seems here that the inference can be drawn that E, a bully, was aware of F's vulnerability and therefore the likely effect of the threat on him. It is my view that the offence of blackmail has been committed by E.

b) *Burglary/theft*

F's taking of money from the till in the shop in which he worked at weekends amounts potentially to the offences of burglary or theft. If a person enters a building with an ulterior intent, for which the occupier has not granted permission, that entry will be trespassory: see *R* v *Jones and Smith* (1976). If he had decided to steal before entering the shop he would have, subject to any defence, committed the offence of burglary under s9(1)(b) of the Theft Act 1968. However, as establishing the stage at which F formed the intent to take the money would be difficult, a charge of theft is unlikely, F would have a number of arguments amounting to a defence to theft.

A person is guilty of theft if he dishonestly appropriates property belonging to another with the intention of permanently depriving the other of it. An offence is not committed if F can show that he never had the intention permanently to deprive his employer of the money. Under s6(1) of the Theft Act 1968 a person treating another's property as his own to dispose of regardless of the other's rights may amount to theft even though there is no intention to permanently deprive that other of it, but only if the lending or borrowing of the money is in circumstances amounting to an outright taking or disposal. If it is accepted that F did intend to repay the money (albeit using different coins or notes) no offence will have been committed. F will also have a defence to theft because of the lack of mens rea in the form of dishonesty; this is embodied in s2(1)(b) of the Theft Act 1968 whereby a belief that the owner would consent to the taking of the property amounts to a defence. Unless the prosecution disprove F's alleged belief beyond reasonable doubt he must be acquitted. In any event, under common law, regardless of whether F raised the s2(1)(b) defence, F must be shown to have been dishonest. The test for dishonesty is provided by the case of *R* v *Ghosh* (1982). Thus, even if F's actions were considered dishonest according to the ordinary standards of reasonable and honest people, if F had not realised that taking money from one's employer in order to pay a blackmailer was dishonest, he did not have the mens rea to have committed the offence.

Lastly, F might raise the defence of duress, if he could show that he had acted as he did because he reasonably believed that E would kill, or severely injure him. Such a threat must have this effect on a person of reasonable firmness sharing the same characteristics as F, or the defence will fail. It seems improbable that a person of reasonable firmness would think E likely to cause severe injury, although the risk of some injury is more probable. In any event this defence is likely to fail because F had the opportunity to escape following E's threat of imminent harm: see *R* v *M'Growther* (1746).

c) *Criminal damage*

When F deliberately let the air out of E's bicycle tyre, he has potentially committed the offence of criminal damage, contrary to s1 of the Criminal Damage Act 1971. No offence will have been committed, however, under s9 of the Criminal Attempts Act 1981 for interference with a vehicle as a bicycle is not a motor vehicle. For criminal damage the principal question is whether or not letting air out of a tyre constitutes damage. Whether property is damaged is a question of fact and degree. Temporary physical harm, which can usually be perceived by the senses, that impairs the value or usefulness of the property can amount to 'damage': see *Cox* v *Riley* (1986). In the case of *Gayford* v *Choulder* (1898) the trampling down of grass was considered enough. Clearly the usefulness of E's bike will be impaired with a flat tyre. In addition, some effort will be required to restore the bicycle to a useful state, therefore F has committed the offence of criminal damage.

If F's letting down of E's tyre was intended to endanger life or created an obvious risk of endangering life and F was reckless as to whether or not life were endangered, F will have committed the more serious offence of criminal damage intending to endanger life or being reckless as to whether life will be endangered, under s1(2) of the Criminal Damage Act 1971. The test of F's recklessness is objective, as adumbrated in *Metropolitan Police Commissioner* v *Caldwell* (1982). In view of the minimal nature of the damage it would seem that no obvious risk is created and no s1(2) charge can lie.

d) *Grievous bodily harm/assault*

As a consequence of F letting down E's tyre E was severely injured. If F intended to cause really serious injury to E he would have committed the offence of causing grievous bodily harm with intent contrary to s18 of the Offences Against the Person Act 1861 if there were no novus actus interveniens. Secondly, if F knew severe injury was a virtually certain consequence of his intended action in letting down the tyre, he would also be guilty of an offence under s18. On the evidence provided it appears that F neither intended to cause grievous bodily harm, nor was it a virtually certain consequence of his intended actions from which intention can be inferred. A lesser degree of intent is required for the offence of inflicting grievous bodily harm, under s20. Under this section the infliction of harm must be unlawful and malicious. F's unlawful act in damaging the bicycle would be enough. F would be deemed to be malicious if he foresaw some harm although not necessarily really serious harm: see *R* v *Savage*; *R* v *Parmenter* (1992). However, the cases of *R* v *Wilson* (1984) and *R* v *Martin* (1881) make it clear that some direct force must be applied. F's letting down of a bicycle tyre will not amount to direct force. Similarly F will not have committed the lesser offences against the person, those of assault occasioning actual bodily harm and common assault, because there has been no assault. In conclusion, unless it can be shown that F intended to cause grievous bodily harm by his actions he will not have committed a further offence by virtue of E's severe injury.

e) *Manslaughter*

If E died as a result of the injuries he sustained from the bicycle accident F may be guilty of constructive manslaughter. Constructive manslaughter requires an unlawful and dangerous act directed at the victim causing death. If F's criminal damage to the bicycle was likely to cause some physical harm and a reasonable and sober person would recognise the risk of some harm to E then E's death would amount to manslaughter: *R* v *Church* (1966). Some doubt does exist, however, as to whether criminal damage can in principle be a sufficient peg on which to hang liability for manslaughter (particularly in the light of s1(2)(b) of the Criminal Justice Act 1991 which draws a sharper distinction between property offences and offences against the person, albeit in the sentencing context). However, in the case of *DPP* v *Newbury* (1977) it appears that the offence of criminal damage, although not specifically identified by the House of Lords, was a sufficient unlawful and dangerous act to found a charge of manslaughter. If *Newbury* were followed F will have committed manslaughter. Alternatively, F may be liable for manslaughter by gross negligence as defined in *R* v *Adomako* (1994).

9 INCHOATE OFFENCES

9.1   Introduction

9.2   Key points

9.3   Recent cases and statutes

9.4   Questions

9.1 Introduction

In addition to the substantive offences looked at in the preceding chapters, it remains to consider those offences which are committed on the way to the commission of a full offence.

Traditionally crimes of incitement and conspiracy are recorded under this heading.

However in this book those offences have been examined under the chapter dealing with participation (Chapter 3) and therefore we are concerned here with criminal attempts.

9.2 Key points

a)   The reason behind offences covering attempts, both under individual statutes (eg s5 Road Traffic Act 1988) and under s1 of the Criminal Attempts Act 1981, must be appreciated.

    There is a need for laws which will punish offenders and potential offenders who fully intend to commit crimes and take purposeful steps, beyond mere preparation, towards doing so.

b) *The actus rea of attempt*

    To commit an attempt under s1 of the Criminal Attempts Act 1981 the accused must do an act which is 'more than merely preparatory' towards the commission of the offence. This is a question of fact which should be debated by the candidate in the examination if necessary. In *R* v *Gullefer* [1990] 3 All ER 882 it was held that an accused does an act which is more than merely preparatory when he 'embarks on the crime proper or the actual commission of the offence'.

c) *Mens rea*

    The accused must intend to bring about the full consequences of the offence – one cannot recklessly attempt to commit an offence: *R* v *Mohan* [1975] 2 All ER 193.

d) *Impossibility*

    It should be noted that the previous complex rules on impossibility are redundant due to s1(2) of the 1981 Act which provides to the effect that impossibility is no longer a defence to a charge of attempt: see also *R* v *Shivpuri* [1986] 2 All ER 334.

9.3 Recent cases and statutes

There have been no major recent developments in this area.

9.4 Questions

QUESTION ONE

'Impossibility is no longer a defence.'

Discuss.

Adapted from University of London LLB Examination
(for External Students) Criminal Law June 1982 Q3

General Comment

This question appeared in the June 1982 paper and, although students would be lucky to get such a straightforward essay in the future it is a useful title to expound the law concerning criminal attempts.

Skeleton Solution

Section 1(1) and (2) Criminal Attempts Act 1981 – recent cases.

Suggested Solution

The Criminal Attempts Act 1981 has made substantial alterations in relation to the defence of impossibility in conspiracy and attempt. However, in order to see the full effects of these alterations the position pre-1981 must be considered.

There are three types of inchoate offence, incitement, conspiracy and attempt. Impossibility in relation to incitement can quickly be dealt with by saying that impossibility never was a defence. In *R* v *McDonough* (1962) the accused was convicted of incitement to receive certain stolen lamb carcasses even though there was no evidence that the carcasses existed at the relevant time. However, in order to be incitement the rule at common law is the act incited must be one which when done would be a crime by the person incited. Therefore, if the offence would never amount to a crime were it to be performed by the person incited, then it can be no crime of incitement. This common law rule has been altered by s54 of the Criminal Law Act 1977 in relation to certain sexual offences, however, the general rule is not affected.

The position in relation to attempt and conspiracy prior to the 1981 Act was governed by *Haughton* v *Smith* (1975). In *Haughton* v *Smith* a van loaded with stolen corned beef was captured by the police. It was allowed on its way with the addition of two officers and rendezvoused with the defendant who unloaded the beef in the belief that he was dealing with stolen property. D was not charged with handling stolen goods as the prosecution conceded that the goods were in police possession and by virtue of s24(3) of the Theft Act 1968 were not stolen goods. He was found liable for attempt. However, since the goods were no longer stolen goods it was legally impossible for him to attempt the offence and the House of Lords quashed the conviction.

Although *Haughton* v *Smith* was a case concerning legal impossibility the House of Lords expressed obiter opinions on other types of impossibility. Lord Hailsham drew distinctions between three particular types of impossibility:

i) Physical impossibility due to ineptitude or insufficiency of means. Providing that the accused had done an act which was proximate to the full offence then the fact that the means could not possibly succeed was immaterial. (The proximity test has now been replaced by a new requirement contained in the Criminal Attempts Act 1981 that in order to amount to an attempt an act must go 'beyond preparation'.)

ii) Physical impossibility because the object of the crime is not there. This type of impossibility would be a complete defence to any charge of attempt because the act was not one which if completed could ever amount to a crime. Thus if a defendant took steps towards stealing a picture which was not in fact there, he could not be liable for attempted theft because the crime was physically impossible to commit.

iii) Legal impossibility, where unknown to the accused the facts which the accused believed to exist are not shown. An example of legal impossibility is shown in *Haughton* v *Smith* where although the defendant believed the goods to be stolen goods, they were not since the police had regained custody. Legal impossibility was a defence under the principles stated in *Haughton* v *Smith*.

Haughton v *Smith* had in effect overruled an earlier decision in *R* v *Ring* (1892) where one of the defendants was found liable for attempted theft when he put his hand into a man's pocket with intention to steal but in fact found there was nothing in the pocket.

Haughton v *Smith* was criticised for the very obvious reason that it allowed those with criminal intentions who took steps towards performing an offence to be acquitted because of the existence of facts unknown to them. The Law Commission examined the question of impossibility and recommended that impossibility no longer be a defence to a charge of attempt.

Haughton v *Smith* was concerned solely with attempt, however, the principles that it laid down in relation to attempt were applied to conspiracy in the House of Lords case in *DPP* v *Nock* (1978). The Law Commission sought to bring a uniform approach to impossibility for both attempt and conspiracy and recommended similarly that in relation to conspiracy, impossibility should no longer be a defence. Thus the Law Commission recommended that conspiracy and attempt be brought into line with the third inchoate offence of incitement.

The Criminal Attempts Act 1981 contains the provisions relating to impossibility for both conspiracy and attempt. Section 1(1) of the Act provides that a person is guilty of attempt where he does an act which is more than merely preparatory to the commission of the offence.

Section 1(2) goes on to deal with impossibility: 'a person may be guilty of attempting to commit an offence even though the facts are such that the commission of the offence is impossible.'

Similar provisions relate to conspiracy so that s1(1) of the Criminal Law Act 1977 is amended by s5(1) of the Criminal Attempts Act 1981 so that an offence of statutory conspiracy is committed:

i) 'if a person agrees with any other person or persons that a course of conduct shall be pursued which, if the agreement is carried out in accordance with their intentions either:

a) will necessarily amount to the commission of any offence or offences by one or more of the parties to the agreement; or

b) would do so but for the existence of facts which render the commission of the offence or any of the offences impossible.'

The effect of these provisions is that the three inchoate offences are now similarly treated where the question of impossibility arises.

Following the passing of the 1981 Act, however, the House of Lords decided that attempting to do what was in fact legal but what would have been unlawful had the facts been as the accused believed them to be, – Lord Hailsham's 'legal impossibility' – did not become a criminal attempt by virtue of s1(2): *Anderton* v *Ryan* (1985).

Nevertheless, in 1987 their Lordships reversed their opinion on this matter, holding that where an accused attempted to bring what he believed to be controlled drugs into Britain but they turned out to be innocuous powder, he was guilty of a criminal attempt: *R* v *Shivpuri* (1987).

The argument that had swayed their Lordships in *Anderton* v *Ryan*, namely that in cases of 'legal impossibility' there was no actus reus but only mens rea, did not so persuade them on this occasion. Therefore, generally, it is true to say that impossibility is no longer a defence. However, it should be remembered that in all instances whether it be in relation to incitement, conspiracy or attempt, a defendant can never be convicted where he has made a mistake as to what amounts to a crime and where he imagines certain conduct to constitute an offence when this does not. For example, if B believes adultery to be an offence, he cannot be convicted of attempting to commit such an offence if the crime itself is imaginary.

This was the case in *R* v *Taaffe* (1984) where the accused imported foreign currency believing that, by so doing, he was committing an offence. In fact there was no such offence at the time and the accused was acquitted.

From a moral standpoint it is difficult to distinguish the two cases but such a jurisprudential quandary will not avail a defendant!

QUESTION TWO

John believes that he can produce 'crack', a controlled drug by mixing bicarbonate of soda with weedkiller. In order to make a large quantity, John buys 2lbs of each powder and several plastic containers and puts them in a laboratory which he has set up to make the drug in this way.

John is told that Royal Jelly – a health food obtained from bees, is now a controlled drug having been found to contain morphine. This is untrue. However, John believes it to be true and puts small quantities of Royal Jelly in packets and sells them to people in his local nightclub.

Advise John of his criminal liability if any.

Written by Editor

General Comment

The question examines a student's understanding of the Criminal Attempts Act 1981 particularly in relation to impossibility.

Skeleton Solution

Criminal Attempts Act 1981 ss1(1) and 1(2) 'impossibility' – interpretation in recent cases.

Suggested Solution

John commits no substantive criminal offence when he buys the powder and containers but he may be guilty of an attempt under s1 of the Criminal Attempts Act 1981 which states:

If, with intent to commit an offence to which this section applies – ie triable an indictment – a person does an act which is more than merely preparatory to the commission of the offence he is guilty of attempting to commit the offence.

John has 'done an act' in buying the items and setting up a laboratory and he has done with an intention of committing an offence under the Misuse of Drugs Act 1971.

However, his actions appear to fall within the proviso of the section, being 'merely preparatory'.

Whether they are merely preparatory is a question of fact for a jury: *R* v *Campbell* (1991).

The former test requiring an accused to have 'crossed the Rubicon and burnt his boats': *DPP* v *Stonehouse* (1978) has been disapproved and it is no longer necessary to prove that the accused has gone beyond the point of no return: *R* v *Gullefer* (1990).

Having regard to cases determined before the 1981 Act but dealing with the same question eg *Comer* v *Bloomfield* (1970) where the accused hid his van and wrote to the insurers asking whether he could claim on the policy – it would seem that John's acts were only preparatory and therefore without more, he is not guilty of attempting to produce a controlled drug.

John's liability in relation to the Royal Jelly is not so straightforward.

John sells packets of the substance believing it to contain morphine. This is not the case and therefore John does not commit an offence of unlawfully supplying a possessing of controlled drug.

However, s1(2) of the 1981 Act states that a person may be guilty of attempting to commit an offence even though the facts are such that the commission of the offence is impossible. Further, s1(3) provides that, in any case where:

a) apart from this subsection a person's intention would not be regarded as having amounted to an intent to commit an offence; but

b) if the facts had been as he believed them to be, his intention would be so regarded, then he shall be regarded as having an intent to commit that offence.

These subsections removed the 'defence' of impossibility which had existed at common law: *Haughton* v *Smith* (1975); *DPP* v *Nock* (1978).

Under subs (2) and (3), the fact that supplying Royal Jelly is not an offence will not save John who carried out the act of selling the substance believing it to contain a controlled drug. That belief is sufficient to attract liability for 'attempting' the offence: *R* v *Shivpuri* (1987).

Had John believed that selling Royal Jelly *per se* was an offence and had gone on to do so, he would not be liable for 'attempting' an offence. This is because his belief would relate to the existence of an imagined offence and therefore there would be no actus reus: *R* v *Taaffe* (1984).

In the instant case the offence of supplying morphine unlawfully does exist and as John believes – albeit erroneously – that that is what he is doing, he is guilty of an attempt notwithstanding the fact that the commission of the completed offence is impossible.

QUESTION THREE

H wrote to his friend, J, in France suggesting that they should rob a bank in London. The letter never arrived. H sent a similar letter to K in England who wrote to H agreeing to his proposal. K's letter never arrived at H's address. H contacted L and together they went to rob a bank but, on the way, H's car which was being driven by L was involved in a motoring accident and L was blinded. The accident resulted from a defect in the brakes which H knew about.

Advise the parties of their criminal liability.

University of London LLB Examination
(for External Students) Criminal Law June 1990 Q6

General Comment

A complex question in which careful planning of the answer is of great importance. Deal with the liabilities of the parties separately. The question requires specific knowledge of the relationship between inchoate offences. It is not necessary to detail the statutory duty to maintain a motor vehicle as this offence is not on the syllabus.

Skeleton Solution

Liability of H for attempted incitement and the completed crime – conspiracy with K and L – attempted robbery – attempted murder of L, injury to L, based upon failure to act – liability of K for conspiracy – liability of L for conspiracy and attempted robbery.

Suggested Solution

The incitement of another to commit an offence is itself an offence at common law. Normally the incitement must reach the mind of the incitee, but where this does not happen the defendant can still incur liability for attempted incitement. In *R* v *Banks* (1873), the defendant was convicted of attempted incitement where his letter was intercepted and never reached the incitee. See also *R* v *Ransford* (1874). There seems no doubt that H had the necessary mens rea for incitement to rob. He intended the suggestion to be acted upon by K. It should be noted that the charge would have to be one of attempted incitement to rob, rather than attempted incitement to conspire to rob, since incitement to conspire was abolished as an offence by s5(7) of the Criminal Law Act 1977. Provided the letter containing the incitement was posted in England, the English courts would have jurisdiction over the offence. As regards the letter sent to K, the incitement obviously reaches the mind of the incitee, who realises that what is being suggested is a criminal offence; see *R v Curr* (1968). It appears to have been the intention of H that the suggestion should be acted upon. There are no jurisdictional problems in this case. It is submitted, therefore, that H could be convicted of inciting K to commit robbery.

As noted below, H commits the offence of statutory conspiracy when he agrees to rob the bank with L. It is questionable whether or not their action constitutes an attempt to commit the offence; see below.

The prosecution may consider a charge of attempted murder in light of the fact that H allowed L to drive the car knowing it had defective brakes. A major stumbling block to liability would be that there is no evidence of a positive act, on the part of H, that causes death. He has not, for example, tampered with the brakes. If liability for failing to service the brakes is to be imposed, there must be a positive legal duty to act. In the present case the prosecution may wish to rely on the statutory duty resting upon a car owner to maintain the vehicle in a roadworthy condition. If one assumes for the sake of argument that the actus reus of the offence is made out (as to which see *R v Gullefer* (1990)), the problem would lie in establishing intent. Some older authorities, such as *R v Whybrow* (1951), suggest that the defendant must have the death of the victim as his purpose. It is submitted that there would at least have to be evidence that H foresaw the death of L as virtually certain before the jury could infer such intent. Note that intent to commit grievous bodily harm would not be sufficient on a charge of attempted murder. It is submitted that since he was also a passenger in the car, it may difficult to establish this intent.

It is worth noting that when the Road Traffic Act 1991 comes into force there will be a new offence of causing death by dangerous driving and that, in assessing whether driving is 'dangerous', regard will be had to the condition of the vehicle concerned. This new offence has been enacted specifically to deal with the type of situation above.

The blinding of L constitutes grievous bodily harm; see *R v Saunders* (1985). To begin to establish liability it would again be necessary to show that H had culpably failed to maintain his vehicle. The prosecution would then have to show that this failure to act caused the harm.

For the purposes of both s18 and s20 of the Offences Against the Persons Act 1861, this would involve proof that the injury was reasonably foreseeable. The fact that the injury was indirectly caused by H is no bar to liability; see *R v Martin* (1881). Under s18, H will have to be shown to have intended the grievous bodily harm; see *R v Belfon* (1976). If this cannot be established, a charge under s20 would require proof that he at least foresaw the possibility of some physical harm occurring to L, albeit slight; see *R v Cunningham* (1957), and *R v Mowatt* (1967). it is submitted that a charge under s20 is likely to succeed.

K agrees to carry out the robbery with H but his letter signifying this is never delivered. K could be charged with statutory conspiracy contrary to s1(1)(a) of the

Criminal Law Act 1977. The act of posting the letter is evidence of his agreement. The fact that the letter is never delivered to H does not provide K with any form of defence based upon impossibility; see Criminal Attempts Act 1981. The prosecution have no choice but to proceed against K with a full charge of conspiracy, since the offence of attempted conspiracy was abolished by s5(7) of the 1977 Act.

In agreeing to rob the bank with H, L commits the offence of statutory conspiracy contrary to s1(1) of the 1977 Act. The parties clearly agree upon a course of conduct which if carried out in accordance with their intentions will necessarily result in the commission of a criminal offence. It is submitted that H and L could not be charged with attempted robbery on the basis that although they are on their way to rob the bank, they may not have committed any acts more than merely preparatory to the offence; see s1(1) of the Criminal Attempts Act 1981, as interpreted in *R* v *Gullefer*. In the final analysis the question of whether or not they have gone beyond mere preparation will be a question of fact for the jury.

10 DEFENCES

10.1 Introduction

10.2 Key points

10.3 Recent cases

10.4 Analysis of questions

10.5 Questions

10.1 Introduction

In answering any question concerning a person's criminal liability it must be remembered that, although a prima facie case may appear to be made out, that person may well have a general or specific defence.

Certain specific defences have been reviewed in the appropriate preceding chapters:

Consent, lawful correction: Chapter 4 – non-fatal offences against the person; provocation and diminished responsibility: Chapter 5 – homicide.

Lawful excuse: Chapter 8 – criminal damage.

Such defences are usually only applicable to a particular crime – eg provocation in murder cases. There are however, general defences which may appropriately be raised in a number of circumstances and it is these defences which are examined here.

10.2 Key points

a) *Infancy or minority*

It is an irrebuttable presumption that a child under ten years of age cannot commit a criminal offence.

For children between ten and 14 years there is a rebuttable presumption that a child is similarly incapable of committing an offence. This presumption may be rebutted by proof of mischievous discretion, ie proof of knowledge that what was done was morally or legally wrong: *R v Gorrie* (1918) 83 JP 136; *McC v Runneckles* [1984] Crim LR 499; *C (a minor) v DPP* [1994] Crim LR 523.

b) *Mistake*

The accused's mistaken belief may allow an acquittal either where it negates the mens rea or, if the facts were as the accused believed them to be, the accused would be entitled to raise a defence (for example self-defence): *R v Williams (Gladstone)* [1983] 3 All ER 316.

c) *Intoxication*

Principally, intoxication is associated with alcohol, although the effects of drugs other than alcohol should also be considered.

Students should note that where drugs are known to produce aggressive or unpredictable behaviour, such drugs will be classed with alcohol for 'intoxication' purposes: *R* v *Hardie* [1985] 1 WLR 64.

i) Note that intoxication generally is not a defence. It may, however, negate the required mens rea.

Where a specific or ulterior intent is required, self-induced intoxication may preclude that intent: *R* v *Bailey* [1983] 2 All ER 503. Drunkenness may, for instance, prevent D from forming the intent required for murder – *R* v *O'Connor* [1991] Crim LR 135.

However note the decision in *Attorney-General for Northern Ireland* v *Gallagher* [1963] AC 349 in relation to drinking for 'dutch courage', having already formed the relevant intention.

ii) Voluntary intoxication will not be a defence for crimes of basic intent: *DPP* v *Majewski* [1977] AC 443.

Such offences are capable of being committed recklessly, a criterion which is itself met by the accused's becoming voluntarily intoxicated.

Where D because of self-induced intoxication forms a mistaken belief that he is using force to defend himself that plea of self-defence will fail: *R* v *O'Grady* (1987) 85 Cr App R 315.

However, an accused may form an honest belief whilst so intoxicated and thereby find a statutory defence such as 'lawful excuse' to damage another's property: *Jaggard* v *Dickinson* [1981] QB 527.

iii) Where intoxication is through a drug such as a sedative: *R* v *Hardie* – or failure to take a drug such as insulin: *R* v *Bailey* – that intoxication may provide a defence even for crimes of basic intent.

iv) Involuntary intoxication may be a defence to a charge of basic intent. The House of Lords in *R* v *Kingston* [1994] Crim LR 846 held that involuntary intoxication may also be a defence to a charge of specific intent, but only where the intoxication deprived the accused of the requisite mens rea: it would not be an adequate defence for the accused to show that, although he still had the requisite mens rea, he would not have committed the offence were he sober.

d) *Insanity and automatism*

The three limbs of the definition of insanity provided in *M'Naghten's Case* (1843) 10 Cl & F 200 must be understood:

i) the accused must be suffering from a 'defect of reason' (*R* v *Clark* [1972] 1 All ER 219),

ii) arising from 'a disease of the mind' (note that any condition which produces the required defect of reason may amount to a disease of the mind – the brain itself need not be affected): *R* v *Kemp* [1956] 3 All ER 249. Further, a disease of the mind giving rise to the defence of insanity must arise from an *internal* cause (such as disease or psychological illness) and not an *external* cause (such as injury or the consumption of drugs): *Bratty* v *Attorney-General for Northern Ireland* [1961] 3 All ER 523.

iii) The 'disease of the mind' must produce either of two effects and the candidate in an examination should specify which he thinks is appropriate: *either* the accused did not know what he was doing *or*, if he did, that he did not know that it was wrong.

The relationship between insanity and automatism is a complex area which is often examined. A person who does not know what he is doing may claim the defence of insanity or automatism. The determinative criteria for distinguishing between the two defences appear to be whether the condition causing the accused to commit the offence is likely to recur (insanity) or not (automatism) and whether the cause of the condition is internal (insanity) or external (automatism): *R* v *Bratty* (above).

See especially: *R* v *Quick & Paddison* [1973] 3 All ER 347 and *R* v *Hennessy* (1989) 89 Cr App R 10 (diabetes); *Bratty* v *Attorney-General for Northern Ireland* [1961] 3 All ER 523 and *R* v *Sullivan* [1984] AC 156 (epilepsy); *R* v *Burgess* [1991] 2 All ER 769 (sleepwalking); *R* v *Rabey* 37 CCC (2d) 461 (Ont) and *R* v *T* [1990] Crim LR 256 (psychological trauma); *Attorney-General's Reference (No 2 of 1992)* [1993] 3 WLR 982 (driving without awareness).

e) *Necessity*

Note the early cases which establish the general rule that necessity may be a factor put forward in mitigation of sentence, but will not provide a defence: *R* v *Dudley and Stephens* (1884) 14 QBD 273; *Southwark London Borough* v *Williams* [1971] 2 All ER 175; and *Buckoke* v *Greater London Council* [1971] Ch 655.

Note the limited circumstances in which the beginnings of a defence of necessity have emerged: s5(2) Criminal Damage Act 1971 (defence to a charge of criminal damage to show that this was necessary to prevent greater damage to property); *R* v *Willer* (1986) 83 Cr App R 225, *R* v *Conway* [1988] 3 All ER 1025 and *DPP* v *Harris* (1994) The Times 15 March (acting in order to avoid a threat of death or serious personal injury may provide a defence to a *traffic offence* – the defence was termed 'duress of circumstances').

The case of *R* v *Cole* [1994] Crim LR 583 is potentially very important in that it held that 'duress of circumstances' (necessity) may be a defence to a charge of robbery – perhaps forming the foundation for an emerging defence of necessity.

f) *Duress*

Note the basic definition of the defence provided in *R* v *Graham* (1982) 74 Cr App R 235 – 'where the accused acted as he did as a result of what he reasonably believed E had said or done and had good cause to fear that if he did not so act E would kill him or cause him serious personal injury'.

The nature of the threat – the threat must be to cause death or serious personal injury (*Graham* above). A threat to damage property or expose immoral behaviour will be insufficient: *R* v *Valderrama-Vega* [1985] Crim LR 220.

The threat must be to the accused's spouse, common law wife or 'immediate family': *R* v *Hurley and Murray* [1967] VR 526.

The accused must have 'good cause' for fear: *DPP* v *Pittaway* [1994] Crim LR 600.

Note the extent to which the threat must be immediate and the accused not have the opportunity of contacting the police: *R* v *Hudson & Taylor* [1971] 2 QB 202; *R* v *Cole* [1994] Crim LR 583.

Duress is *not* available to a person charged with murder (*Abbot* v *R* [1977] AC 755), attempted murder (*R* v *Gotts* [1992] 1 All ER 832) or as an accessory to murder (*R* v *Howe* [1987] 1 All ER 771).

Where the accused voluntarily participates in a criminal offence with another person whom he knows to be violent and likely to demand that he commit other criminal offences, the accused cannot rely on the defence of duress: *R* v *Ali* [1995] Crim LR 303.

g) *Self-defence*

Self-defence allows reasonable force to be used to defend oneself, another person or property from attack or damage.

Note the overlap between self-defence at common law and s3 of the Criminal Law Act 1967 which allows reasonable force to be used in the prevention of crime.

The force used must be commensurate with the level of the perceived attack: *R* v *Oatridge* [1992] Crim LR 205.

The reasonableness of the force must be considered in the light of the fear and pressure the accused was under at the time of the attack: *Palmer* v *R* [1971] AC 814.

The victim of an attack does not necessarily have to wait for the first blow to be struck: *R* v *Beckford* [1988] 1 AC 130.

Where the accused is charged with murder and raises the defence of self-defence or the use of reasonable force to prevent a crime or effect an arrest under s3 Criminal Law Act 1967 the accused is entitled to a full acquittal if the force used was reasonable. If the force used was unreasonable then, even though the use of some force may have been justified, the accused must be convicted of murder. In other words, under the law as it now stands, the use of excessive force where some force is justified is not a partial defence which can mitigate what would have been a conviction for murder to one of manslaughter: *R* v *Clegg* [1995] All ER 80.

Note that an accused who mistakenly believes that he is under attack may still be able to raise the defence of self-defence: *R* v *Williams (Gladstone)* [1983] All ER 316.

10.3 Recent cases

Attorney-General's Reference (No 2 of 1992) [1993] 3 WLR 982

R v *Kingston* [1994] Crim LR 846

DPP v *Harris* (1994) The Times 15 March

R v *Cole* [1994] Crim LR 583

DPP v *Pittaway* [1994] Crim LR 600

R v *Ali* [1995] Crim LR 303

R v *Clegg* [1995] All ER 80

10.4 Analysis of questions

Questions on general defences will appear either in essay form or among the facts of a problem question and when answering the latter, students should always consider circumstances or facts which may provide a defendant with such a defence. However, that is not to say that a defence will be available in every case.

Occasionally questions will be split into an essay part and a problem part (see Question 3). This can help a student clarify the relevant law before applying it to specific situations and it is suggested that the essay part of such questions is tackled first.

10.5 Questions

QUESTION ONE

'The law regarding the defences of self-induced and insane automatism and voluntary intoxication is hopelessly confused.'

Discuss and illustrate your answer by reference to the relevant case law.

Adapted from University of London LLB Examination
(for External Students) Criminal Law June 1982 Q8(b)

General Comment

Students could almost spend the entire examination answering this question in depth. Whereas it is difficult to keep an answer such as this concise as well as dealing with all the major issues, it is a good revision aid on a complex subject.

Skeleton Solution

Self-induced automatism – insane automatism – voluntary intoxication – overlap *inter se* and cases illustrating difficulties.

Suggested Solution

Insane automatism may provide an accused with a defence to a crime providing the accused can show that he falls within the *M'Naghten* (1843) rules. The law on insanity is still governed by these rules of 1843 which provide that it is a defence for the accused to prove 'that at the time of committing the act, the party accused was labouring under such a defect of reason, from disease of the mind, so as not to know the nature and quality of the act he was doing or if he did know it, that he did not know that what he was doing was wrong'.

In *R* v *Sullivan* (1984) the House of Lords accepted that the rules have been a comprehensive definition of insanity since 1843.

CRIMINAL LAW

The term 'defect of reason' connotes that the accused must be deprived of reasoning. Simply a failure to use the reasoning powers that the accused possesses due to confusion or absent mindedness is not sufficient: *R v Clarke* (1972).

The question of whether or not the accused is suffering from a 'disease of the mind', is a legal question and not a medical question, although medical evidence is obviously relevant. In *R v Quick and Paddison* (1973), the Court of Appeal held that 'disease of the mind' meant a 'malfunctioning of the mind caused by disease'. It was not simply limited to a disease of the brain, but the term does not cover the transitory effect of such external matters as violence, drugs, alcohol and hypnosis. The term however does cover physical diseases which affect the mind. Thus in *R v Kemp* (1956) arterio sclerosis caused congestion of the blood in the defendant's brain and consequent lack of consciousness. It was claimed on the defendant's behalf that there was no insanity until degeneration of the brain cells occurred and in the absence of this, the defendant was merely suffering from automatism. The court rejected this argument. 'The law is not concerned with the brain but with the mind, in the sense that "mind" is ordinarily used. The mental facilities of reason, memory and understanding. If one reads for "disease of the mind", "disease of the brain", it would follow that in many cases, pleas of insanity would not be established because it could not be proved that the brain had been affected in any way.' The defendant was found to be insane.

'Nature and quality' refers to the physical quality of the act not to its moral or legal quality: *R v Codere* (1916).

'Wrong' means 'legally' wrong. If the accused knew that his act was contrary to the law or that it was wrong according to the ordinary standard of a reasonable man, he cannot be heard to say that he did not know the act to be wrong, even if he believes his action to be morally right: *R v Windle* (1952).

The effect of a successful plea of insanity is the verdict of 'not guilty by reason of insanity' Criminal Procedure (Insanity) Act 1964 s1. The defendant will then be sentenced to an indefinite period in a criminal mental hospital.

There has, for many years, been some problem in distinguishing circumstances where the defence of insanity should be available. Automatism has generally been regarded as a defence where the accused shows that his conduct was not 'willed'. An example given in *Hill v Baxter* (1958) would be where the defendant, while driving, was attacked by a swarm of bees and was disabled from controlling the vehicle. In these circumstances, it would be held that he would no longer be 'driving' because the movement of the defendant's limbs was involuntary. In *R v Boshears* (1961), the accused was acquitted of murder where he contended that he had killed a girl in his sleep. Similarly, in *R v Scott* (1967) the accused was held not liable for acts done while he was unconscious through concussion.

The effect of a successful plea of automatism is a complete acquittal. Obviously, this is preferable to a finding of 'not guilty by reason of insanity', which although a type of acquittal, results in the accused being incarcerated for an indefinite period in a criminal mental hospital. Therefore where possible, an accused would always wish to rely on the general defence of automatism rather than that of insanity. In *Bratty v Attorney-General for Northern Ireland* (1961), the appellant was charged with murder of a girl. There was evidence that he suffered from a form of epilepsy which could result in no recollection of acts done. The defence raised two possible defences,

170

automatism which would result in acquittal or insanity. The trial judge refused to leave the defence of automatism to the jury and the appellant was found guilty of murder after the jury rejected the plea of insanity. He appealed unsuccessfully to the Court of Appeal for Northern Ireland and, thereafter to the House of Lords.

Viscount Kilmuir accepted that if a defence of insanity was raised unsuccessfully, there could, in certain circumstances be room for an alternative defence based on automatism, for example, a jury might reject evidence of a defect of reason from disease of the mind, but accept evidence that the accused did not know what he was doing, in which case the jury should find him not guilty. However, such a defence could only succeed where there had been positive evidence of something other than a defect of reason.

'Where the only cause alleged for the unconsciousness is a defect of reason from disease of the mind, and that cause is rejected by the jury, there can be no room for the alternative defence of automatism.' On the facts before the House, there was nothing to suggest any other pathological causes for automatism and the accused's appeal was dismissed.

This case outlined the link and also the difference between insane automatism and non-insane automatism. However, it did not cover every situation and it was accepted by the courts that there would be borderline situations. Nevertheless, it did outline the considerations which a court should bear in mind in considering whether both defences should be available to an accused or merely one of them.

Until 1973, there was never any suggestion in a case that the defence of automatism would not be available to an accused if it was shown that the automatism arose from the defendant's fault. However, in the case of R v *Quick and Paddison* (1973), the Court of Appeal proposed a new rule which did require the court to consider whether or not the accused was to blame for his automation state (obiter).

The general rule that the Court of Appeal laid down provides:

'A self-induced incapacity will not excuse, see R v *Lipman* (1969), nor will one which could have been reasonably foreseen as a result of either doing or omitting to do something, as, or for example, taking alcohol against medical advice after using certain prescribed drugs, or failing to have regular meals while taking insulin.'

However, in R v *Bailey* (1983) the Court of Appeal held that the defence of automatism may be open to an accused who fails to take the required amount of food after insulin. In such cases, the court must decide whether the accused has been proved to have been reckless in not taking sufficient food and, if he knows that by failing to do so he will become aggressive, unpredictable or uncontrolled, with the result that he may cause injury to others, he may be found to be reckless.

It is not clear whether a case such as R v *Bailey* is one of 'self-induced' automatism, although it is arguable that his omission to take food, combined with his knowledge of the attendant consequences, could make any ensuing automation state 'voluntary' or 'self-induced'. If an accused does not know that his failing to take the food will have those consequences then, according to the decision in R v *Bailey* the defence of automatism will be open to him.

A more clear-cut area of self-induced automatism is that of voluntary drunkenness and 'dangerous' drugs. The distinction between sedatives and the drugs with a merely soporific effect, and those drugs which induce aggressive or unpredictable behaviour appears to have been introduced by the Court of Appeal in *R* v *Bailey* and *R* v *Hardie* (1984).

In the latter case the accused took Valium pills and then, whilst under their influence, went on to damage property. The judge directed that such 'intoxication' was no defence, equating it with alcohol and the *DPP* v *Majewski* (1976) rule (below). However, the Court of Appeal made a distinction between drugs such as Valium and 'dangerous drugs' or alcohol.

In such cases as *R* v *Bailey* and *R* v *Hardie* the question will be one of recklessness and the *DPP* v *Majewski* restrictions will not be imposed upon the accused's raising the defence of intoxication.

Generally, voluntary drunkenness is not a defence to a criminal charge. The term 'drunkenness' includes a state of mind induced by voluntary drug taking: *R* v *Lipman* (1969).

There are difficulties surrounding 'voluntariness' here. In *R* v *Tandy* (1988) it was argued that a woman who was an alcoholic did not drink 'voluntarily' prior to committing a murder but had been driven to it by her alcoholism. Her argument failed to impress the Court of Appeal who held that at least her first drink of the day was taken voluntarily.

Similarly, in *R* v *Allen* (1988), where the accused argued that he did not know the strength of the drink he had consumed and that therefore his consumption of it was involuntary, the court held this to be voluntary intoxication.

However, in certain circumstances, drunkenness may be a defence:

1) If it causes a disease of the mind, eg delirium tremens. In these circumstances the accused will be entitled to an acquittal providing he can satisfy the requirements of the *M'Naghten* (1843) rules.

2) It may enable the defendant to establish a mistake of fact incompatible with criminal responsibility, eg *R* v *Letenock* (1917) (provocation).

3) Drunkenness may provide a defence to a crime, where the drunkenness totally negatives the specific intent necessary for the crime. In *DPP* v *Majewski* (1976), the accused who was drunk assaulted a police officer, who arrested him. The defendant's appeal against conviction for assault occasioning actual bodily harm was dismissed by the House of Lords, because the defence did not involve specific intent and his drunkenness was consequently immaterial.

This rule laid down in *DPP* v *Majewski* is plainly one of policy and is not one that has its roots in logic. Plainly, a sufficient degree of intoxication can negative mens rea totally but this will only be a defence where it negatives the mens rea in a crime of specific intent, not a crime of basic intent. The situation is further complicated, because a crime of 'specific intent' for the purposes of drink and drugs, will not necessarily be classified for other criminal law purposes as a crime of specific intent. Furthermore, a crime which might generally be classified as a crime of specific or ulterior intent for the purposes of criminal law generally may not be classified as a crime of specific intent for the purposes of the defence of drink and drugs. It is necessary to look to case law to discover what are crimes of specific intent for the purposes of drink and drugs and what are crimes of basic intent. This rather arbitrary classification by the courts is obviously subject to review and re-classification of offences which were previously held to be crimes of specific intent to crimes of basic intent have occurred. In the case of *MPC* v *Caldwell* (1981), the House of Lords considered the effect of *DPP* v *Majewski* on a charge under s1(2) of the Criminal Damage Act 1971, where the accused was charged with causing criminal damage, being reckless as to whether life was endangered. The court considered that the effect of *DPP* v *Majewski* was that if an accused was charged with causing criminal damage under s1(2) of the Criminal Damage Act with intent to endanger life, he would have a defence where he could show that voluntary intoxication made him unable to form the necessary mens rea. However, he would not have a defence where he was charged under s1(2), with being reckless as to whether life was endangered. *DPP* v *Majewski* provides that all crimes of recklessness must be crimes of basic intent and therefore, this anomalous situation arises.

The effect of this decision is to overturn a previously accepted rule that where an accused was voluntarily intoxicated to the extent that he was unable to form mens rea, he would have a defence under s1(2) of the Criminal Damage Act 1971, because this is a crime of specific intent, but he would not have a defence under s1(1) of the Criminal Damage Act 1971 as this is a crime of basic intent.

The rules laid out in *DPP* v *Majewski* have been severely critizised on the basis of their arbitrary and illogical nature. *MPC* v *Caldwell* serves to emphasise this as criticism and it is to be hoped that there will shortly be some clarification in this area.

A final area of self-induced intoxication is where the accused deliberately gets drunk in order to give himself 'dutch courage' to carry out a crime that he has formed the intention to commit. It was held in *Attorney-General for Northern Ireland* v *Gallagher* (1963) that 'he cannot rely on this self-induced drunkenness as a defence to a charge of murder, nor even as reducing it to manslaughter ... the wickedness of his mind before he got drunk is enough to condemn him' (per Lord Denning).

As with *DPP* v *Majewski* there is a strong element of policy evident in this decision which appears to contradict the general requirement that mens rea must coincide with actus reus and that an intention to commit some future act is not mens rea: *R* v *Jakeman* (1983).

QUESTION TWO

Una, a terrorist, forced Vernon into her car at gun point. Una said, 'We have your wife and children. Carry out your instructions and they will be safe.' Vernon was given a pistol, a photograph and detailed instructions which involved killing the person in the photograph when he came out of the nearby cathedral, 45 minutes later Una placed an electronic 'bug' under Vernon's watch and told Vernon 'If you take this off or contact the police, your children will die.' Vernon was dropped off at the cathedral. He did not know what to do. He telephoned his home but received no answer. Finally, Vernon walked up the cathedral steps and shot the victim as he was leaving. The victim was not killed but was severely wounded.

Advise Una and Vernon of their criminal liability. Would it make any difference to your advice if the victim had died or if Una never had Vernon's wife and children in her custody?

University of London LLB Examination
(for External Students) Criminal Law June 1982 Q8

General Comment

The core of this question concerns the offence of attempted murder and the general defences which may be available to it. It is also concerned with the rather difficult principle of innocent agency and liability for an offence where the principal is not present. The two defences which have to be considered in relation to murder are duress and mistake. These are difficult defences in their own right and become exceptionally difficult when they are intermingled.

Skeleton Solution

Assault – threats to kill: s16 CLA 1977 – false imprisonment – incitement, procurement of murder – attempted murder: s1 CAA 1981 – gbh, s18 OAP 1861.

Defence – duress: applicability to murder/attempt murder – mistake.

Suggested Solution

When Una forced Vernon into the car at gun point she commits a common law assault in that she puts a person in fear of being then and there subjected to force. By making threats to kill Vernon's children she commits an offence contrary to s16 of the Criminal Law Act 1977 which states that a person who without lawful excuse makes to another a threat intending that that other would fear that it would be carried out to kill the other or a third person shall be guilty of an offence.

By forcing Vernon into her car she may commit the offence of false-imprisonment where the victim is unlawfully and intentionally or recklessly restrained from moving freely from a particular place. There may, furthermore, be the offence of kidnapping which is a particular type of false imprisonment involving the removal or secreting of a victim against his will.

However, the most serious offence that she commits is that concerning the plan to kill. By requiring Vernon to carry out this plan to kill she is at least inciting a murder. It is an offence under the common law to incite another to commit an indictable or summary offence. However, the incitement must be more than the mere expression of desire. It must be shown that Una urged or spurred Vernon on by advice, encouragement, persuasion, threats or pressure: *Race Relations Board* v *Applin* (1973). To be liable for incitement it is not necessary that the offence is actually committed. The crime is complete at the time of the persuasion even if the full offence never occurs. However, if the person incited does commit the offence the inciter becomes a participant in that offence and is guilty of counselling the offence.

It may be that Una is more than just an inciter or counsellor to the offence. It is possible that under the doctrine of innocent agency Vernon could be relieved of liability and Una would be deemed to be the principal offender in the offence.

However, this doctrine will be considered at greater length when Vernon's liability and possible defences have been discussed.

When Vernon shoots at the victim severely wounding him, he performs the actus reus of attempted murder. For there to be an attempt it must be shown that there is an act beyond preparation towards the commission of the offence. Section 1 Criminal Attempts Act 1981. The mens rea for an attempt is generally the same as for the full offence. However, in a charge of attempted murder it must be shown that Vernon had intention to kill. Any lesser mens rea is insufficient for the charge although had Vernon actually killed he could have been liable for murder with a lesser mens rea. If Vernon did not intend to kill but merely intended grievous bodily harm he will have committed an offence contrary to s18 of the Offences Against the Person Act 1861 in that he caused grievous bodily harm with intent to cause grievous bodily harm.

It may be possible for Vernon to claim that he was acting under duress. For the defence to be operative it must be shown that Vernon committed the offence only because of an overriding threat of death or serious personal injury: *DPP for Northern Ireland* v *Lynch* (1975).

The threat must be 'immediate' in the sense that the accused had no reasonable opportunity to render it ineffective by seeking police protection. On the facts in question it should be noted that there was opportunity for Vernon to contact the police although he had been told that this would bring about his children's death. The jury would therefore have to decide whether or not the opportunity should have been taken by Vernon to contact the police. It should be noted that in *R* v *Hudson and Taylor* (1971) the accused was still able to claim the defence of duress even though they had not thought to contact the police because the police protection offered to them would have been ineffective.

It is not necessary that the threat be directed towards the accused. In *R* v *Hurley and Murray* (1967) the Supreme Court of Victoria (Australia) held that the threats to kill or seriously injure the defendant's common law wife were sufficient for duress, and this principle would clearly extend to an accused's family, and it was opined in *R* v *Shepherd* (1988) that there was nothing in principle to exclude threats made against an accused's relatives.

The test to be applied by the jury in deciding whether the defence is shown was outlined in the case of *R* v *Graham* (1982), the Court of Appeal stated that the jury should be directed to ask themselves 'whether the defendant was, or might have been, impelled to act as he did because of the result of what he reasonably believed the partner had said or done, the defendant had good cause to fear that, if he did not so act the partner would kill him'. If that was so, the jury must further be satisfied that a sober person of reasonable firmness sharing the defendant's characteristics would have responded to the situation by taking part in the killing. The test therefore is two limbed. The first limb is subjective – was the accused responding to a reasonably perceived threat to kill himself? The second limb is objective – would the ordinary man have responded to that threat by taking part in the killing?

However, the fact that Vernon has committed an attempted murder complicates the matter.

The House of Lords in *R* v *Howe* (1987) held the defence of duress not to be available in murder cases.

Addressing the question of attempted murder Lord Hailsham said that in such a case the defence would need to be reconsidered. Lord Griffiths felt that the defence would not be available and Smith and Hogan argue that if it were otherwise, the situation would be absurd (6th ed p233), with the law providing a defence for an act when it was done and then removing it after a year and a day if the victim died within that period. In *R* v *Gotts* (1992) the House of Lords confirmed that duress is not available as a defence to a charge of murder or attempted murder.

Had the victim died, Vernon would not have the defence of duress open to him following *R* v *Howe* as Vernon would be either the principal offender or a secondary party.

It is unlikely then that Vernon will be able to bring himself within the ambit of 'innocent agency' thereby imputing liability as principal offender to Una.

Una would appear to be guilty of procuring the murder (s8 Accessories and Abettors Act 1861) and therefore would also be liable to be tried as a principal offender.

Had Una never had Vernon's family in custody, that fact alone should not deprive Vernon of any defence of duress which might otherwise be available to him. It will be a consideration in deciding whether or not his belief of the threat was reasonable and whether his reaction to the threat was one which might be expected of a sober person of reasonable firmness (per *R* v *Graham*) so, for instance, if it would have been almost impossible for Una to have had the family in custody eg they were abroad at the time – then Vernon's submitting to Una's threat would not meet the Graham requirements.

However, we are told that Vernon tried to contact his family without success.

If he could have expected them to be there, and had taken all reasonable steps open to him to ascertain the truth of Una's claim then it is submitted that he would be able to argue that he was acting under duress even though there was no threat to his family.

It is also submitted that, following *R* v *Williams (Gladstone)* (1987) (private defence) that Vernon should be judged on the facts as he believed them to be, whether reasonably or not (see Smith and Hogan 6th Ed p236).

QUESTION THREE

Mistake operates by considering the position the accused thought he was in and on that assumption examines the legal significance of his acts.

Discuss.

University of London LLB Examination
(for External Students) Criminal Law June 1984 Q3(a)

General Comment

Bearing in mind the recent case law and the academic discussion surrounding the defence of mistake and the problems that arise from it this question should be one that a well-prepared student would have been able to answer well and possibly would even have been pleased to see. The fact that it is half essay/half problem in its format may also assist a student because the essay aspect of the question will often help a student to recall clearly and accurately the necessary cases and principles that are to be applied in relation to the problem part of the question.

Skeleton Solution

Mistake: negation of mens rea – 'honest and reasonable' – recent cases: removal of 'reasonableness' requirement except in certain cases.

Suggested Solution

a) A mistaken belief held by an accused may be as to fact or as to law (either civil or criminal). It is necessary always to distinguish what particular type of mistake an accused may be labouring under as a mistake of law is usually to be regarded as no defence. In *R* v *Bailey* (1800) the mistaken belief that conduct was not criminal when in fact it was, was held to be no defence, although it went to mitigation. A mistake of fact may be a defence providing it negates the particular mens rea necessary to prove the crime charged.

A mistake which does not preclude the mens rea cannot provide a defence as it is irrelevant.

The difficulty for many years has been in settling what particular type of mistake of fact should enable an accused to be judged according to the position he thought he was in. Some early case law, for example *R* v *Rose* (1884), suggested that the mistake had to be both honest and reasonable. However, in *DPP* v *Morgan* (1975) a purely subjective approach was adopted. In that case D had invited three friends to have sexual intercourse with his wife. He told them that she would put up a struggle as this would increase her sexual pleasure. The men had intercourse with the wife and were convicted of rape. The men appealed against conviction to the House of Lords on a question of whether an honest though unreasonable belief in consent to intercourse was a defence. The House of Lords held that since rape required intercourse without consent, if an accused honestly (though unreasonably) believed that his victim was consenting the prosecution had failed to prove the necessary mens rea for the crime.

More recently there have been a number of cases which have suggested that in certain cases a mistake has got to be both honest and reasonable before it enables the accused to be judged on the basis of what he thought. For example in *Albert* v *Lavin* (1980) the Divisional Court considered the question of mistake in relation to a charge arising under s51 of the Police Act 1964. It was held that it was necessary to distinguish between mens rea required for the basic elements of the offence and the mental element required for a defence. In the former case an honest, albeit unreasonable, mistaken belief may negative mens rea; in the latter, only an honest and reasonable mistake would suffice. For example in the case of an assault charge under s51 a mistaken belief by the defendant that the victim had no right to detain him related to the nature of a defence and applying *Albert* v *Lavin* would have needed to have been reasonable as well as honest. However, more recently there has been a move away from this approach. In *R* v *Kimber*

(1983) it was stated that, on a charge of indecent assault, if an accused honestly believed a victim was consenting then he would be entitled to be acquitted. The question of whether his belief was reasonable or unreasonable was irrelevant save in so far that it might have assisted the jury to decide whether an accused did believe what he said he did. Furthermore in R v *Williams (Gladstone)* (1984) it was held to be a material misdirection when it was not made clear to the jury that it was for the prosecution to eliminate the possibility that the appellant was acting under a genuine mistake of fact. Once again the Court of Appeal stated that the question of reasonableness of the appellant's mistaken belief was material only to the question of whether or not the belief was in fact held.

In *Beckford* v R (1987), where the Privy Council described Morgan as 'a landmark decision in the development of the Common law', the court approved the decision in R v *Williams (Gladstone)* (1984). That decision was that, in relation to assaults, 'the mental element necessary … is the intent to apply unlawful force' and that if the accused believed, reasonably or otherwise, in the existence of facts which would justify his using that force in self-defence, then he did not have the required mens rea.

Since *Beckford* v R then, the distinction made in *Albert* v *Lavin* (1981) between elements of the offence and these of a defence has been removed.

It is therefore true to say that mistake generally operates by considering the position the accused thought he was in and on that assumption examines the legal significance of his acts. There do appear to be exceptions to this rule, for example in *DPP* v *Morgan* (1976) the House of Lords refused to overrule R v *Tolson* (1889). In that case the accused had been deserted by her husband for five years and believed him to be dead. She remarried whereupon her first husband reappeared. Her conviction for bigamy was quashed because her belief was not only an honest one but also based upon reasonable grounds. Lord Hailsham stated in *DPP* v *Morgan* that he viewed R v *Tolson* as a narrow decision based on the construction of a statute which prima facie seemed to make an absolute statutory offence with a proviso of the statutory defence. In Lord Hailsham's view there was a distinction between R v *Tolson* and other cases based on statute and the more general situation in *DPP* v *Morgan*.

This view is supported by *Westminster City Council* v *Croyalgrange* (1986).

However, in R v O'Grady (1987) it was held that where D, because of self-induced intoxication, formed a mistaken belief that he was using force to defend himself his plea (of self-defence) failed.

Finally, where a crime is one capable of commission by negligence, the requirement of reasonableness in mistake persists as an unreasonably held mistaken belief is itself negligent.

QUESTION FOUR

I was a plain clothes policeman arresting a violent criminal dressed as an old lady. J saw the incident and honestly believed that I was attacking an old lady. J hit I over the head with his bag.

Advise J.

Adapted from University of London LLB Examination
(for External Students) Criminal Law June 1984 Q3(b)

General Comment

A simple test of the application of the principles relating to mistake and justified use of force.

Skeleton Solution

Assault: s51 Police Act 1964 – prevention of crime s3 CLA 1967 – mistake.

Suggested Solution

I should be advised that J may have committed a number of serious offences against him. In particular, s51 of the Police Act 1964. However, it may be open to J to claim the benefit of s3 of the Criminal Law Act 1967 in conjunction with his genuine mistake of fact.

Under s51 of the Police Act 1964 a person who assaults a constable in the execution of his duty shall be guilty of an offence. It is not necessary that an accused knows that it is a constable he is assaulting provided that the constable is acting 'in execution of his duty'. In order for J to be convicted of an offence contrary to s51 it must be shown that the initial arrest being effected by I was lawful: *Riley* v *DPP* (1989). I would seem to be acting in the execution of his duty as his conduct falls within the general scope of preventing crime and catching offenders: *R* v *Waterfield* (1964). J could not be liable under s51(2) for wilfully obstructing a constable in the execution of his duty because on the facts in question he was not acting wilfully as he did not know I was a policeman.

J will wish to claim the defence contained in s3 of the Criminal Law Act 1967 in conjunction with the defence of mistake. The facts in question are very similar to those contained in *R* v *Williams (Gladstone)* (1984). In that case the accused saw M knock a youth to the ground. M said that he was arresting the youth for mugging a woman. The accused did not believe his story and the struggle ensued during which the accused punched M who sustained injuries to his face. The accused was charged under s47 of the Offences Against the Person Act 1861 and put forward the defence that he had honestly believed M was unlawfully assaulting the youth. The trial judge directed that the accused could only rely on his mistake if it was both honest and reasonable. The accused was found guilty and appealed to the Court of Appeal where it was held that there had been a material misdirection in that it had not been made clear to the jury that it was for the prosecution to eliminate the possibility that the appellant was acting under a genuine mistake of fact. The question of whether or not that mistake was reasonable was relevant only in deciding whether the belief was honestly held.

Furthermore, following the Privy Council decision in *Beckford* v *R* (1987) the question to be asked will be did the accused believe, reasonably or not, in the existence of facts which would justify his use of force under the circumstances?

Applying that principle to the facts in question, providing J honestly believed that I

179

was attacking an old lady his criminal liability must be judged on the basis of what he perceived the facts to be.

He would therefore be able to claim the defence contained in s3 of the Criminal Law Act 1967 which provides that a person may use such force as is reasonable in the circumstances in the prevention of crime. This defence will not be available to him if he used excessive force in the light of all the circumstances.

The test of what is 'reasonable' here will be an objective one: *Farrell v Secretary of State for Defence* (1980), however, account will be taken of the 'heat' of the situation and allowances made therefor.

J will be judged, in respect of his use of force, by the standards of a reasonable man under those particular circumstances and not by those of a reasonable man who is able to exercise detached reflection in the cold light of day: *R v Whyte* (1987).

QUESTION FIVE

R was climbing with his friends S and T. They were roped together and were climbing a particularly dangerous Welsh mountain. T, who was on the bottom of the rope, fell away from the face and dragged S off. R was supporting S and T but they were heavy. R was not able to hold their weight for long so he shouted to S to cut the rope below him. S said, 'But this would be murder.' R said, 'Unless you do so I will cut you both free and you will both be killed.' Reluctantly, S cut the rope and T, who was unconscious, plunged to his death several thousand metres below.

Advise the parties of their criminal liability.

University of London LLB Examination
(for External Students) Criminal Law June 1987 Q6

General Comment

This question appeared in the June examination of 1987 and, in view of the recent appeal cases in this area, such a question was to be expected.

This question was relatively straightforward, although the aspect of causation was not easy. The link between necessity and duress required careful consideration.

Skeleton Solution

S   Murder – causation, necessity, duress – availability to murder.

R   Aid/abet murder – necessity.

Suggested Solution

The question requires consideration of a number of difficult aspects of the law of homicide. The type of extreme situation described has never come before the courts in practice and much of the law to be considered in this situation may at first glance appear incongruous in its application as the case law involved is more obviously 'criminal' than the facts in question.

The core of the question concerns whether or not R and S can be liable under the criminal law for the death of T. There is nothing in the question to indicate that R and S have acted recklessly in relation to the mountaineering itself. Nor is there anything to indicate that they did anything that would amount to a crime in itself separate from possible liability for the death. Therefore killing by reckless conduct and constructive manslaughter do not appear to be in any way appropriate on the facts.

The most obvious charge that could apply is that of murder. Murder is established when a person unlawfully kills another with 'malice aforethought'. The technical term 'malice aforethought' encompasses two particular types of mens rea – intention to kill and intention to do grievous bodily harm. Either one of these states of mind will be sufficient mens rea for murder: *R v Moloney* (1985); *R v Hancock and Shankland* (1986); *R v Nedrick* (1986).

The term intention includes direct intent (desiring a particular result) and oblique intent (knowledge that a particular result is certain or virtually certain to occur). On the facts in question the prosecution would allege that S had oblique intention to kill, ie he knew that it was certain to occur as a result of what he did even though he did not desire it.

However S could only be liable if he was regarded as the legal cause of T's death. Causation is a mixed question of fact and law. Undoubtedly it must be shown that S's act is a sine qua non of the event. This is a question of fact and in the facts in the question it would seem indisputably satisfied. Even so in law S's act may not be regarded as the cause of the death. Sometimes it is stated that the act must be 'substantial' before it can be regarded as the legal cause of a result. However this is now regarded as being too favourable to the accused. Generally all that need be established is that the accused is a cause of the death and that his contribution is not so trivial that it should be ignored.

Killing a person is merely accelerating an inevitable event. A very trivial acceleration should be ignored and will not be regarded as a legal cause of death. It could therefore be argued that by cutting the rope thus allowing T to fall to his death, S has merely hastened T's death by a matter of seconds and such a slight speeding up of death could not be regarded as the legal cause of the death.

There is therefore a strong argument for suggesting that S is not the legal cause of T's death and therefore is not liable for murder. However in order to examine all aspects of the question it will be assumed that S is the legal cause of T's death and could be liable for murder because he kills intending to kill. In this event it is necessary to consider whether S would be able to claim a defence.

The most obvious defence to consider on these facts is that of necessity. In essence this is a plea that S's intentional conduct, which otherwise would be criminal, was not criminal because what he did was necessary to avoid some other greater evil. However English law does not recognise a general defence of necessity. Thus in *R v Dudley and Stevens* (1884) the necessity for self-preservation was no defence to a charge of murder, arising out of the killing and eating of a cabin-boy by shipwrecked sailors adrift on an open boat and without food.

Furthermore, Lord Denning in *Southwark London Borough v Williams* (1971) dismissed the notion of such a defence ever existing in English law in relation to certain crimes.

However there has emerged recently a trend in the courts toward a recognition of a defence of 'duress of circumstances' which is a type of necessity. The Court of Appeal accepted such a defence to a charge of reckless driving in *R* v *Willer* (1986) and similarly, the defence was accepted in *R* v *Conway* (1988) as a type of duress.

Whatever the nomenclature, in *R* v *Martin* (1989) the Court of Appeal held that necessity and duress overlapped and that:

i)   in extreme circumstances the law does recognise the defence of necessity;

ii)   it is a defence which is only available if, objectively viewed, the accused can be said to be acting reasonably and proportionately in order to avoid a threat of death or serious injury; and

iii) if the defence is available to the accused, the issue should be left to the jury.

They must be directed to determine whether the accused was impelled – or may have been impelled – to act as he did because, as a result of what he reasonably believed, he had good cause to fear that death or serious injury would otherwise ensue.

If that were the case, the question will then be 'would a sober person of reasonable firmness, sharing the characteristics of the accused, have responded to that situation by acting as the accused did? Although the cases of *R* v *Martin* and *R* v *Conway* on their facts have only extended the defence of necessity to a person charged with driving offences, the recent case of *R* v *Cole* (1994) indicated that necessity may be a defence to a charge of robbery. However, as the law now stands there is no authority to support that necessity may be a defence to homicide and *R* v *Dudley and Stephens* suggests that it is not.

Here, it is submitted that the above criteria are met, at least by S and possibly by R, although, as the defence of duress is not available in cases of murder (see below), the overlapping concept of 'duress of circumstances' or necessity is unlikely to be open to S and R.

Duress is a further example of what might be regarded as a limited defence of necessity. Duress may be available where S has committed the offence only because of a threat of death or serious personal injury: *DPP for Northern Ireland* v *Lynch* (1975).

For many years it was unclear whether or not duress was available to a principal charged with murder. In *DPP for Northern Ireland* v *Lynch* the House of Lords had allowed a plea of duress where an aider and abettor had taken part in a murder under duress. In *Abbott* v *R* (1976) the Privy Council held by a majority that the defence was not available to a principal charged with murder. The minority view was that since there was no compelling authority or public policy to the contrary, the defence should be available to a principal offender.

The lack of clarity on this area of law was further emphasised in *R* v *Graham* (1982) where the prosecution conceded that the defence could raise a plea of duress even though the accused was charged as a principal to murder.

Recently the House of Lords had opportunity to review the law in this difficult area. In *R* v *Howe* (1987); *R* v *Bannister* (1962); *R* v *Burke* (1987) and *R* v *Clarkson* (1987) the House, after much deliberation, departed from its own decision in *DPP for Northern Ireland* v *Lynch* and held that the defence of duress was no longer available to an accomplice to murder, including an aider and abettor. Indeed it was not available to a principal or accomplice charged with murder as there was no proper distinction that could be drawn between a principal and an accomplice. The inconsistency of approach in this area has therefore been corrected. Furthermore the House affirmed the approach as stated in *R* v *Graham* that in any event a defence of duress would fail if the prosecution proved that a person of reasonable firmness sharing the characteristics of the defendant would not have given way to the threats as did the defendant.

Thus it is clear that S could not plead duress. Had S been able to plead duress R would have become a principal offender via the doctrine of innocent agency. However his only possible liability now must be an an aider and abettor. An aider and abettor is one who is present at the scene of the offence assisting or encouraging: *R* v *Coney* (1882); *R* v *Clarkson* (1971). To be an aider and abettor an accused must have full knowledge of the facts that amount to the crime: *Johnson* v *Youden* (1950). Patently this is established on the facts in question. R would be unable to claim any defence in law. Self defence is only available where an accused is countering a threat from a person. Necessity is not available as a defence in English criminal law. R, like S, would appear to be liable for murder. However, it must be remembered that this application of the law would not be appropriate if S was not the legal cause of T's death.

QUESTION SIX

G had invited H to a party given at G's house. H was a well known total abstainer. G believed that H had walked to the party whereas in fact H had come by car. G laced H's drink to see how H would react. In fact H became ill and decided to drive home. H was aware that he was not himself but he did not know that his disability was the result of the laced drink. H drove home and on the way collided with a parked car damaging it and causing severe anger to its owner who was some distance away. When H arrived home he found an intruder in his house and chased him intending to catch him. The intruder fell down stairs whilst being chased and broke a leg.

Advise the parties of their criminal liability.

University of London LLB (Examination)
(for External Students) Criminal Law June 1990 Q5

General Comment

A question requiring a good knowledge of automatism and intoxication. The question raises the interesting issue of non-reckless intoxication. Far more space should be devoted to H's liability than that of G.

Skeleton Solution

Liability of H – criminal damage, automatism and non-reckless intoxication – injuries to intruder – causation – consider mens rea for ss18, 20, and 47 – defence under s3 1967 Act – liability of G – administering a noxious substance – accessorial liability.

Suggested Solution

H has obviously damaged property belonging to another, contrary to s1(1) Criminal Damage Act 1971. The difficulty surrounding his liability for this offences stems from the fact that he was unwell/intoxicated at the time and thus may have a defence based on the submission that he was not responsible for his actions at the time. The most attractive argument to rely on from H's point of view, is that because of the effect of the alcohol on his nervous system he was in a state of automatism at the time of the collision. If this argument were to succeed it would result in H being totally relieved of all criminal liability for the collision. Automatism has been defined, in cases such as *Bratty* v *Attorney-General for Northern Ireland* (1963), as 'something done by the muscles without the control of the mind'. It is generally accepted that it takes the form of some external factor operating upon the brain, such as hypnotism. In theory the effect of alcohol upon the brain could come within this category, although there are two difficulties with this line of argument.

The first difficulty is that there must be evidence that H was really in an automatic state. If there is evidence that he was actually conscious of his actions, for example that he knew he was driving, the defence will not be available to him; see *Broome* v *Perkins* (1987). Secondly, there is evidence to suggest that he knew he was feeling unwell. The court may take the view that he should not have attempted to drive at all in such a situation, and that there is a degree of fault to be found in his deciding to drive; see *R* v *Bailey* (1983). A possible distinction between 'Bailey' and the present case is that H did not know the cause of his illness, and thus may not have been expected to know its possible consequences.

If the defence of automatism is not available to H, the defence of intoxication will have to be considered. It is well established that the defence of intoxication is normally only available to defendants charged with crimes of specific intent. Criminal damage contrary to s1(1) of the 1971 Act is a crime of basic intent. Following the House of Lords' decision in *DPP* v *Majewski* (1976), the mens rea required for the crime of basic intent, i.e recklessness, is to be found in the defendant's recklessness, or fault, in becoming intoxicated in the first instance. At this point a possible distinction between most cases of intoxication and the case of H emerges. H may contend that he was not at fault in becoming intoxicated since there was nothing that would have alerted him, or even the reasonable person, to the fact that his drink had been laced with alcohol. The concept of so-called 'non-reckless intoxication' was considered by the Court of Appeal in *R* v *Hardie* (1984). There the court held that where there is evidence that a defendant charged with a basic intent crime may not have been reckless in becoming intoxicated, the issue ought to be left to the jury. On this basis it is submitted that H may succeed with the defence of intoxication.

It is submitted that there will be no criminal liability for causing the car owner to be enraged. Such a condition is unlikely to constitute actual bodily harm contrary to s47 of the Offences Against the Persons Act 1861, as defined in *R* v *Miller* (1954), neither is it a common assault as the owner did not apprehend immediate physical violence.

In suffering a broken leg, the intruder in H's house incurs grievous bodily harm, as defined in *R* v *Saunders* (1985). H will be regarded as having caused the injury on the basis that the intruder's reaction, ie that of running away in haste, was a reasonably foreseeable consequence of his being chased by H; see *R* v *Roberts* (1971). There is no evidence of the intruder doing anything 'daft' that would break the chain of causation.

For liability under s18 of the 1861 Act, H will have to be shown to have intended to cause the intruder some grievous bodily harm; see *R* v *Belfon* (1976). On the facts this may be difficult to prove, as H will claim that his intention was to catch the intruder. More likely perhaps is a charge of inflicting grievous bodily harm contrary to s20 of the 1861 Act. For this offence it would have to be shown that H was 'malicious', ie that he foresaw at least the possibility of some physical harm occurring to the intruder albeit slight; see *R* v *Cunningham* (1957), and *R* v *Mowatt* (1967). H could escape liability under s20 if he can show that he never foresaw the possibility of any physical harm occurring to the intruder. It is submitted that if this proves to be the case, H might still be guilty of an offence contrary to s47 of the 1861 Act. The mens rea for the s47 offence is that required for an assault as defined in *R* v *Venna* (1976). In *R* v *Savage*; *R* v *Parmenter* (1991) the House of Lords held that no mens rea is required as to the actual bodily harm caused. It will therefore be irrelevant that H may not have intended or foresaw injury to the intruder.

By way of defence H can contend that he was using reasonable force in effecting or assisting in the lawful arrest of a suspected offender; see s3 Criminal Law Act 1967. It is submitted that his intoxication is irrelevant here since there is no evidence of his having misjudged the use of force necessary in the circumstances.

By placing alcohol in H's drink G may have committed either the offence of maliciously administering a noxious substance so as thereby to endanger life, contrary to s23 of the 1861 Act, or the offence of maliciously administering a noxious substance, with intent to injure aggrieve or annoy, contrary to s24 of the 1861 Act. Alcohol can be a noxious substance in certain circumstances; see *R* v *Cato* (1976), and *R* v *Marcus* (1981). A charge under s23 would be appropriate if the collision is seen as placing H's life in danger. Under s23, G does not need to have foreseen the collision, merely that there was a risk that H would suffer some physical harm; see *R* v *Cunningham*. It is submitted that H probably did have the mens rea required by s24, namely the intent to injure annoy or aggrieve.

H cannot be regarded as the innocent agent of G, as he was aware of his actions at the time of the collision, and when chasing the intruder. By causing H to become intoxicated, however, G may incur liability as an accessory to the criminal damage; see *Attorney-General's Reference (No 1 of 1975)* (1975).

11 UNIVERSITY OF LONDON LLB (EXTERNAL) 1994 QUESTIONS AND SUGGESTED SOLUTIONS

UNIVERSITY OF LONDON
LLB EXAMINATIONS 1994
for External Students
INTERMEDIATE EXAMINATION (Scheme A) and
FIRST AND SECOND YEAR EXAMINATIONS (Scheme B)

CRIMINAL LAW

Tuesday, 4 June: 10am to 1pm

Answer *FOUR* of the following SEVEN questions

1 K, a bank clerk, was working late when he was telephoned by L and told to switch off the alarm at the bank that evening or else L would kill K's daughter, whom L had abducted. K was instructed not to contact anyone and to place an explosive device on a strong room door which L would blow by remote control. K was to take certain bonds from the strongroom and throw them out of his office window to a car waiting below. K did as he was instructed though he knew that others working late in the bank might be seriously injured or even killed by the explosion. A security guard, M, died from a heart attach from shock. The bonds were never recovered.

Advise K and L of their criminal liability.

2 A was very angry because he had just been fired from his job. He arrived back home to find that his wife had left a note for him stating that she had taken their two children and was leaving him. He was upset and decided to go for a walk to calm down. He had been walking for an hour when he called into a public house and ordered a glass of mineral water. By mistake he was given a large glass of vodka by the landlord. He gulped down the drink without tasting it. Outside he was approached by two homeless youngsters, B and C, who were asking for money. He thought they were going to attack him and he hit out at B, the one nearer to him, and by mistake, hit C. C fell back and hit his head on the pavement and was concussed.

Advise A of his criminal liability. What difference, if any, would it make to your advice if C had died from the fall because he had a thin skull?

3 E had been given a stolen building society cheque by F to pay for a car which E had sold to him. E did not know that the cheque was stolen and, by the time that this was discovered, F had sold the car to H for £500 cash. E went to the address that F had given and climbed in through an open window of F's flat. He removed two items which he estimated were worth £500. These he intended to

186

sell, 'to get his own back'. On the way out he knocked over a vase. He pushed past the caretaker who tried to stop him. The flat did not belong to F.

Advise E and F.

4   G was given to lapses of concentration and was driving home from work on a dual carriageway after a night shift. G started to overtake the car in front on the inside. But the road rapidly started to narrow. Taking into account his experience as a driver, G concluded that there was no chance of his failing to get through. In fact, because the road was wet, G crashed into the car but the driver was not injured.

Advise G. What difference, if any, would it make to your advice if the driver of the other car was seriously injured?

5   H, aged 13 years, felt that J, his teacher, was trying to make a fool of him in front of his fellow pupils. He poured a quantity of acid into a bucket which he placed above the door of J's study. J entered the study and the acid spilled onto the carpet (which it burned) but did not come into contact with J. The bucket grazed J's head and the acid fumes made J's eyes water for a couple of hours and gave him a choking sensation.

Advise H of his criminal liability.

6   M and N agreed to rob a local building society branch. N drove M to the branch. M went in to see if it could be broken into on a subsequent occasion. M threatened an assistant with a replica pistol. He said, 'Your money or your life.' She handed over the cash before M pistol-whipped her. Next M ran out and jumped into the car throwing the money into the back. When N realised that M had used violence he refused to drive away. M then ran off and before driving off N threw the money out of the car window.

Advise M and N of their criminal liability.

7   P was walking home his girlfriend, Q, when they started to kiss. P was kissing her goodnight when he bruised her lips and Q gave him a love bite which drew blood. Q suggested that P return later and climb into her bedroom. In the middle of the night P climbed into what he though was Q's bedroom. In fact, it was her twin sister R's bedroom. P did not know that Q had a twin sister. He climbed into R's bed. She did not wake fully because she had taken a sleeping tablet. P penetrated her before she woke up and screamed in alarm.

Advise P of his criminal liability.

QUESTION ONE

K, a bank clerk, was working late when he was telephoned by L and told to switch off the alarm at the bank that evening or else L would kill K's daughter, whom L had abducted. K was instructed not to contact anyone and to place an explosive device on a strong room door which L would blow by remote control. K was to take certain bonds from the strongroom and throw them out of his office window to a car waiting below. K did as he was instructed though he knew that others working late in the bank might be seriously injured or even killed by the explosion. A security guard, M, died from a heart attach from shock. The bonds were never recovered.

Advise K and L of their criminal liability.

University of London LLB Examination
(for External Students) Criminal Law June 1994 Q1

General Comment

The substantive offences and the defence of duress are relatively straightforward, the only complication being the extent to which K and L can be charged as accessories to the offences committed by each other. This latter aspect should be approached by dealing with the liability of each party as a principal offender first, and then discussing the liability of the other as an accessory.

Skeleton Solution

L's liability: Kidnapping – threats – incitement – criminal damage – arson-aggravated criminal damage – theft – causation – constructive manslaughter – reckless manslaughter – murder.

K's liability: Conspiracy – theft – aiding and abetting the offences committed by L – defence of duress.

Suggested Solution

When L abducts K's daughter he will have committed the offence of kidnapping which was defined in *R* v *D* (1984) as where the accused takes or carries away a person without their consent, by force or fraud and without lawful excuse.

When L tells K to switch off the alarm, place an explosive device and throw the bonds out of the window, he may have committed the offence of inciting K to commit theft and criminal damage. An incitement was defined in *Race Relations Board* v *Applin* (1973) as where the accused urges or spurs on another to commit an offence by advice, encouragement, threats, persuasion or pressure. L would clearly fall under this definition as he has threatened to harm K's daughter unless K goes along with the plan.

By detonating the explosive device L will have damaged the strongroom door and will consequently be guilty of criminal damage contrary to s1 of the Criminal Damage Act 1971. If any fire ensued L may also be guilty of arson contrary to s1(3) of the same Act. L may also be guilty of the offence under s1(2) of the 1971 Act of damaging property, intending or reckless as to whether life is endangered. Although there is no evidence that L intended to injure anyone, it is sufficient under s1(2) that he was reckless in the *Caldwell* (1981) sense as to whether the life of another will be endangered. This would require the prosecution to prove that L took an unjustifiable risk (which is clearly the case here) and either that L was aware of the risk or had given no thought to the matter.

L may also be liable for the homicide of the security guard. The first issue to establish is whether L is the legal cause of the guard's death. L may argue that the average person would not have died of a heart attack and that perhaps the guard died because he had a weak heart. Such an argument will fail since it is established law that 'you take your victim as you find him', which means that an assailant is responsible for whatever injuries he causes to the victim even if these are exacerbated by defects in the victim's own state of health (*R* v *Blaue* (1975)).

It is unlikely that L would be liable for the murder of the guard as this would require the prosecution to prove that L intended to kill someone or cause grievous bodily harm (*R* v *Hancock & Shankland* (1986)) and there is no evidence of this.

L may, however, be guilty of constructive manslaughter, which was defined in *R* v *Church* (1966) as where the accused commits an unlawful act which all sober and reasonable people would inevitably recognise must subject the other person to the risk of some harm resulting therefrom, albeit not serious harm. It is submitted that detonating a bomb clearly fulfils the first of these requirements in that the planting of a bomb is unlawful. In respect of the second requirement, it has been established in *R* v *Dawson* (1985) that although the question as to whether reasonable and sober people would inevitably foresee that the accused's act would expose another to the risk of some harm is an objective one, it must be considered only in the light of the knowledge possessed by the accused at the time of the offence. Although *K* knew that there were other people working late in the bank there is no evidence that *L* was so aware. If this is so, a reasonable person may not foresee that planting a bomb late at night in a bank would inevitably expose another person to the risk of harm.

However, L may still be guilty of manslaughter by gross negligence as defined in the recent House of Lords case of *R* v *Adomako* (1994) which is a landmark case in the law of homicide. *Adomako* held, in effect, that the offence of reckless manslaughter no longer existed and that it was superseded by manslaughter by gross negligence. Although the latter offence has existed for some time the House of Lords redefined it. According to this definition the first requirement is that the accused owed the deceased a duty of care. Lord Mackay said that everyone must be under a duty not to do acts imperilling the lives of others. Under this definition, it would appear that a duty can be established in this (and almost all) cases. Secondly, it must be established that the accused breached this duty, which L has done by detonating the bomb. Finally, the prosecution must prove that the accused is guilty of 'gross negligence' which was defined as:

'... supremely a jury question, [the issue is] whether, having regard to the risk of death involved, the conduct of the defendant was so bad in all the circumstances as to amount in their judgment to a criminal act or omission.'

It is submitted that the risk of death following the detonation of a bomb is so considerable and unjustifiable as to meet this requirement.

If K is guilty of the theft of the bonds, then L may have committed the offence of handling stolen goods contrary to s22 of the Theft Act 1968 when he received them after K threw them out of the window. If, however, K is entitled to the defence of duress as discussed below, then L will be guilty as a principal offender of the substantive offence of theft since he acted through an 'innocent agent'.

K may be guilty of theft of the bonds contrary to s1 of the Theft Act 1968. K clearly has appropriated property belonging to another with the intention of permanently depriving the other of it.

K may also be guilty of aiding and abetting the offences committed by L, contrary to s8 of the Accessories and Abettors Act 1861. Under s8 a person who assists another to commit an act may be liable as an accessory to any offences committed by that other which were within his 'common design' (R v Bainbridge (1960)). K obviously knew that the bomb would cause damage which is therefore within his common design and he may therefore be an accessory to the criminal damage committed by L.

Since K foresaw that the people working late in the bank might be seriously injured or killed in the ensuing explosion, under the Bainbridge principle K may be liable as an accessory to the manslaughter committed by L.

A more interesting question, however, is whether K may be liable as an accessory to murder even though the principal offender (L) is only guilty of manslaughter. It was established in R v Roberts (1992) that although the mens rea required of a principal offender in murder was an intention to kill or cause grievous bodily harm, the mens rea required of an accessory was merely that the accessory foresaw that death or grievous bodily harm might occur. Therefore, it is technically possible that although L may only be guilty of manslaughter, K may be convicted as an accessory to murder!

However, K may be able to plead the defence of duress to some of the above offences. At the outset one might note that it has been established by the House of Lords in R v Howe (1987) that duress is not available to a person charged with murder or being an accessory to murder. Therefore if, under Roberts, K was charged with murder under s8 of the 1861 Act he could not raise the defence of duress.

However, if K is charged with being an accessory to the manslaughter committed by L, he may raise the defence of duress. Duress may be a defence to a charge of manslaughter provided the requisite requirements of the defence are met. In R v Graham (1982) it was established that an accused may raise the defence of duress if he believed that his life or that of his immediate family was in immediate danger. Since L has threatened to kill K's daughter it would appear that this requirement is satisfied. It was also held that the jury should consider 'whether a sober person of reasonable firmness sharing the defendant's characteristics would have responded in the same way to the threats'. It is submitted that although the point is arguable, a reasonable person whose daughter had been threatened in this way might have given in to the threats. It is established law that the fact that the accused could have summoned help instead of giving in to the threat does not automatically deprive him of the defence of duress (R v Hudson & Taylor (1971)).

QUESTION TWO

A was very angry because he had just been fired from his job. He arrived back home to find that his wife had left a note for him stating that she had taken their two children and was leaving him. He was upset and decided to go for a walk to calm down. He had been walking for an hour when he called into a public house and ordered a glass of mineral water. By mistake he was given a large glass of vodka by the landlord. He gulped down the drink without tasting it. Outside he was approached by two homeless youngsters, B and C, who were asking for money. He thought they were going to attack him and he hit out at B, the one nearer to him, and by mistake, hit C. C fell back and hit his head on the pavement and was concussed.

Advise A of his criminal liability. What difference, if any, would it make to your advice if C had died from the fall because he had a thin skull?

University of London LLB Examination
(for External Students) Criminal Law June 1994 Q2

General Comment

The substantive fatal and non-fatal offences against the person are relatively straightforward; the more tricky areas of the question revolve around the defences of self defence, mistake and involuntary intoxication. With the recent Court of Appeal decision in *R v Kingston* a question on the latter defence was almost inevitable (although the answer below will use the more recent House of Lords' decision in *Kingston* which students may not have been aware of at the time of taking the examination).

Skeleton Solution

Assault against B – offences against the person against C – self-defence – mistake – involuntary intoxication – causation – murder – constructive manslaughter.

Suggested Solution

When A hit out at B he may have committed an assault against B even though he did not make contact with him. This is because an assault was defined in the case of *R v Venna* (1975) as where the accused intentionally or recklessly causes the victim to apprehend immediate and unlawful personal violence. Thus A may have committed the actus reus of assault when he struck out at B and put him in fear of violence even though he did not actually strike him. A certainly has the mens rea of the offence as he intended to strike B.

The more difficult question is whether A may be liable for assault and battery against C since he only intended to strike B. A may be held liable for the offence in either of two ways. First, one may use the doctrine of transferred malice established in *R v Latimer* (1886) under which an intention to cause harm to one person may be transferred to another if the latter is mistakenly injured. Alternatively, one may argue that by hitting out at B, A was reckless as whether he might put C in fear of violence. However, it was held in *Venna* itself that *Cunningham* (1957) recklessness applied to the offence of assault and this has been confirmed by the House of Lords in *R v Savage; R v Parmenter* (1991). Effectively, this means that to secure a conviction of assault against C on the basis of A's recklessness it would have to be established that when A struck out at B he was aware that he might hit or put C in fear of violence. Proof of this subjective awareness may be difficult and it is submitted that the doctrine of transferred malice would be more appropriate.

A may also have committed the offence of assault occasioning actual bodily harm contrary to s47 of the Offences Against the Person Act 1861. Actual bodily harm

191

was defined in *R* v *Chan Fook* (1994) as any hurt or injury which interferes with the health or comfort of the victim, provided it is more than trivial. Concussion would obviously interfere with the health and comfort of C. It was established by the House of Lords in *R* v *Savage; R* v *Parmenter* that once it has been proved that the accused has assaulted the victim and that the assault has occasioned actual bodily harm, no further mens rea is necessary. Consequently, it is submitted that since an assault can be established under the doctrine of transferred malice as discussed above, and this assault clearly caused C concussion, A will be guilty of the s47 offence.

It is submitted that it is unlikely that A would be guilty of the more serious offences under ss18 and 20 of the 1861 Act of intentionally or recklessly causing grievous bodily harm as it is unlikely that concussion per se would be held to amount to grievous bodily harm.

To the charges of assault, battery and the offence under s47, A may raise the defence of self-defence. Although it appears that he was not in fact under attack from the two youngsters, he may be entitled to rely on the defence because of the doctrine of mistake. It has been established in *R* v *Williams* (1983) that if an accused responds to circumstances which he mistakenly believes to have occurred or are about to occur his liability should be assessed according to the facts as he believed them to be *even if such a belief is unreasonable*. It is important to understand that mistake does not provide a defence in itself but may allow the accused to plead another defence (in this case self-defence).

In the case of *R* v *Oatridge* (1992) it was held that an accused might be entitled to the defence of self-defence if the 'response was commensurate with the degree of risk which the defendant believed to be created by the attack under which he believed himself to be'. It is submitted that if A was under attack by two youngsters, as he so believed, it would be reasonable to strike one of them. In this respect it should be noted that it has been established in *R* v *Beckford* (1988) that one does not have to wait for an assailant to strike the first blow – 'circumstances may justify a pre-emptive strike'.

An interesting question is whether A can raise the defence of involuntary intoxication to any of the above charges. In *DPP* v *Majewski* (1976) it was held that intoxication may be a defence to a charge of basic intent but not one of specific intent. Therefore, if A was so drunk that he did not form the intent required for any of the above charges it follows that he must be acquitted of them. The more interesting question is whether A is entitled to a defence if, although he still had the requisite intent despite his intoxication, he would not have acted as he did were it not for the fact that he was intoxicated *through no fault of his own* (ie involuntary intoxication). The Court of Appeal held in *R* v *Kingston* (1993) that the criminal law should not punish a person who is not at fault. Consequently, if the evidence is that although the accused still had the intent necessary for the offence despite his intoxication he would not have been inclined to commit the offence had he not been involuntary intoxicated, the accused must be acquitted of the offence because such an intent is not a 'criminal intent'. The House of Lords in *Kingston* (1994) reversed the decision of the Court of Appeal and held that the only question was whether at the time of the offence the accused had the requisite mens rea. If the accused had the mens rea required for the offence he must be convicted. If the evidence is that he was intoxicated through no fault of his own, but that he would not have committed the offence were he not so intoxicated, this is a factor to be taken into consideration in mitigation of sentence only.

If C had died from the fall because he had a thin skull, it is submitted that A could be charged with the homicide of C under the doctrine of transferred malice as discussed above. The fact that C died because he had a thin skull, whereas any 'normal' person would have survived, will not absolve A from liability since it has been established in *R v Blaue* (1975) that 'one takes one's victim as one finds him'. It is unlikely that A would be convicted of the murder of C because the prosecution would have difficulty in proving that by throwing the punch A intended to kill or cause grievous bodily harm as required by *R v Hancock and Shankland* (1986). However, A may be guilty of the constructive manslaughter of C, which was defined in *R v Church* (1966) as where the accused commits an unlawful act which all reasonable and sober people would inevitably recognise would expose others to the risk of harm, albeit not serious harm. Unless A was acting in self-defence, striking out at B was an unlawful act (assault) which would expose another to danger.

QUESTION THREE

E had been given a stolen building society cheque by F to pay for a car which E had sold to him. E did not know that the cheque was stolen and, by the time that this was discovered, F had sold the car to H for £500 cash. E went to the address that F had given and climbed in through an open window of F's flat. He removed two items which he estimated were worth £500. These he intended to sell, 'to get his own back'. On the way out he knocked over a vase. He pushed past the caretaker who tried to stop him. The flat did not belong to F.

Advise E and F.

University of London LLB Examination
(for External Students) Criminal Law June 1994 Q3

General Comment

The second part of the question on burglary, theft and criminal damage is relatively straightforward, but the question is complicated by some of the more difficult aspects of the offence of handling stolen goods.

Skeleton Solution

F: Theft – handling stolen goods in relation to the cheque – obtaining property by deception – evasion of liability by deception – handling stolen goods in relation to the sale of the car to H.

E: Burglary – theft – mistake – criminal damage – assault and battery.

Suggested Solution

F has used a stolen cheque to buy a car from E. We do not know how he has come by the cheque or even whether F knew that it was stolen. If F has stolen the cheque he may be charged with theft contrary to s1 Theft Act 1968. If he was not the thief, but was given the cheque by someone else, he may be guilty of handling stolen goods contrary to s22 of the 1968 Act (assuming that he knew it to be stolen). The difficulty in bringing the latter charge is that s32 of the 1968 Act which defines 'goods' makes no mention of whether intangible property (such as the money represented by the cheque rather than the piece of paper which forms the cheque itself) can constitute 'goods' for the purposes of the offence under s22. However, it has been established in *Attorney-General's Reference (No 4 of 1979)* (1980) that intangible property does fall under the definition of goods in s34 and, consequently, F may be convicted of this offence.

By paying for the car with a stolen cheque, F may have committed the offence of obtaining property by deception contrary to s15 of the Theft Act 1968. It would have to be established under s15(4) that F has deceived E. Since the cheque is stolen, the building society will not pay out on it and consequently F will have deceived E into believing that he will be paid when he presents the cheque to the building society for payment (this is, of course, again assuming that F is aware that the cheque is stolen). It must also be established that the deception caused F to obtain the car from E (*Metropolitan Police Commissioner* v *Charles* (1977)) and it is submitted that this is the case since it is unlikely that E would have parted with the car had he known that the cheque he was paid with would not be met. It would also have to be established whether F acted dishonestly within the meaning stated in *R* v *Ghosh* (1982). Under *Ghosh* F will be dishonest if reasonable and honest people would regard what he has done as dishonest and he is aware that they would so regard it. It is submitted that if F knew he was paying for the car with a stolen cheque a jury would almost certainly find that this was dishonest.

Under s24 of the 1968 Act goods *representing* the goods originally stolen may be regarded as stolen goods. Therefore, since F bought the car with a stolen cheque, the car itself may now be regarded as stolen. It would appear that F could be charged with handling stolen goods on the basis that he has disposed of the notionally 'stolen' car. However, it is laid down in s22 that a person can only commit the offence of handling by disposal if the disposal is for *another's* benefit and this has been confirmed by the case of *R* v *Bloxham* (1981). Accordingly, since F sold the car for his own benefit, he fails this requirement and cannot be convicted under s22 in relation to the car.

When E entered the flat it appears that he had an existing intention to steal and consequently may be guilty of burglary under s9(1)(a) of the 1968 Act in that he has entered the building as a trespasser with the intention of stealing.

When E removed the two items from the flat he may have committed theft contrary to s1 of the Theft Act 1968, which provides that a person shall be guilty of theft if they dishonestly appropriate property belonging to another with the intention of permanently depriving that other of it. The only point of debate here is whether E has acted dishonestly. He estimated that the items he stole were worth £500 – the same value that F cheated him out of. E may argue that he falls under s2(1)(a) of the 1968 Act which provides that a person cannot be dishonest if he believes that he has the right in law to deprive the other of the property taken. It is submitted that even though E may have felt justified in taking property from F (or from whom he believed to be F), it is unlikely that he believed that he had the legal right to do so. E's dishonesty would therefore be assessed under the *Ghosh* test described above. In this case it should be noted that the issue is whether reasonable and honest people would regard what E did as dishonest. The fact that E may have believed that what he was doing was right is irrelevant, although it must be proven that E knew that other people would regard what he has done as dishonest.

It should also be noted that the possible arguments mentioned above which E may put to counter the allegation of dishonesty may still be raised, despite the fact that the flat eventually turns out not to belong to F. This is because it has been established in *R v Williams* (1984) that where a person makes a mistake his liability should be assessed according to the facts as he believed them to be.

By knocking over the vase E may have committed the offence of criminal damage contrary to s1 of the Criminal Damage Act 1971. Under this section a person is guilty of criminal damage if he intentionally or recklessly damages property belonging to another. There is no evidence that E intended to damage the vase and the prosecution will therefore have to establish that he did so recklessly within the meaning laid down in *R v Caldwell* (1981). According to the definition of recklessness in *Caldwell* it must be proved that E took an obvious risk of damaging the vase and either that he was aware of the risk or had given no thought to the matter (per Lord Diplock). Whether or not E took an obvious risk of damaging the vase would depend on a number of factors; for example, where the vase was situated, whether it was securely fixed and how fast E ran past it.

In pushing past the guard E will probably have committed the offence of assault which was defined in the case of *R v Venna* (1975) as where the accused intentionally or recklessly caused the victim to apprehend immediate personal violence. There is no evidence that E intended to put the guard in fear, and the prosecution will therefore have to establish that he did so recklessly in the sense laid down in *R v Cunningham* (1957). For *Cunningham* recklessness the prosecution will have to prove that E was aware that he might put the guard in fear. E may also be charged with battery against the guard in that he made unlawful physical contact with the guard.

QUESTION FOUR

G was given to lapses of concentration and was driving home from work on a dual carriageway after a night shift. G started to overtake the car in front on the inside. But the road rapidly started to narrow. Taking into account his experience as a driver, G concluded that there was no chance of his failing to get through. In fact, because the road was wet, G crashed into the car but the driver was not injured.

Advise G. What difference, if any, would it make to your advice if the driver of the other car was seriously injured?

University of London LLB Examination
(for External Students) Criminal Law June 1994 Q4

General Comment

An unusually narrow question in that it focuses very much on an in-depth analysis of the meaning of recklessness in the context of criminal damage and offences against the person. The temptation might be to discuss the offences of dangerous driving and causing death by dangerous driving. Neither would be relevant as the former is not on the syllabus and the driver of the other motor vehicle was not killed, thereby eliminating the latter.

Skeleton Solution

Criminal damage – meaning of recklessness – the 'lacuna' in the meaning of recklessness – maliciously wounding or causing grievous bodily harm.

Suggested Solution

G may be guilty of criminal damage to the other car contrary to s1 of the Criminal Damage Act 1971. Section 1 provides that it is an offence to intentionally or recklessly damage property belonging to another. It is clear that the car belongs to another and it is probable that it was damaged when G crashed into it (although this is not expressly stated in the facts given). Since it is also clear that G did not intend to damage the other car the only debatable issue is whether G damaged the other car recklessly.

To be reckless, the accused must have taken an unjustifiable risk. Overtaking another vehicle on the inside is a breach of the Highway Code and since there appears to be no good reason why G did so, it would appear that the risk is unjustifiable.

In *R v Caldwell* (1981) Lord Diplock held that a person was reckless as to whether they destroyed or damaged property if they created an obvious risk that they would destroy or damage property and either that they were aware of the risk or that they had never given any thought to the matter. The first question, therefore, is whether G drove in such a way that he created an obvious risk that property might be damaged. It has been confirmed in *Elliot v C* (1983) that the question is whether the risk would have been obvious to a reasonable person. Therefore, it will not be open to G to argue that the risk was not obvious to him as he suffered from lapses of concentration or because he was tired after working a night shift. Whether or not the risk would have been *obvious* to a reasonable person is impossible to say on the facts given. The fact that overtaking on the inside is generally prohibited and that the road was wet indicates that the risk may have been obvious but more detailed information about the incident would be necessary before a more definite conclusion could be made.

The next issue is whether G has the mens rea required for *Caldwell* recklessness. It would appear that G was not aware of the risk because we are told that on 'account of his experience as a driver' he believed there was no chance of his not getting through. Neither could it be said that G had never thought about the possibility of there being any risk because we are told that he *concluded* that there was no chance of his not being able to get through (ie indicating that he has addressed his mind to the possibility of there being a risk, but come to the incorrect conclusion that there was none). In other words, it would appear that G may fall under what has come to be termed the 'lacuna' in the law of recklessness (at least as far as *Caldwell* recklessness is concerned) in that he had addressed the possibility of there being a risk (therefore not falling under the second limb mentioned above) and concluded, wrongly, that there was no risk (and therefore was unaware of the risk and does not fall under the first limb).

It is unclear whether such a state of mind will constitute recklessness or not. The Queen's Bench Division in *Chief Constable of Avon v Shimmen* (1986) was of the opinion (obiter dicta), that it would not. The House of Lords in *R v Reid* (1992) also held (obiter dicta) that a person who considers the potential risks of his acts but concludes that there are none would fall outside the mens rea of recklessness stated by Lord Diplock in *Caldwell* and might therefore be acquitted

In conclusion, it is submitted that it is likely that G falls under the 'lacuna', and on the balance of the authorities is likely to be held to be outside the scope of *Caldwell* recklessness and therefore acquitted of criminal damage.

If the driver of the other car was seriously injured G may be charged with the offence of maliciously wounding or inflicting grievous bodily harm contrary to ss18 or 20 of the Offences Against the Person Act 1861.

In order to sustain a charge under either section it must be established that the injuries suffered by the driver amount to 'grievous bodily harm' which was defined in *DPP* v *Smith* (1960) as 'really serious harm' or 'wounding' which, under the authority of *C (a minor)* v *Eisenhower* (1984) requires that both the outer and inner layers of the skin are broken. No information is given about the nature of the injuries sustained by the other driver but since they are said to be serious, I will assume that they do constitute grievous bodily harm or wounding. The main difference between ss18 and 20 lies in the mens rea required. In order to secure a conviction under s18 the prosecution would have to prove that the G intended to cause the other driver a serious injury. The facts of this question make it clear that the crash is unintentional and it is therefore submitted that a charge under s18 can be ruled out. In order to secure a conviction under s20 the prosecution must prove that G maliciously wounded or inflicted grievous bodily harm. It has been held by the House of Lords in *R* v *Savage; R* v *Parmenter* (1991) that this means that the prosecution must prove that the accused intended to cause the victim some harm or was reckless as to whether he would cause some harm. Since there is no evidence that G intended to cause the driver of the other vehicle any harm at all, the only possible way that G may be convicted under s20 is to establish that he was reckless. *R* v *Savage; R* v *Parmenter* also held that recklessness under s20 applies in the *Cunningham* (1957) sense. This means that the prosecution must prove that at the time of committing the alleged offence the accused was *aware* of the possibility of causing injury to another. Since we are told that G believed that there was no chance that he would fail to get through it would appear that he was not aware of any possibility that he might cause injury, and therefore must be acquitted of a charge under s20.

QUESTION FIVE

H, aged 13 years, felt that J, his teacher, was trying to make a fool of him in front of his fellow pupils. He poured a quantity of acid into a bucket which he placed above the door of J's study. J entered the study and the acid spilled onto the carpet (which it burned) but did not come into contact with J. The bucket grazed J's head and the acid fumes made J's eyes water for a couple of hours and gave him a choking sensation.

Advise H of his criminal liability.

University of London LLB Examination
(for External Students) Criminal Law June 1994 Q5

CRIMINAL LAW

General Comment

A relatively straightforward question on offences against the person and the defence of infancy. In the latter respect students could demonstrate their knowledge of the recent case of *C v DPP*. The main dangers lie in missing the possible charges of administering a poison contrary to ss23 or 24 of the Offences Against the Person Act 1861 and the sheer amount of material which could be put into the answer.

Skeleton Solution

Assault – assault occasioning actual bodily harm – grievous bodily harm – attempting to cause grievous bodily harm – criminal damage – aggravated criminal damage – administering a poison or noxious substance contrary to ss23 or 24 of the 1861 Act – defence of infancy.

Suggested Solution

By causing the bucket to fall on his teacher, H may be guilty of an assault, which was defined in the case of *R v Venna* (1975) as where the accused intentionally or recklessly causes the victim to apprehend immediate personal violence. It is also likely that H would be guilty of battery, which is defined as the unlawful application of force to another person: *Collins v Wilcock* (1984). The civil case of *Scott v Sheppard* (1773) and the criminal case of *R v Martin* (1881) establish that it is not necessary for the accused to touch the victim directly.

H may also be charged with assault occasioning actual bodily harm contrary to s47 of the Offences Against the Person Act 1861. Actual bodily harm was defined in the case of *R v Chan Fook* (1994) as including any hurt or injury which is more than trivial. It is submitted that the grazing of J's head, the choking sensation and the watering of his eyes due to the acid fumes would fulfil this requirement. H may argue that the falling of the bucket onto J does not constitute an assault because it does not cause him to fear *violence* as opposed to merely being hit by a falling bucket. If this argument were to succeed it might appear that H could not be guilty of the offence of *assault* occasioning actual bodily harm. However, the case of *DPP v Little* (1992) has held that for the purposes of a charge under s47 an 'assault' shall include a 'battery'. It has been established in *R v Savage*; *R v Parmenter* (1991) that the offence under s47 is constituted when the prosecution proves that the accused committed an assault or battery and that the assault or battery caused actual bodily harm – it is unnecessary for the prosecution to prove that the accused had any mens rea in relation to the harm (although in this case it is clear that H did intend to cause J harm).

It is unlikely that H would be convicted of wounding or causing grievous bodily harm with intent contrary to s18 of the 1861 Act as 'grievous bodily harm' would require a 'really serious injury' (*DPP v Smith* (1960)) and 'wounding' would require that both layers of the skin be broken (*C (a minor) v Eisenhower* (1984)). A graze would probably only have broken the outer layer of skin, and it is unlikely that a choking sensation or making J's eyes water for a couple of hours would be held to constitute 'a really serious injury'.

However, H may be guilty of attempting to cause grievous bodily harm contrary to s1 of the Criminal Attempts Act 1981. Under s1 it is an offence to do an act which

198

is more than merely preparatory towards the commission of the full offence, with the intention of committing that offence. Placing the bucket of acid above the door is clearly more than merely preparatory. The prosecution would also have to prove that H intended to cause J a really serious injury which it is submitted they would be able to do if they could prove that H was aware of the effects acid would have if it fell on a person (although this may also depend on how strong the acid was, or H believed it to be). There is authority in the case of *R* v *Walker & Hayles* (1990) to suggest that a person may be guilty of an attempt if he merely foresaw that his act would 'highly probably' lead to the prohibited consequence. Thus H may be convicted of this charge if he merely foresaw that the acid was highly probable to cause J a really serious injury.

H may be guilty of criminal damage contrary to s1 of the Criminal Damage Act 1971 which provides that it is an offence to intentionally or recklessly damage property belonging to another. It appears that H intended to injure J but not damage property. However, he may have been *Caldwell* (1981) reckless as to whether he would cause such damage. To establish such recklessness the prosecution must prove that H created an obvious risk of damage (which it is submitted he has) and either that he was aware of the risk or he never gave the matter any thought.

It would appear that H may also have committed the offence of aggravated criminal damage contrary to s1(2) of the 1971 Act in that he damaged property, intending by that damage to endanger the life of another. The problem here is that it has been held in *R* v *Steer* (1988) that the accused must intend that or be reckless as to whether life is endangered *by the damage caused*. H may argue that in this case life has been endangered by the fumes from the acid but not from the damage to the carpet. However, in *R* v *Dudley* (1989), where the accused firebombed a house intending to injure the occupants inside, the court distinguished itself from *Steer* and held in effect that it was sufficient that the accused damaged property intending that or reckless as to whether life was endangered, it being unnecessary that life is endangered by the damage itself. Since H intended to injure J, it is submitted that he would fall under the latter case and would consequently be convicted of the offence under s1(2).

H may also be charged with the offence of maliciously administering or causing to be taken a poison or noxious substance with the intent to injure, aggrieve or annoy contrary to s24 of the 1861 Act. It is clear that acid is a noxious substance. In the case of *R* v *Gillard* (1988) it was held that the word 'taken' as used in s24 implies that the accused has ingested the noxious substance. This requirement would appear to be fulfilled as J has inhaled some of the fumes from the acid. It was also held in *Gillard* that the word 'administer' in s24 goes beyond ingestion and includes 'bringing a noxious substance into contact with the victim's body'. The latter would also be met by the fumes making contact with J's eyes causing them to water. It would appear that H did have the mens rea of the offence in that he intended to injure or annoy J. It is unlikely that H would be guilty of the more serious offence under s23 of administering a noxious substance so as thereby to endanger the life of the victim or to cause the victim grievous bodily harm, since it would appear that neither of these requirements are met.

The final issue is whether H's age may afford him the defence of infancy. It used to be the case that a person between ten and 14 years of age was presumed to be 'doli incapax', ie incapable of forming a 'guilty mind' (*JM* v *Runeckles* (1984)). In order to rebut this presumption the prosecution needed to prove that the accused had 'mischievous discretion' in addition to committing the actus reus of the offence with the mens rea. In the case of *C v DPP* (1994) the Divisional Court abolished this rule and held that the guilt of an accused between ten and 14 was established when the prosecution proved that he committed the actus reus of the offence with requisite mens rea, there being no need to prove any additional elements in order to secure a conviction. However, this was overruled by the Court of Appeal, which, although agreeing with the sentiments of the Divisional Court, held that the abolition of the this long-standing rule raised issues of public policy and could only be altered by Parliament.

QUESTION SIX

M and N agreed to rob a local building society branch. N drove M to the branch. M went in to see if it could be broken into on a subsequent occasion. M threatened an assistant with a replica pistol. He said, 'Your money or your life.' She handed over the cash before M pistol-whipped her. Next M ran out and jumped into the car throwing the money into the back. When N realised that M had used violence he refused to drive away. M then ran off and before driving off N threw the money out of the car window.

Advise M and N of their criminal liability.

University of London LLB Examination
(for External Students) Criminal Law June 1994 Q6

General Comment

The parts of the question involving offences against the person and robbery are relatively straightforward. Care has to be taken, however, when answering the aspect of the question on accessories which involves some difficult issues relating to the level of foresight required for accessorial liability and the issue of withdrawal from a common enterprise. As always when discussing accessorial liability, the liability of the secondary party should be discussed *after* that of the principal offender.

Skeleton Solution

Conspiracy to commit robbery and burglary.

M: Burglary – assault – robbery – battery – actual bodily harm – grievous bodily harm – theft – blackmail.

N: Accessorial liability for the above offences.

Suggested Solution

Both M and N may be guilty of a conspiracy to commit robbery and burglary which is defined in s1 Criminal Law Act 1977 as where two or more people agree on a course of conduct which will necessarily amount to the commission of an offence.

Burglary is defined under s9(1)(a) Theft Act 1968 as where a person enters a building as a trespasser intending to steal, rape, commit criminal damage or grievous bodily harm. Since it appears that M entered the building society intending to see if it could be broken into at a later date it seems he lacked the intention to steal at the moment of entry and, therefore, cannot be guilty of burglary at this stage. When he changed his mind and decided to rob the building society, he still had not committed burglary under s9(1)(a) as he had not 'entered a building or part of a building' with the requisite intent – he only formed the intent once he was already inside the building.

When M said to the assistant 'your money or your life' and threatened her with a replica pistol he committed an assault which is defined in *R* v *Venna* (1975) as where the accused intentionally or recklessly causes the victim to apprehend immediate personal violence.

When M pistol-whipped the assistant he may also have committed the offences of causing actual bodily harm or causing grievous bodily harm (intentionally or recklessly) contrary to ss47, 18 and 20 of the Offences Against the Person Act 1861. Which offence he is actually guilty of will depend on the level of injury caused and the mens rea he had in respect of that injury. In order to be convicted of the offence under s47, M must have caused the assistant actual bodily harm, which was defined in *R* v *Chan Fook* (1994) as including any injury which is more than trivial. Since M hit the assistant with a gun it is likely that he caused her such harm. Once it is established that M assaulted the assistant, and that this assault caused actual bodily harm, it is unnecessary to prove that M had any mens rea in relation to the harm he caused (*R* v *Savage*; *R* v *Parmenter* (1991)).

If the injuries sustained by the assistant are more serious, M may have committed the offence of causing grievous bodily harm contrary to ss18 or 20 of the 1861 Act. If this is so, M will also have committed the offence of burglary contrary to s9(1)(b) of the Theft Act 1968 in that 'having entered a building as a trespasser he inflicts or attempts to inflict on any person therein any grievous bodily harm'. To secure a conviction under s9(1)(b) it is not necessary to prove that the accused had the intention to cause grievous bodily harm at the moment of entry. Additionally, since at the time of committing this burglary M had with him an imitation gun, he will also be guilty of the more serious offence of aggravated burglary contrary to s10 of the 1968 Act.

When M threatened the assistant, he also committed the offence of robbery contrary to s8 of the 1968 Act in that he committed theft (by taking the money) and 'at the time of doing so', and in order to do so, he threatened the assistant with the use of force. It should be noted that although M only used force *after* he had obtained the money he may still be convicted of robbery because the *threat* of force alone is sufficient, provided it precedes the theft (*R* v *Clouden* (1987)).

Since M made a demand with menaces he may also have committed the offence of blackmail contrary to s21 of the 1968 Act, although in these circumstances it is submitted that the charges mentioned above would be more appropriate.

N may be liable as an accessory to the crimes committed by M. It is established law that a person may be liable as an accessory for any acts committed by the principal offender provided they are within the 'common design' of himself and the principal offender (*R* v *Bainbridge* (1960) and *DPP for Northern Ireland* v *Maxwell* (1978)). Since burglary, theft and robbery are clearly within N's common design he will be liable as an accessory to these offences.

A more debatable issue is whether N may be liable as an accessory to the offences against the person committed by M. On the one hand, since we are told that M and N agreed to rob the building society and since robbery by definition involves the use of force or at least the threat of force, one may argue that M's act of pistol-whipping the assistant is within M and N's joint enterprise or common design. In addition, it should be noted that the House of Lords held in *Maxwell* that it was sufficient that the offence committed was *one of a range in the accused's contemplation* even if the accused did not know exactly which offence was to be committed. On the other hand, it is also established law that a person is not an accessory to offences committed by the principal offender which are outside his contemplation (*Davies* v *DPP* (1954), as confirmed by *R* v *Carberry* (1994)). It may be argued that if N was unaware that M was carrying an imitation gun and unaware that he was actually going to use violence as opposed to merely the threat of violence, N is not liable as an accessory to the offences arising from the pistol-whipping as these are outside the scope of what he saw the joint enterprise to be.

Because N refused to drive off when he discovered that M had used violence he may try to escape liability for being an accessory to this violence by arguing that his act of refusing to drive off amounted to a withdrawal from the joint enterprise. However, it was established in the case of *R* v *Becerra* (1975) and confirmed in the recent case of *R* v *Baker* (1994) that an accused may only withdraw from a joint enterprise *before* the offence has been committed by unequivocally communicating to the other party his withdrawal from the enterprise, making it clear that if the other party continues he does so without the accused's assistance. Since N's act of refusing to drive away from the scene has occurred only after M committed the offences against the assistant, it cannot amount to a valid withdrawal from the enterprise.

QUESTION SEVEN

P was walking home his girlfriend, Q, when they started to kiss. P was kissing her goodnight when he bruised her lips and Q gave him a love bite which drew blood. Q suggested that P return later and climb into her bedroom. In the middle of the night P climbed into what he though was Q's bedroom. In fact, it was her twin sister R's bedroom. P did not know that Q had a twin sister. He climbed into R's bed. She did not wake fully because she had taken a sleeping tablet. P penetrated her before she woke up and screamed in alarm.

Advise P of his criminal liability.

University of London LLB Examination
(for External Students) Criminal Law June 1994 Q7

General Comment

An unusual question combining a discussion of offences against the person, the defence of consent, and rape. It should be noted that although Q kissed P 'which drew blood' it is unnecessary to discuss the potential liability of Q as the question asks only for advice as to P's liability.

Skeleton Solution

Bruising – whether amounts to battery or actual bodily harm – defence of consent – rape – mistake – burglary.

Suggested Solution

The first issue is whether P may have committed an assault or battery when he kissed Q so hard as to bruise her lips. It is unlikely that a charge of assault could be sustained as this requires that the victim apprehend immediate personal violence (*R v Venna* (1975)). Since the bruise appears to have been caused in the throws of an act of passion it is unlikely that Q apprehended any personal violence.

It is possible, however, that P has committed the actus reus of battery. Battery was defined in *Venna* as 'where the defendant intentionally or recklessly applies force to the person of another'. The act of kissing Q was done intentionally, although whether this could be said to amount to force is questionable.

Potentially, P could be guilty of the offence of assault occasioning actual bodily harm contrary to s47 of the Offences Against the Person Act 1861. Although the statutory definition of the offence mentions only an assault, it has been held in the case of *DPP v Little* (1992) that the offence under s47 is complete if the accused committed an assault or battery which occasioned actual bodily harm. A bruise on the lip may well amount to actual bodily harm since this was defined in *R v Chan Fook* (1994) as any hurt or injury which is more than trivial. It is possible that the court would regard a bruise, depending on its severity, as insignificant. It is likely that P did not intend to cause Q any injury at all but inflicted the bruising when he (and, judging by her love bite, Q), got carried away in their romantic encounter. However, it has been established in *R v Savage; R v Parmenter* (1991) that the offence under s47 is constituted when the prosecution proves that the accused committed an assault (or in this case battery) which caused actual bodily harm, it being unnecessary to prove that the accused had any mens rea in relation to the actual bodily harm caused.

If it is established that P has committed the actus reus and mens rea of battery and/or assault occasioning actual bodily harm, he may attempt to raise the defence of consent. It would first of all have to be established whether Q did consent to the bruising or the possibility of bruising, as opposed to merely kissing. When someone responds positively to the kiss of another, they impliedly consent to contact by the other person, but this does not necessarily mean that they consent to being bruised. In this case, however, it may be argued that Q's love bite, which was so powerful as to draw blood, indicated that she consented to a more aggressive form of kissing, including the possibility of bruising.

If it is the case that following the discussion above P is guilty only of battery, it is likely that the defence of consent will succeed. This is because it was held in *R v Donovan* (1934) that consent is an absolute defence to a charge of assault or battery provided no injury is caused. This proposition has been confirmed by the House of Lords in *R v Brown* (1993).

However, if a charge of assault occasioning actual bodily harm is sustained the situation is more problematic. *Brown* held that whether consent can amount to a defence to charges involving injury to the 'victim' must be determined as a matter of public policy and public interest. In *Brown* it was held that consent was not a defence to charges involving the infliction of non-permanent injuries in the course of sadomasochistic acts. It is a question of degree as to how far the courts are likely to apply this principle. It may well be that the courts will hold that consent is a defence to such a minor injury inflicted in the course of 'normal' sexual activity.

P may be charged with the rape of R contrary to s1 of the Sexual Offences Act 1956. The actus reus of this offence is that the accused had unlawful sexual intercourse with a woman without her consent. Although it was held in *R v Mayers* (1872) that a man could not be guilty of rape if he had sexual intercourse with a woman who was asleep as the intercourse was not against the woman's will in a positive sense, this will no longer apply as the case was decided before the 1956 Act, which clearly requires the woman to 'consent'. The prosecution will also have to establish either that P knew that R was not consenting or was reckless as to whether she consented. It would appear that P believed that he was entering Q's bed room and that Q had invited him to do so. If P believed that this invitation included consent to sexual intercourse, it could not be said that he 'knew' that the victim did not consent.

The prosecution may then argue that P was reckless as to whether the victim was consenting, on the basis that he should have taken steps to ensure the identity of his proposed 'partner'. In *R v Satnam* (1983) it was held that the accused was reckless as to whether the woman consented or not if his attitude was one of 'I could not care less whether she is consenting or not, I am going to have intercourse with her regardless'. The exact meaning of this type of recklessness is unclear but it would appear that the accused must at least be aware of the possibility that the woman may not be consenting, ie more similar to *Cunningham* recklessness than *Caldwell* (see the views expressed by Smith & Hogan, *Textbook on Criminal Law*, 7th edition, at p458). If P *believed* that Q's invitation to her bedroom included an implied consent to sexual intercourse he would lack this awareness and therefore have to be acquitted. This is the case even if his belief is unreasonable.

It is submitted that he could not be guilty of burglary under s9(1)(a) Theft Act 1968 because he has not entered the building with the intention of raping or committing theft, criminal damage or grievous bodily harm.

HLT Publications

HLT books are specially planned and written to help you in every stage of your studies. Each of the wide range of textbooks is brought up-to-date annually, and the companion volumes of our Law Series are all designed to work together.

You can buy HLT books from your local bookshop, or in case of difficulty, order direct using this form,

The Law Series covers the following modules:

Administrative Law	Evidence
Commercial Law	Family Law
Company Law	Jurisprudence
Conflict of Laws	Land Law
Constitutional Law	Law of International Trade
Contract Law	Legal Skills and System
Criminal Law	Public International Law
Criminology	Revenue Law
English Legal System	Succession
Equity and Trusts	Tort
European Union Law	

The HLT Law Series:

A comprehensive range of books for your law course, and the legal aspects of business and commercial studies.

Each module is covered by a comprehensive six-part set of books

- Textbook
- Casebook
- Revision Workbook
- Suggested Solutions, for:
  - 1985-90
  - 1991-94
  - 1995

Module	Books required	Cost
To complete your order, please fill in the form overleaf	Postage	
	TOTAL	

Prices (including postage and packing in the UK): Textbooks £19.00; Casebooks £19.00; Revision Workbooks £10.00; Suggested Solutions (1985-90) £9.00, Suggested Solutions (1991-94) £6.00, Suggested Solutions (1995) £3.00.

For Europe, add 15% postage and packing (£20 maximum). For the rest of the world, add 40% for airmail (£35 maximum).

ORDERING

By telephone to 01892 724371, with your credit card to hand

By fax to 01892 724206 (giving your credit card details).

By post to:

HLT Publications,
The Gatehouse, Ruck Lane, Horsmonden, Tonbridge, Kent TN12 8EA

When ordering by post, please enclose full payment by cheque or banker's draft, or complete the credit card details below.

We aim to dispatch your books within 3 working days of receiving your order.

Name

Address

Postcode

Telephone

Total value of order, including postage: £

I enclose a cheque/banker's draft for the above sum, or

charge my ☐ Access/Mastercard ☐ Visa ☐ American Express

Card number

Expiry date

Signature

Date

Publications from **The Old Bailey Press**

Cracknell's Statutes

A full understanding of statute law is vital for any student, and this series presents the original wording of legislation, together with any amendments and substitutions and the sources of these changes.

Cracknell's Companions

Recognised as invaluable study aids since their introduction in 1961, this series summarises all the most important court decisions and acts, and features a glossary of Latin words, as well as full indexing.

Please telephone our Order Hotline on 01892 724371, or write to our order department, for full details of these series.